This book is concerned with what it was like to be a slave in the classical Roman world, and with the impact of the institution of slavery on Roman society at large. It shows how and in what sense Rome was a slave society through much of its history, considers how the Romans procured their slaves, discusses the work roles slaves fulfilled and the material conditions under which they spent their lives, investigates how slaves responded to and resisted slavery and argues that, paradoxically, slavery as an institution became more and more oppressive over time under the influence of philosophical and religious teaching. The book stresses the harsh realities of life in slavery and the way in which slavery was an integral part of Roman civilisation.

KEY THEMES IN ANCIENT HISTORY

Dr P. A. Cartledge
Clare College Cambridge

Dr P. D. A. Garnsey
Jesus College, Cambridge

Key Themes in Ancient History aims to provide readable, informed and original studies of various basic topics, designed in the first instance for students and teachers of Classics and Ancient History, but also for those engaged in related disciplines. Each volume is devoted to a general theme in Greek, Roman, or where appropriate, Graeco-Roman history, or to some salient aspect or aspects of it. Besides indicating the state of current research in the relevant area, authors seek to show how the theme is significant for our own as well as ancient culture and society. By providing books for courses that are oriented around themes it is hoped to encourage and stimulate promising new developments in teaching and research in ancient history.

Other books in the series

Death-ritual and social structure in classical antiquity, by Ian Morris
Literacy and orality in ancient Greece, by Rosalind Thomas

KEY THEMES IN ANCIENT HISTORY

Slavery and society at Rome

A captive German woman and her son surrounded by Roman troops, on the
Column of Marcus Aurelius. Photo: DAI 95–1171.

SLAVERY AND SOCIETY
AT ROME

KEITH BRADLEY

Professor of Classics, University of Victoria

CAMBRIDGE
UNIVERSITY PRESS

Published by the Press Syndicate of the University of Cambridge
The Pitt Building, Trumpington Street, Cambridge CB2 1RP
40 West 20th Street, New York, NY 10011–4211, USA
10 Stamford Road, Oakleigh, Melbourne 3166, Australia

First published 1994

Printed in Great Britain at the University Press, Cambridge

A catalogue record for this book is available from the British Library

Library of Congress cataloguing in publication data

Bradley, K. R.
Slavery and society at Rome / Keith Bradley.
p.   cm. – (Key themes in ancient history)
Includes bibliographical references and index.
ISBN 0–521–37287–9 (hardback) – ISBN 0–521–37887–7 (paperback)
1. Slavery – Rome – History.   2. Rome – History – Republic, 265–30
BC   3. Rome – History – Empire, 30 BC–284 AD   I. Title.
II. Series.
HT863.B7   1994
306.3′62′09376 – dc20   93–42802   CIP

ISBN 0 521 37287 9 hardback
ISBN 0 521 37887 7 paperback

For
Stephen J. D. Bradley

Contents

Preface

This book is a study of slavery in the central period of Roman history that pays particular attention to what it was like – or to what I think it was like – to be a Roman slave. By 'central period' I mean the four centuries from roughly 200 BC to roughly AD 200, though I wander freely beyond these chronological limits as I think appropriate. Edward Gibbon described the slave population of Rome as that 'unhappy condition of men who have endured the weight, without sharing the benefits, of society'. My interest lies in emphasising the structural importance of slavery in Roman society and culture and in trying to recreate the realities of the slave experience. The results are not always edifying, but they are in my view essential to a proper understanding of Roman antiquity. I hope that readers will find them arresting and absorbing as well, even if a trace of the 'unhappy' must always remain.

In keeping with the aims of the series to which it belongs, the book is primarily intended for students who are examining Roman slavery for the first time. Accordingly I attempt to combine a reasonable amount of basic material and explanation with analysis and interpretation. If more advanced readers find the book useful so much the better. I must stress, however, that I have written for those whose interests are genuinely historical and wide-ranging, free that is to say from the conservatism that conventionally dominates the practice of ancient history. It has been inevitable that I draw on and expand ideas about Roman slavery which I offered in *Slaves and Masters in the Roman Empire: A Study in Social Control* and *Slavery and Rebellion in the Roman World, 140 B.C.–70 B.C.* But I have consciously avoided excessive duplication of material (mostly for my own sake), and in particular I have given no detailed account of the major slave uprisings that belong to the first half of Rome's central period. I do not assume that readers of this book will

xi

necessarily have read its predecessors, but I hope that they will be prepared to follow up specific topics in them when this seems fitting.

Finally, I must express my very deep gratitude to Paul Cartledge and Peter Garnsey, both for the confidence implicit in their original invitation to contribute to their series, and for their constant, but not obtrusive, support and interest while the book was in progress (especially on the part of Paul Cartledge). I trust that they will clearly recognise where their editorial advice has proved beneficial and that they will accept my thanks accordingly. I must also thank my colleague Patricia Clark for her willingness to comment on a draft of the book and, more importantly, for her general encouragement throughout, particularly on the bad days. I am grateful, too, to the Social Sciences and Humanities Research Council of Canada and to the University of Victoria Research and Travel Fund for a series of awards that facilitated my research and, of even greater significance, made available the invaluable resource of time in which to write. My deepest, and unpayable, debt, however, remains all that I owe to Diane Bradley, whose continuing support of my work in all manner of circumstances I find, like her, to border on the miraculous.

Victoria, British Columbia   KRB

Abbreviations

A Class	Acta Classica
AE	L'année épigraphique
AJAH	American Journal of Ancient History
ANRW	Aufstieg und Niedergang der Römischen Welt
AntJ	Antiquaries Journal
ArchClass	Archeologia Classica
BCH	Bulletin de Correspondance Hellénique
BGU	Aegyptische Urkunden aus den Staatlichen Museen zu Berlin, Griechische Urkunden
CAH²	Cambridge Ancient History (2nd edn)
C & M	Classica et Mediaevalia
CIL	Corpus Inscriptionum Latinarum
CPh	Classical Philology
CPL	Corpus Papyrorum Latinorum
CQ	Classical Quarterly
CRAI	Comptes rendus de l'Académie des Inscriptions et Belles-Lettres
DArch	Dialoghi di Archeologia
EMC	Echos du Monde Classique/Classical Views
HSPh	Harvard Studies in Classical Philology
ILS	Inscriptiones Latinae Selectae
JESHO	Journal of the Economic and Social History of the Orient
JRS	Journal of Roman Studies
JThS	Journal of Theological Studies
LEC	Les études classiques
MAAR	Memoirs of the American Academy at Rome
MBAH	Münstersche Beiträge zur Antiken Handelsgeschichte
MH	Museum Helveticum
PBSR	Papers of the British School at Rome

_P & P_	_Past and Present_
P C PhS	_Proceedings of the Cambridge Philological Society_
P. Cair. Masp.	_Catalogue général des antiquités égyptiennes du Musée du Caire; Papyrus grecs d'époque byzantine_
PIR²	_Prosopographia Imperii Romani_ (2nd edn)
P. Oxy.	_The Oxyrhynchus Papyri_
P. Turner	_Papyri, Greek and Roman; edited by various hands in honour of Eric Gardner Turner_
P. Wisc.	_Papyri at the University of Wisconsin_
_RD_	_Revue historique de droit français et étranger_
ZPE	_Zeitschrift für Papyrologie und Epigraphik_
ZRG	_Zeitschrift der Savigny-Stiftung für Rechtsgeschichte (Romanistische Abteilung)_

CHAPTER I

Confronting slavery at Rome

In the late spring of 53 BC the Roman orator and politician M. Tullius Cicero received a letter from his brother Quintus who was then occupied with Julius Caesar in the conquest of Gaul. The letter (*Epistulae ad Familiares* 16.6) began as follows:

My dear Marcus, as I hope to see you again and my boy and my Tulliola and your son, I am truly grateful for what you have done about Tiro, in judging his former condition to be below his deserts and preferring us to have him as a friend rather than a slave. Believe me, I jumped for joy when I read your letter and his. Thank you, and congratulations.

The source of Quintus' pleasure was Cicero's decision, taken shortly before, to set free a family slave named Tiro, a cultured man of considerable literary capacity. The pleasure was intense. Quintus spoke in his letter of Tiro, his own son and Cicero's children – all in one breath as it were – without communicating any sense of unease, for the manumission was a joyous affair, almost, it seems, a family event. Also intense was Cicero's personal regard for the slave, as a number of other letters that passed between the two show: just prior to the manumission for instance Cicero had been very concerned about Tiro's ill-health. Tiro was a valued slave whom Cicero thought fit to translate to a condition that better suited his accomplishments and the esteem in which he was held. In Roman Italy of the first century BC, it was evidently possible for the slave to achieve individual distinction despite his lowly origins and to be happily received into the free, civic community.[1]

Somewhat later a slave experience far different from Tiro's manumission took place in a very remote part of the Roman world, the province of Pamphylia in central southern Asia Minor. There,

[1] Ill-health: Cic. *Fam.* 16.10. Tiro: see in general, Treggiari 1969: 259–63.

in the coastal city of Side in the summer of A D 142, as a papyrus document (*P. Turner* 22) reveals, a ten-year-old slave girl named Abaskantis was sold by a certain Artemidoros to a new owner, Pamphilos, in a transaction bound by the Roman law of sale. The document opens thus:

> In the consulship of L. Cuspius Rufinus and L. Statius Quadratus, at Side, before L. Claudius Auspicatus, demiurge and priest of the goddess Roma, on 26 Loos. Pamphilos, otherwise known as Kanopos, son of Aigyptos, from Alexandria, has purchased in the marketplace from Artemidoros, son of Aristokles, the slave girl Abaskantis, or by whatever other name she may be known, a ten-year-old Galatian, for the sum of 280 silver denarii. M. Aelius Gavianus stands surety for and guarantees the sale. The girl is healthy, in accordance with the Edict of the Aediles . . . is free of liability in all respects, is prone neither to wandering nor running away, and is free of epilepsy . . .

From this text the early history and the ultimate fate of Abaskantis cannot be known. All that is certain is that she was once sold by herself at a tender age in a city far from her place of birth in Galatia to the north. It looks as if she had been taken from her family of origin to become a victim of what the Roman jurist Papinian (*Digesta Iustiniani* 41.3.44 pr.) once called 'the regular, daily traffic in slaves', and was perhaps now being exchanged between slave-dealers: Pamphilos was from Alexandria at least, and so Abaskantis was probably destined for Egypt. Evidently the buying and selling of human merchandise was an ordinary, prosaic aspect of Roman life that among the free caused little consternation.

A more fortunate figure than Abaskantis, it seems, was the Roman slave Musicus Scurranus, a man known from an inscription (*ILS* 1514) set up to commemorate him when he died in the early first century A D. The inscription begins like this:

> To the deserving Musicus Scurranus, slave of Tiberius Caesar Augustus, accountant (*dispensator*) of the Gallic Treasury in the province of Gallia Lugdunensis, from those of his underslaves (*vicarii*) who were with him when he died at Rome . . .

Although himself a slave, that is to say, Musicus Scurranus had a personal slave retinue of his own, and his inscription actually continues with the names and job-titles, save in one case, of sixteen of its members. They include a business agent, an accountant, three secretaries, a doctor, two chamberlains, two attendants, two cooks, and three slaves who were respectively in charge of Scurranus' clothes, gold and silver. In law the Roman slave was allowed to own nothing, so although he was their owner in effect, technically the *vicarii* of Musicus Scurranus belonged to Scurranus' own master, the emperor Tiberius. Ownership of slaves by slaves seems strange at first sight, but in societies like that of Rome where slaveowning was a critical mark of any individual's social standing it has been far from unusual. Here it immediately exposes a hierarchy among Rome's servile population close to the top of which Musicus Scurranus apparently rose. He himself was one of the hundreds of imperially owned slaves who played an important role in the administration of the Roman empire under the new system of government introduced by Augustus. The fact that he was a financial official presupposes that he was reasonably well-educated and trustworthy, and his position obviously brought him substantial material rewards. In many ways, therefore, Musicus Scurranus was a great success.[2]

Another glimpse of slave life can be seen, though less brilliantly, in a legal text preserved in the *Digest of Justinian*, the great compilation of Roman law that belongs to the second quarter of the sixth century AD. When a slave was sold – the case of Abaskantis is a good example – the law required that certain procedures be followed, one of which was that the seller should declare whether the slave was diseased or defective in any way in case the slave's capacity to perform was at all diminished. In consequence jurists frequently had to rule on what constituted disease or defect because disputes often arose about the effects on performance of specific complaints. A startling decision of this kind is the following ruling from Ulpian, usually regarded as one of the greatest of the Roman jurists, who flourished in the early third century AD (*Dig.* 21.1.8):

The question arises whether one whose tongue has been cut out is healthy. This problem is dealt with by Ofilius in respect of a horse. His opinion is in the negative.

Now it is difficult to imagine circumstances under which a slave's tongue had been cut out unless a slaveowner had opted to punish the slave in a particularly brutal way or had engaged in a sadistic act of unwarranted violence against him. However, Ulpian could plainly take the severing of a slave's tongue as a realistic event that

---

[2] Unusual: Karasch 1987: 211.

from a legal point of view had to be dealt with pragmatically. He recognised that any Roman slave, as a matter of course, could become the object of physical abuse or injury at any time, and in so doing reflected the strong association between slavery and violence that always held a place in the Roman mind.

As an introduction to the study of slavery in Roman antiquity, the four images of slave life with which I have begun are variously instructive. They illustrate first the great complexity of Roman slavery, for although manumission and sale, the achievement of material success and physical violation were all common features of servile experience at Rome, they are features which hardly seem to fit comfortably together. It is as if they were pieces of two jigsaw puzzles that have been indiscriminately tossed together with no hope of ever being sorted out – or to put it another way one can hardly imagine Cicero the kindly benefactor of Tiro cutting out a slave's tongue, Tiro's or anyone else's. The truth is, however, that there were many variations and contradictions in the way slaves were treated at Rome and in how they lived their lives, and incongruity could easily manifest itself in the actions of a single individual. In a letter written to his friend Atticus when a favourite slave boy had died, Cicero made the revealing remark (*Epistulae ad Atticum* 1.12.4) that the event had touched him 'more than the death of a slave perhaps ought to do'. The Roman slavery system cannot be understood, therefore, without at once acknowledging its enormous diversity and variability, and any attempt to define its general features must constantly allow for the unanticipated and the exceptional.

Secondly, the opening images show that slavery at Rome has to be approached above all as a social institution. Individual slaves were set free, sold, rewarded or punished by their owners, the men, women and at times children who utterly dominated their lives, which means that the institution itself has to be approached primarily in terms of the social relationship which bound slave and slaveowner together. The relationship was just one, as it happens, of a sequence of asymmetrical relationships in Roman society that tied individuals together, comparable to the relationships between emperor and citizen-subject, father and son, teacher and pupil or officer and soldier, a set of examples used by the younger Seneca (*de Clementia* 1.16.2) in the middle of the first century AD in a work composed for the emperor Nero. The point Seneca wanted to make was that, although forms of authority could differ in degree, all relationships were best served if the superior party treated the inferior with clemency. The idea was that traditional social bonds, all dependent upon injunction and deference, served to perpetuate the established order of society and had to be preserved: if some people were given power over others, the best interests of all would be met, at least from the standpoint of those who exercised control. The master–slave relationship at Rome, therefore, was not altogether a social peculiarity.[3]

On another occasion (*de Beneficiis* 3.18.3) Seneca compared the relationships between king and subject and commander and soldier with that between master and slave, and towards the close of the central period the Christian writer Tertullian (*Apologeticus* 3.4) took the relationships between husband and wife, father and son, and master and slave as the basic structures of authority around him. It was a conventional mode of thought. But if the master–slave relationship was only a variation on a theme in the Roman mind, the degree of variation in this case was highly significant, for in no other circumstance was power exercised by one over the other in such an all-embracing manner. The Roman emperor passed laws that affected all his citizen-subjects, but his powers of enforcement were limited. The Roman father retained formal authority over his sons until his death, but in real life adult sons were in many respects fully independent. The powers of the schoolteacher and military officer were also circumscribed by time and situation. In the master–slave relationship, however, there were no restricting factors: the slave was at the complete and permanent disposal of the master and except by an act of resistance could never find relief from the necessity of obeying because there were no countervailing · rights or powers in the condition of slavery itself to which the slave had recourse. From the slave it was complete submission that the master expected, the kind of submission that, ironically enough, sometimes made slaves better patients than the free, according to Celsus (3.21.2): sick slaves could put up with harsh remedies because they were used to coercion. Slavery consequently occupied an extreme place in the spectrum of Roman social relationships in which it was expected that authority should flow from one and

[3] Asymmetrical relationships: see in general, Saller 1982: 7–39.

dutifulness be exhibited by the other. It is not surprising, therefore, that Cicero (*de Republica* 37) should have distinguished it from all other conventional associations by pointing out that, while a son could be expected to obey his father willingly, the slave had to be coerced and worn down into obedience by his master: his spirit had to be broken. The master–slave relationship was not a social contract that bound each side to a set of mutual and reciprocal obligations and benefits in any mutually acceptable manner; it was an arrangement intended to benefit one side only.

Thirdly, the opening items give a good idea of the varied nature of the evidence available for the study of Roman slavery. The images extend chronologically from the middle of the first century BC to the early third century AD, indicating that it is in the central period of Roman history that most is known about the institution. By the central period, I mean the four centuries from roughly 200 BC to AD 200, a span of time which constitutes a distinct historical epoch despite the political and constitutional developments involved, and it is on this period that I shall for the most part concentrate. At the same time the images illustrate the range of conventional sources – literature, papyri, inscriptions, law – from which information has to be drawn (and to which evidence from archaeology can at times be added), and because they range geographically, from Rome and Italy on the one hand (the Roman heartland) to Asia Minor and Egypt on the other, they also serve as a useful reminder that over time, and especially through the central period, Rome subjugated and brought under imperial rule a vast diversity of peoples and lands, uniting all under a single political and administrative framework. This means that when the historian speaks of Rome and of Roman society the terms are constantly redefining themselves, referring at one extreme to a single city in Italy and at the other extreme to the whole of the empire. The shift is one from a geographical to a cultural designation, from the city in a narrow sense to wherever the city's culture came to impose itself. Thus when evidence becomes available from beyond the heartland, as for example from Egypt, allowance has to be made for the possibility of regional variations in slavery practices. Certainly the volume of evidence on slavery at 'Rome' becomes greater over time.[4]

---

[4] Central period: cf. Brunt 1988: 9–12.

All historians are the victims of their sources. But the historian of Roman slavery is at a special disadvantage, for although a great volume of information is on hand it is all subject to the fundamental flaw that there is no surviving record, if indeed any ever existed, of what life in slavery was like from a slave's point of view. To be sure, some inscriptions that slaves or former slaves set up are still extant, as too a few writings by men who had once been slaves – the fabulist Phaedrus and the philosopher Epictetus for instance. But there is nothing in the ancient evidence comparable to the collections of interviews with former slaves that historians of modern slavery systems can turn to, and nothing resembling the autobiographies of former slaves such as those of the American fugitives Frederick Douglass and Harriet Jacobs, works that provide, as one modern historian has put it, 'a window into the "inside half" of the slave's life which never appears in the commentaries of "outsiders"'. By contrast Roman slavery is almost entirely represented from what the historian of a modern slave culture would call proslavery sources, items of evidence that reflect the attitudes and prejudices of the slaveowning sectors of society and that contain at most only minimal sensitivity to the servile perspective of events. What it actually felt like as a Roman slave to be set free or to be sold is difficult to recover when slaves like Tiro and Abaskantis appear in the sources not as historical agents or actors, but as individuals who were acted upon.[5]

The point is critical enough to warrant elaboration. In December 54 BC, some time before the receipt of Quintus' letter concerning Tiro, Cicero wrote to his brother to give him news in his absence of what was happening in Rome. Having disposed of political business, he continued (*Epistulae ad Quintum fratrem* 3.9.4):

Thank you very much for your promise of slaves. As you say, I am indeed short-handed, both in Rome and on my estates. But, my dear fellow, please don't consider anything to do with my convenience unless it's absolutely convenient and easy for *you*.

To enslave prisoners-of-war was standard policy throughout Roman history, so there was nothing untoward about the connection Cicero made between successful warfare in Gaul or Britain and the maintenance of the slave supply at Rome. He simply assumed

---

[5] Modern historian: Blassingame 1979: 367.

that mechanisms were available for transporting newly acquired slaves from northern to southern Europe and that he could, as it were, place an order for them at any time. What is not evident, however, is any interest in what was involved in the process, especially the emotional process of suddenly being converted from a state of freedom to a state of servitude – of being forcibly separated from kin and a familiar physical environment, of being relocated in a completely alien setting, of being compelled to work for or serve a stranger into whose ownership the captive had fallen, of losing all control over one's existence. From Cicero's rather blasé tone one would doubt that the issue had ever presented itself to him as worthy of consideration. But in its attitudinal deficiency his text, as an item of evidence, typifies practically all the evidence that now remains on Roman slavery.

To overcome this obstacle evidence of every description has to be exploited, and not just conventional evidence. Here a considerable amount of attention will be given to the evidence of Roman law, especially the law of the *Digest*, and to the evidence of those works of imaginative literature composed in the second half of Rome's central period variously styled romances or novels. The first procedure is not all that unusual of course, but it is always potentially problematical, given that Roman law often dealt with the possible rather than the factual. The *Digest*, however, was not compiled for antiquarian or academic reasons but with the practical end in view of law being used and applied, and its authors drew on earlier legal works that in their own time had been derived from the world of reality around them. The words of the jurist Celsus, who flourished in the early second century AD, are important in this respect (*Dig.* 1.3.4–5):

Out of those matters whose occurrence in one kind of case is a bare possibility, rules of law do not develop. For the law ought rather to be adapted to the kinds of things which happen frequently and easily, than to those which happen very seldom.[6]

More unusual, and perhaps controversial, is to use as historical evidence fictional narratives such as Longus' *Daphnis & Chloe* and Apuleius' *Metamorphoses*, works that have been taken to reflect primarily the ambience of the Hellenistic world in which the literary

---

[6] See further, Bradley 1988. For the lack of sympathy towards slaves displayed by some Roman jurists in the late Republic, see Watson 1968.

form of the romance first developed. Yet in their assumptions of what is plausible and credible in everyday life, as too in their depictions of psychological response to crisis, these narratives also reflect aspects of contemporary reality that can provide valuable historical information. The Lesbos in which *Daphnis & Chloe* is set, it should be noted, is a Lesbos that betrays signs of first-hand knowledge of the island on the author's part, while the Roman provincial milieu of the *Metamorphoses* is unmistakable.[7]

More controversial still is to draw on the evidence of other historical slave regimes, those for example of the New World in the eighteenth and nineteenth centuries, on the assumption that Roman slavery can be profitably illuminated by comparison or contrast with them. The objection is obvious: the historical conditions involved are far too different to make juxtaposition of ancient and modern worthwhile. In my view, however, it is misguided to pretend that the major slave societies of the past have not shared common features and to believe that nothing useful for the ancient world can be learned from modern history, at least as a corrective to simplistic judgements, even as regard is maintained for historical particularity. As appropriate, therefore, reference will be made throughout this book to slavery in later history as a means of compensating for the inadequacy of the Roman sources. Success will depend on replacing images with more durable impressions of slavery and Roman society.

[7] Hellenistic world: Hägg 1983. Contemporary reality: Bowie 1977; Reardon 1991; cf. Boswell 1988: 95–100. Lesbos: Bowie 1985: 86–90. Provincial milieu: Millar 1981.

CHAPTER 2

The slave society of Rome

In 2 BC a law was passed at Rome which regulated the number of slaves a slaveowner was allowed to set free in his will. The *lex Fufia Caninia* was one element of what is customarily called the Augustan social legislation, a sequence of measures enacted in the principate of Augustus intended by and large to arrest a decline in civic responsibility that contemporaries perceived in the world around them. In this case the object was to oblige slaveowners to use their powers of manumission wisely and to set free only those slaves who had proved that they deserved freedom: indiscriminate and irresponsible manumission was to be avoided. A fragment of a Latin will found in Egypt (*CPL* 174) shows a slaveowner late in the central period about to give details on the slaves he proposed to set free. It begins: 'Since I know that I am not permitted by will to manumit a greater number than provided by the *lex Fufia Caninia* ...' The law was followed, even in much later times and far removed places, and made an impact on society.

The point of immediate interest, however, is not the issue of setting slaves free but the scale of slaveownership that the authors of the *lex Fufia* understood to be typical of their society when they framed it. According to the jurist Gaius (*Institutiones* 1.43) in the second century AD, the law provided as follows:

Someone who has more than two but not more than ten slaves is permitted to free up to half their number; someone who has more than ten but not more than thirty is permitted to free up to one-third. Someone who has more than thirty but not more than one hundred is allowed to free up to a quarter. Finally, someone who has more than one hundred but not more than five hundred is permitted to free not more than one-fifth; nor does the law take account of someone owning more than five hundred to select a proportion from that number, but it prescribes that no one may lawfully free more than one hundred slaves. But if someone has only one slave in all, or two, this law does not apply and so he has full power to free.

It is evident from Gaius' summary that the number of slaves a slaveowner possessed might fall anywhere along a broad range of possibilities. Six categories of holdings are imagined in all: 1–2 slaves, 3–10 slaves, 11–30 slaves, 31–100 slaves, 101–500 slaves, 501 and more slaves. It appears therefore that slaveowning was not confined in the central period, as might at first be expected, to the wealthiest members of society, the socially and politically elite, but that many people of lesser rank and fortune, perhaps even those of minimal wealth, could also own at least a small number of slaves.

Other evidence tends to confirm this view. At times very large complements of slaves are heard of in literary sources – the 400 domestics of the senator L. Pedanius Secundus in the middle of the first century AD, the 400 slaves given to the sons of her first marriage by Pudentilla, wife of the littérateur Apuleius in the middle of the second century, the 4,116 slaves owned at the time of his death in 8 BC by the wealthy freedman C. Caecilius Isidorus, the 8,000 set free in the fifth century AD by the younger Melania when she took up a life of Christian asceticism. In all but one of these examples the number cited represents not the total number of slaves owned but only a proportion, and while three of the owners were from the upper reaches of society, and in Pudentilla's case upper-class provincial society, one had begun life as no more than a slave himself. An inscription (*ILS* 2927) reveals that the younger Pliny, who died early in the second century AD, provided in his will for the manumission and maintenance of 100 slaves, which implies that he owned at least 500. In contrast, however, C. Longinus Castor, a veteran of the Roman fleet at Misenum, provided in his will, which is known from a papyrus (*BGU* 326), for freeing only three slaves, two of whom were a mother and daughter. The will was made in the Egyptian village of Karanis in AD 189 and was opened a few years later. Although it names four other people who seem to be slaves, Longinus Castor's holdings were clearly not extensive. The niggardly moneylender Milo in Apuleius' *Metamorphoses* owned just one slave, the very capable Photis. From an upper-class perspective three slaves could be taken as an indication of their owner's poverty.[1]

---

[1] L. Pedanius Secundus: Tacitus, *Annales* 14.43. Pudentilla: Apuleius, *Apologia* 93. C. Caecilius Isidorus: Pliny, *Naturalis Historia* 33.135. Melania: Palladius, *Historia Lausiaca* 61. Photis: Ap. *Met.* 1.21; 1.22; 1.23. Cf. Plin. *Nat.* 7.54 on the cheap slave Serapio who once belonged to a pig-dealer. Poverty: Ap. *Apol.* 17.

Roman slaveholdings then were characterised by great numerical variation and owning slaves was typical of many levels of society. The same was true in the New World. A pattern of slave-ownership is apparent in fact which suggests that in the central period of its history Rome should properly be termed a 'slave society', a phrase that has a good deal of currency in slavery studies. But what does it mean to describe Rome this way? In what sense was Rome a slave society? These are the central questions of this chapter. To discuss them is to show at once how deeply embedded within the fabric of Roman society the institution of slavery always was.[2]

As a point of departure, three recent methods of determining a slave society may be considered. The first applies a demographic test. An arbitrary but sensible proportion of slaves in a given population can be postulated as a basic minimum for providing a significant source of economic power and for distinguishing a true slave society from a society in which some slaves have simply been present. A slave society consequently is 'a society in which slaves play an important part in production and form a high proportion (say over 20 per cent) of the population'. On this test only five genuine slave societies have existed in all of human history: Brazil, the Caribbean and the United States in the modern era, and Athens and Roman Italy (not the whole of the Roman empire) in classical antiquity. For Rome the fact that the servile proportion of the population of Italy in the time of Augustus can fairly be estimated at 35 per cent, a figure comparable to that for Brazil in 1800 and for the United States in 1820, is the crucial factor.[3]

The second method is qualitative. Since population estimates for antiquity can never be more than estimates (insufficient evidence has survived for accurate quantification or statistical extrapolation), what should be done when judging the role slaves played in a historical society is to determine their 'location'; that is, to determine 'who their owners were' and 'what role they played, in the economy but not only in the economy'. On this test as on the first the same five societies emerge as the only genuine slave societies in world history. But for classical Italy this time (again not the whole

[2] New World: Karasch 1987: 69–70; Fogel 1989: 184–6.
[3] Hopkins 1978: 99–102 (quotation, 99).

of the Roman empire) the reason is because 'slaves dominated, and virtually monopolized, large-scale production in both the country-side and the urban sector', thereby providing 'the bulk of the im-mediate income from property ... of the élites'. Mass ownership of slaves by upper-class Romans, like Pliny, and the extraction of great revenue from them are thus the key elements here.[4]

The third method is much broader than the others. Slavery in a strict sense, it is argued, is only one of many types of dependent labour that may be available for masters of the propertied classes to exploit – from which, that is to say, the wealthy may extract a surplus. There may be, for example, as there were in antiquity, debt bondage and serfdom, and all can be subsumed under the heading of 'unfree labour'. Accordingly because wealthy Romans drew most of their incomes from exploiting unfree labour in this general sense, it is possible to call their world a slave society or a slave economy, loosely at least – 'even though we have to concede that during a large part of ... Roman history peasants and other independent producers may not only have formed the actual ma-jority of the total population but may also have had a larger share ... in production than slaves and other unfree workers'.[5]

Whether in favour of Roman (classical) Italy or the greater Roman world, and despite the 'not only' qualifying phrase of the second approach, the choice these views allow is clearly to be made in economic terms, for it is concepts of production, income and extracting a surplus that predominate among them. Furthermore, if the choice settles on Roman Italy alone, description of Rome as a slave society has to be restricted not just regionally – only a fraction of the Roman world is involved – but chronologically too. On the first option Rome cannot be called a slave society before the middle of the third century BC, when acquisition of an overseas empire began, because the servile proportion of the total population was too small to meet the limit of demographic acceptability; it was only from the second century BC, when Rome was importing vast numbers of prisoners-of-war to Italy and Sicily in the wake of successful foreign wars, that the demographic test was met. On the 'location' method the restriction is less rigid but still present: Rome became a slave society 'not later than the third century BC', when

---

[4] Finley 1980: 9; 80–2; cf. 149 (quotations, 80–2).
[5] Ste Croix 1981: 52–3; 173; 209 (quotation, 209).

the necessary economic determinants – the concentration of land ownership by and among an elite, the availability of commodity markets, the lack of any alternative internal labour supply – had emerged. There is also, however, restriction at the opposite end of the time-scale: Rome was not a slave society in the later imperial period (that is, roughly speaking, from the time of Diocletian on), because 'slavery no longer dominated large-scale production in the countryside' in that era; 'large-scale production in the cities had been reduced to the state factories', it is said; 'slaves no longer provided the bulk of the property revenues of the élites'. With the third approach, moreover, there is the quite obvious danger that slavery in a strict sense will be lost to view given the vagueness of the notion of 'unfree labour'.[6]

It is natural, of course, to associate slavery with profit-making, especially in its New World manifestations, for in Brazil, the Caribbean and the United States production on the grand scale for sale on world markets of staple crops such as cotton, rice, tobacco, indigo and above all sugar, was the primary objective of those who owned slaves. But slaves have not always or exclusively been regarded by their owners as mere sources of compulsory labour and potential profit; rather they have often been kept as expressions of their owners' status and prestige, as for instance in nineteenth-century India, where slaves were owned for reasons that mostly had nothing to do with financial gain. The exercise of power for its own sake, the display of power and influence before one's peers, and the satisfaction of personal, inner demands have been just as important motives for owning slaves in past societies as the desire for additional wealth. When the elderly widower John Newsom of Calloway County, Missouri, purchased the fourteen-year-old slave girl Celia in 1850 to be his concubine – she bore him two children before she killed him – it was not thoughts of his economic well-being that were uppermost in his mind.[7]

The Romans were well aware of the concept of profit-making, as is shown by the practical guidance on obtaining good yields in cereal farming given, across a period of almost three hundred years, by the writers on agriculture Cato, Varro and Columella. The

---

[6] First option: Hopkins 1978: 9; 102. 'Location' method: Finley 1980: 83–6 (quotation, 83); cf. *CAH²* VII.2, 334; 413. Later imperial period: Finley 1980: 149 (quoted).
[7] India: Temperley 1972: 95. Exercise of power: Patterson 1982: 1–14. Celia: McLaurin 1991.

question articulated by Varro (*Res Rusticae* 1.2.8), 'whether the land would yield a fair return (*fructus*) for the investment in money and labour', was a question that all wealthy landowners would have asked themselves. They needed good yields and surpluses after all to provide some security against lean years, to ensure a supply of food for the rural workers on their estates and the domestics in their urban and leisure residences, and to make profitable sales in local markets. All the agricultural writers took the availability of slave labour for granted; the involvement of Roman slaves in primary production for their owners' financial advantage is thus beyond doubt.[8]

Yet it does not follow that landowners sought the greatest possible levels of profit from their possessions in the capitalistic manner of New World slaveowners. The aim of production was to provide food mostly for household and local needs, not to produce crops for sale on highly competitive world markets with profits automatically reinvested to increase yields and the margins of profit still further. Many slaves, moreover, were not directly involved in primary production at all. Domestic slaves furnished their owners with services that often had nothing to do with generating revenue; in fact domestics tended to consume wealth rather than produce it, and revenue-earners, slaves such as field hands, accountants, managers of apartment blocks, bailiffs, even doorkeepers and weavers, were distinguished from those who were kept simply for their owners' personal needs, cooks, bedroom attendants, masseurs and the like. The distinction drawn, however, was not prejudicial but reflective of the combination of values that motivated Roman slaveowning. The ostentatious slave retinues of Roman grandees that could be seen in Rome of the fourth century A D, fifty strong and drawn up in military style, were common enough to arouse the indignation of the historian Ammianus Marcellinus (14.6.16–17; 28.4.8–9), but they were equally effective in advertising their owners' social *éclat* (and there was nothing new about them). In a highly charged political and social environment such slaves were as essential to those who needed to maintain a competitive social profile as those who were more economically productive.[9]

To take a largely economic approach to Roman slavery, then,

---

[8] Yields and surpluses: Spurr 1986: 7.
[9] Distinguished: *Dig.* 50.16.203.

diverts attention from the broad cultural significance slavery held in Roman society at large, a point that can be highlighted by contrasting two formal definitions of slavery. The first comes from a League of Nations committee that in 1926 defined slavery as 'the status or condition of a person over whom any or all of the powers attaching to the right of ownership are exercised'. The second comes from a contemporary sociologist, who describes slavery as 'the permanent, violent domination of natally alienated and generally dishonored persons'. The two formulas are not altogether incompatible, but they differ significantly in orientation: the former, in stressing ownership of property implies that slavery must be principally understood as an economic institution; whereas the latter, in stressing the slave's subjection and isolation, suggests that slavery should be understood principally as a social relationship founded on the exercise of authority over an inferior party by a superior party. For Rome it is the second definition that has most relevance.[10]

Once Roman slavery is approached as a social institution in which the economic aspect, though important, was subsidiary, it becomes possible to appreciate the vast amount of time and space in which the Romans themselves were conscious of the presence of slavery among them and of the impact slavery made upon their culture. For early Roman history investigation is impeded by the lack of contemporary sources. But to judge from what can be reconstructed of the Twelve Tables, Rome's first codified body of law that traditionally belongs to the middle of the fifth century BC, the presence of slaves in the Roman community had quickly established itself as normative and was acknowledged institutionally long before the dates at which modern historians are prepared to identify Rome as a slave society.[11]

The Twelve Tables are known only from excerpts preserved in authors who lived much later than the fifth century, but the details on slavery that they preserve are highly suggestive. First there is a provision that if an ex-slave, a freedman, died intestate and had no

---

[10] League of Nations: Patterson 1982: 21. Contemporary sociologist: Patterso.. 1982: 13. Cf. Blackburn 1988.
[11] Twelve Tables: see Watson 1975: 3–4 and, in general, *CAH*[2] VII.2, 125–6; 209. Note, however, the reservations of Harris 1989: 151–3, and see Harris 1990 on the fourth century BC.

heir, his former owner, who was now his patron, was to collect his estate. For present purposes the vital phrase in this provision is 'the freedman Roman citizen', because it reveals that the capacity both for a slave to be set free and to become part of the citizen community had been created at an early date. Moreover, manumission was available to male and female slaves. A second provision stipulates that a person ordered to be set free in a will on payment of a cash sum to an heir shall be set free even if the heir alienates the slave, provided that the money is paid to the third party. It makes clear the antiquity of the procedure of setting slaves free through testamentary instruction of course, but it also shows that setting a slave free – which is assumed to be a normal occurrence – was not necessarily regarded as a disinterested act of generosity on the part of the testator but rather as a diminution of the heir's estate (or that of a third party) for which reparation had to be made. Thirdly, the rules on thieves caught in the act of stealing lay down that while a free criminal was to be flogged and handed over to the injured party, a slave offender was to be flogged and then executed. A distinction was thus drawn between the worth of a free person and the worth of a slave, obviously to the disadvantage of the latter, an attitude that is seen too in the rule that physical injury to a free person was to have a higher compensatory value than injury to a slave. Finally a sort of religious taboo against slaves seems indicated by the directive that slaves were forbidden to anoint corpses.[12]

Historians agree that the laws of the Twelve Tables were generally not innovative but reflected the customary law of early Rome. The rules just itemised therefore must be taken to mirror aspects of Roman life well in evidence before the middle of the fifth century B C. Moreover, they are predicated on sophisticated conceptual developments, for it is not axiomatic when slaves are present in a given society that means of release from slavery have to emerge, or that the punishment of criminal slaves has to be inherently different from that of free persons guilty of the same crimes, or that slaves must be barred from interfering with burial practices. These ideas seem in fact to indicate in early Rome a critical mass of slaves whose presence was substantial enough to warrant or command methods of treatment appropriate to their inferior social character,

[12] *XII Tabulae* 5.8; 6.1d; 8.14; 8.3; 10.6a. See also 2.1; 5.4–5; 5.8; 11.2a–b.

as it was perceived by others, and the institutionalisation in law of
customary behaviour likewise requires the postulate of a culturally
significant servile element in the early Roman community. The size
of the slave population in fifth-century Rome cannot be determined. But the question of numbers may not be as important as
recognising the institutional devices by which those numbers were
regulated when the place of slavery in Roman society is assessed.
The legal form of conveyance known as *mancipatio*, an imaginary
sale carried out before witnesses by striking ceremonial scales with
a bronze token, is believed to be as old as the Twelve Tables; it
cannot be insignificant that slaves were one of the small number of
items subject to the formality.[13]

The notion that institutions will mark the structural importance
of slavery in a slaveowning society can be taken further by looking
briefly at two aspects of Rome's religious history, in which slaves
again appear to have prompted formal acknowledgement of their
presence at an early date. First there is the ban that was laid
against the participation of slave women in the Matralia, a
women's festival that was held annually in historical times on 11
June – except that during the ceremony a slave girl was ritually
beaten by and then expelled from the company of the free worship-
pers. When the ban and the ritual expulsion originated is beyond
knowledge. But it may well be that they are as old as 400 BC, at
about which date a major redevelopment of the temple of the
goddess Mater Matuta, the principal deity of the Matralia, took
place. Secondly, notice can also be taken of a festival that was
simply called the 'Slave Women's Festival' (*ancillarum feriae*), which
again in historical times was celebrated each year on 7 July. The
traditional explanation of the festival was that it had been instituted to honour a group of slave women who early in the fourth
century had saved the city from external assault. This cannot be
verified precisely, but there is no doubt about the great antiquity of
the festival itself. What is evident and important in both examples,
however, is a primitive religious institutionalisation of a slave
presence that complements the legal evidence.[14]

Cicero recorded (*de Legibus* 2.59) that when he and his brother

---

[13] *Mancipatio*: Gaius, *Inst.* 1.119–22; 2.102–7. Cf. the account of *vindicatio* at Gaius, *Inst.* 4.16.
[14] Matralia: Ovid, *Fasti* 6.551–8; Plutarch, *Camillus* 5.2; *Quaestiones Romanae* 16–17; see
Coarelli 1988: 244–53. Redevelopment: Coarelli 1988: 211. 'Slave Women's Festival':
Plut. *Cam.* 33; *Romulus* 29; Macrobius, *Saturnalia* 1.11.36; see Robertson 1987.

were boys they learned the Twelve Tables by heart as a school exercise. So presumably did many of their contemporaries. It was impossible therefore for Romans of the central period looking back at the early history of their city to conceive of a Rome in which the master-slave relationship had never existed, unless in a semi-mythical past, for it was as natural as the other key relationships in their midst. If they consequently assumed that slavery had played an important part in the early history of Rome they were probably right. Moreover, had they or their contemporaries looked to the future they would hardly have anticipated the 'decline' of slavery that some modern historians have seen in later Roman history, having no reason to expect any substantive change in social structure and social relations. From a mass of evidence, two examples are enough to show the durability of slavery in the later Roman empire.[15]

First, the surviving portion of the history of Ammianus Marcellinus, which covers the third quarter of the fourth century A D, makes clear the vital presence of slavery in the Roman world of that time. Much of the work is given over to long accounts of Rome's wars against foreign forces, and the enslavement of prisoners-of-war is a ubiquitous feature of them, on the part of Rome and of its enemies. Describing the siege of Amida in A D 359, for instance, Ammianus speaks (19.6.2) of the thousands of captives he himself saw the Persians taking into slavery from the centres they had destroyed:

Among them were many feeble old men and aged women. When their strength gave out for various reasons under the hardships of the long march and they lost any desire to live, their calves or hams were severed and they were left behind.

But in a sequence of incidental details, slaves are also seen fulfilling traditional domestic roles, exhibiting both loyalty and disloyalty to their owners at moments of crisis, being put to the torture for evidence in political trials, being punished for trivial offences, being set free in the Circus at Constantinople. The contexts hardly differ from those visible in earlier Roman historians. What is most telling, however, is Ammianus' casual comment (31.2.25) that among the

---

[15] Semi-mythical past: *Dig.* 1.1.4; see Plin. *Nat.* 36.204, the story of the miraculous impregnation of the captive slave Ocresia, the mother of Servius Tullius. 'Decline': see for discussion, Finley 1980: 123–49.

Alans, a people living on the fringe of the Roman world on the Russian steppe, slavery did not exist: for the simple statement reveals how odd the absence of slavery was to an observer whose social frame of reference had never excluded it.[16]

Secondly, the year A D 533, although a late date in Roman history by conventional standards, is memorable as the year in which the *Digest* was published. The work was inspired by the wish of the emperor Justinian to have available for contemporary use a synthesis of classical Roman juristic writings from which all that was obsolete had been excised. That is to say, only what was relevant to the present was to be included. The *Digest* is a work of excerpts, but the amount of detail it contains is staggering and can be explained only on the assumption that the compilers were responding to a genuine need for practical, informed guidance in the dispensation of justice. A number of simple quotations will show that the law of slavery is as complex as any other area of law treated. The fortieth book, for instance, is concerned exclusively with manumission and other ways in which the slave might acquire freedom. Divided into various subsections, it deals with manumission during the slave-owner's lifetime, testamentary manumission, conditional release from slavery, how claims for freedom might be made by the slave, and so on. The following extracts are taken solely from the section on testamentary manumission:

If freedom has been left to the slave in the following terms, 'let Stichus my slave be free in the twelfth year after my death', it is plausible that he is to be free from the beginning of the twelfth year, that being the intention of the deceased. There is a great difference, usually observed in our language, between the phrases 'in the twelfth year' and 'after twelve years'. It is the twelfth year when the smallest part of the twelfth year has come or passed, and if a man's freedom is ordered in the twelfth year it is ordered for every day of that year. (*Dig.* 40.4.41 pr.)

Aristo replied to Neratius Priscus that when a man was ordered by will to be free at the age of thirty and was condemned to penal labour in the mines before reaching that age and subsequently recalled, a legacy made to him along with his freedom undoubtedly belonged to him and that his right was not altered by the penal sentence; so, too, if he had been

---

[16] Details: Amm. Marc. 19.6.1–2; 14.1.7; 14.6.23; 14.11.16; 16.8.8; 16.8.9; 19.9.4; 21.16.6; 22.7.2; 28.1.55; 28.4.16; see Matthews 1989: 57–66; 334–7; 405. Absence of slavery: cf. Plin. *Nat.* 6.89 on Ceylon.

instituted heir conditionally; for he would even be the *heres necessarius.* (*Dig.* 40.4.46)

A man who had a slave Cratistus provided in his will: 'Let my slave Cratinus be free'; could the slave Cratistus attain freedom, when the testator had not a slave Cratinus but only one called Cratistus? He replied that the mistake of a syllable was no bar. (*Dig.* 40.4.54 pr.)

Similarly the eleventh book contains a section on corrupting a slave. These items are typical of its contents:

One also makes a slave worse if one persuades him to commit an injury or theft, to run away, to incite another man's slave, to mismanage his *peculium*, to become a lover, to play truant, to practise evil arts, to spend too much time at public entertainments, or to become seditious; or if by argument or bribe, one persuades a slave-agent to tamper with or falsify his master's accounts, or to confuse accounts entrusted to him; or if one makes a slave extravagant or defiant; or persuades him to be debauched. (*Dig.* 11.3.1.5–11.3.2)

An owner manumitted a slave-steward, and subsequently received the accounts from him; since they did not balance, he discovered that the slave had spent the money on a woman who was not very reputable. The question was asked whether the owner could sue the woman for making a slave worse, when the slave in question was now a free man. I replied that he could, but he could also sue for theft in respect of the money which the slave had handed over to her. (*Dig.* 11.3.16)

The fact that there was need in late antiquity to preserve law of this sort, and in considerable bulk, is evidence enough of the continuing vigour of slavery, even if some allowance has to be made for over-enthusiasm on the part of the compilers. It is in the later imperial period that much is heard of course of the colonate, a form of dependent labour that lowered the status of free peasants almost to the level of slaves; but whatever the extent of the depression of the peasantry, there are no grounds for assuming that the colonate simply replaced slavery. The link between slaveowning in the Roman empire and slaveowning in the early mediaeval world was direct and uninterrupted.[17]

---

[17] Colonate: see for discussion, Ste Croix 1981: 158–60; 249–55; Whittaker 1987. On the social visibility of slavery in post-Diocletianic Egypt, see Bagnall 1993.

If the profile of slavery appears to be relatively high in the two historical eras that act as bookends to the central period of Roman history, the same is true when the growth of Roman power within the four centuries of the central epoch itself is considered from a regional point of view.

When Cato wrote his agricultural manual in the early second century BC, Rome was only one of several major forces in Mediterranean politics. Effective political control over much of peninsular Italy had been acquired, and in the aftermath of two long wars against the Carthaginians an overseas empire had begun to arise. But as yet Roman influence in the Mediterranean was limited. By the time of Augustus, however, the complexion of the Mediterranean world had altered drastically. After two centuries of more or less continuous military expansion Rome came to control an empire of enormous dimensions that ranged from the English Channel to the littoral of North Africa, including Egypt, and from the Pillars of Hercules (Gibraltar) to the Euphrates. It was only across this river, the border between the Roman province of Syria and the empire of the Parthians, that Rome could see any possible rival to its power. In the two hundred years or so after Augustus' death the conquests of the Republican era were consolidated and marginally increased, as a period of peacefulness and stability generally prevailed in Mediterranean affairs. But by the time of Ammianus Marcellinus the complexion of the Roman world had radically changed again. Once more, warfare was endemic but now, under great pressures on its frontiers, Rome laboured to conserve rather than ornament its empire. From a slavery perspective, what is significant in this long process of expansion, consolidation and incipient decline is that wherever Rome went in the Mediterranean world, its representatives either encountered local forms of slaveowning or took with them their own slaveowning practices or both. (And not the least consequential of local slaveowning practices were those of the Greeks.) The result was that geographically as well as chronologically slavery was always an integral element of Roman civilisation and experience.

Consider in this connection, for instance, the remarks of the historian Tacitus (*Germania* 25), written about AD 100, on slavery among the Germanic tribes of northern Europe:

Slaves in general do not have particular duties about the house and estate allotted to them, as our slaves do. Each has control of a holding and a home of his own. The master demands from him a stated quantity of grain, live-stock, or cloth, as he would from a tenant ... To flog a slave, or to punish him by imprisonment and hard labour, is very unusual; yet to kill one outright is quite common.

Tacitus also mentions (*Ger.* 24; 38) the Germans' willingness to sell themselves into slavery to pay off gambling debts and, speaking of the Suebi in particular, details the difference in hairstyle maintained between masters and slaves. To the historian it was of interest to compare and contrast Roman and regional slaveowning practices; but it was not at all remarkable that slavery itself should have been met in Germanic society.[18]

Or take again the report of Tacitus' contemporary the younger Pliny (*Epistulae* 10.74) of a Roman slave who claimed to have been taken prisoner during the first war of the emperor Trajan against the Dacians and sent as a gift by the Dacian king Decebalus to Pacorus, the king of Parthia. The report was written to Trajan himself early in the second century when Pliny was governor of the province of Bithynia-Pontus. The slave was a certain Callidromus, who belonged originally to M'. Laberius Maximus, a figure of some consequence whose exploits in the Dacian war earned him the honour of a second consulship in A D 103. After several years in Parthian hands Callidromus eventually escaped and made his way to Nicomedia in Bithynia, where he entered the service of two bakers. It was as a result of a problem with these men that he came to Pliny's attention.[19]

Because it sounds far-fetched the story of Callidromus has been doubted. However, in the entry in the *Digest* on *postliminium*, the recovery of Roman citizen rights by a former prisoner-of-war, it is taken for granted by the jurists that a slave might find himself transported as a captive from one region of the ancient world to another, and that a slave might escape from enemy detention and return to Rome on his own initiative. Callidromus' story therefore may not be as preposterous as it seems on the surface. The significant point, however, is that Pliny did not doubt the plausibility of an exchange between two kings of a slave being detained in enemy hands for several years. The legal rules on *postliminium* show in fact

[18] Germanic tribes: see Thompson 1957.
[19] M'. Laberius Maximus: see Syme 1988: 508.

that it was common for all peoples to convert captives into slaves, the assumption being that slavery was universal, or near-universal, in the ancient world. To a conventional observer, indeed, the renunciation of slavery by the Essenes in the first century A D was yet another bizarre feature of an unusual religious community.[20]

The cultural and institutional visibility of slavery at Rome, across time and space, implies that for slaveowners slaveowning was a never failing source of personal advantage. The social and economic benefits that accrued to owners derived from their almost limitless abilities to control and coerce human property. From a legal point of view the Latin words for power (*potestas*) and slave-ownership (*dominium*) could be regarded as synonymous, which means that, above all, slaveowning was an expression of power. Two ceremonial events that in the nature of things were common occurrences illustrate what was involved.[21]

The Roman triumph, first, was a spectacular ceremony that honoured a general victorious in war against a foreign enemy. Essentially it consisted of an elaborate parade that made its way through the streets of Rome, starting from the Campus Martius and culminating at the Capitol where sacrifices of thanksgiving were made to Jupiter. Apart from the senate and magistrates, the procession was made up of the victorious general and his army, who displayed to the crowds of onlookers the spoils of war they had taken and representations of the cities they had captured and territories they had conquered. Customarily too the procession included prisoners-of-war, some of whom might be withdrawn and executed before or as the ceremony concluded, no matter what their rank. So the Numidian prince Jugurtha was put to death following the triumph of C. Marius on the first day of January, 104 B C, whereas it was quite unusual when Pompey (Cn. Pompeius) gave orders that none of his captives was to be killed in his triumph of 61 B C. The prisoners were slaves, symbols of Roman power and invincibility whose very lives now lay in the hands of their conquerors, a sorry contrast to the Roman soldiers also in the procession who had

---

[20] Doubted: Sherwin-White 1966: 662–3. *Postliminium*: *Dig.* 49.15.27; 49.15.30. Rules: *Dig.* 49.15.19 pr.; 49.15.24. Cf. Tac. *Ann.* 12.27, Romans recovered from forty years of enslavement in Germany. Essenes: Brown 1988: 39.

[21] Legal point of view: *Dig.* 50.16.215.

been liberated – brought back to life, as it were – from enemy enslavement.[22]

It was also customary, secondly, for newly manumitted slaves to appear in the funeral processions that preceded interment or cremation of the dead. They were in fact slaves who had just been set free in accordance with the wishes of their former owners. The idea was that by appearing in the ceremony as free men and citizens – and again, especially in the case of the elite, the processions could be very elaborate affairs – they would be seen to be living proof of the dead slaveowner's generosity and would ensure that he was well-remembered in the community. Dionysius of Halicarnassus, writing in the late first century BC, complained vigorously (4.24.6) that the practice had become excessive in his day. The most telling point of the practice, however, was that for a few moments in time the almost miraculous capacity of the individual slaveowner to convert the powerless to a state of independence was clear to all who witnessed the passing of his cortege.[23]

In effect, therefore, the power that lay at the disposal of the Roman slaveowner was the power of life and death, and slavery itself was viewed in many ways as a state of living death. The idea is apparent in a number of sources, especially legal texts for instance: 'slavery is equated with death', Ulpian (*Dig.* 35.1.59.2) declared categorically, as if the connection needed no explanation, and again: 'In every branch of the law, a person who fails to return from enemy hands is regarded as having died at the moment when he was captured' (*Dig.* 49.15.18). Ulpian was writing at the close of the central period but the sentiment was by no means unique to his generation. The statement, 'We compare slavery closely with death', appears in a section of the *Digest* (50.17.209) headed *Various Rules of Ancient Law*, and a ruling of Justinian's, that the marriage of a freed person came to an end if reenslavement occurred, just as if death had intervened, continued the association into the Byzantine age. The association was based on the view that slavery originated in warfare:

Slaves (*servi*) are so-called, because generals have a custom of selling their prisoners and thereby *preserving* rather than killing them: and indeed they

---

[22] Triumph: see Versnel 1970: 95–6. Jugurtha: Livy, *Periochae* 67; Plut. *Marius* 12.3. Cn. Pompeius: Appian, *Mithridatica* 117.
[23] Funeral processions: see Toynbee 1971: 46–8.

are said to be *mancipia*, because they are *captives* in the hand (*manus*) of their enemies. (*Dig.* 1.5.4.2)

The victor in battle had the right to kill the vanquished. If, however, the victor spared the vanquished and enslaved him instead, the latter continued to live, but only in a condition of suspended death at the discretion of the former. The slave's very identity, in fact, now depended on his owner. This was the source of the slave-owner's power.[24]

Slaveowners learned the habit of commanding authority at an early age. In schools for example the children of prosperous families were given language exercises as part of their curriculum depicting scenes from everyday life (they were called *colloquia*), which as they were studied and practised transmitted from generation to generation the cultural norm of wielding power over dependants and inferiors. The process was indirect and unconscious but effective. In one recently published example a *colloquium* shows a boy rising in the morning and going off to school, studying for several hours with his teachers and then returning home for lunch. It assumes that the boy will have a string of personal attendants to cater to his needs – someone to dress him, someone to help him wash, someone to feed him, someone to take care of his school supplies – and it assumes that he is already perfectly used to instructing his servants in their duties, even to the extent of using the humiliating form of address Roman slaveowners commonly used of their slaves: 'Get up, boy, see if it's light yet: open the door and window'; 'Give me that; hold out my shoes, unfold my best clothes and put my playclothes away. Hand me my cloak and mantle'; 'Take some clean water to your master my brother, so that he can go with me to school'. Reinforcing, presumably, what had already been observed, absorbed and inculcated at home, the school exercises helped establish in children a structure of authority and an expectation of the capacity, even the right, to give orders that would remain with them for the rest of their lives.[25]

---

[24] Ruling: *Iustiniani Novellae* 22.9, 'tamquam morte secuta'. Cf. Tac. *Ann.* 2.15; Amm. Marc. 31.8.8. Identity: see Varro, *de Lingua Latina* 8.21 on the slaveowner's prerogative of naming the slave. Source: on slavery as a form of social death in general, see Patterson 1982.

[25] Recently published example: see Dionisotti 1982, pointing out (93) that for slaveowners much of the daily routine in antiquity 'could consist of telling others what to do rather than doing it oneself'. Attendants: *nutrix, nutritor, capsarius, scrinarius, paedagogus* are the terms used; cf. Bradley 1991: 13–75. Form of address: *Dig.* 50.16.204.

For slaves, in contrast, the consequence of living in a state of suspended death was that they could claim no human rights or privileges of any kind. By definition slaves were kinless and were permitted no legally sanctioned familial bonds. Nor could they own property of any kind. In reality of course some slaves reproduced, at times perhaps with the open encouragement of their owners (the benefits were often obvious), but the slaveowner was under no obligation to respect any quasi-familial ties that may have come into being among them. It was common too for many slaves to have a *peculium*, property in kind or cash at their effective disposal; but its contents, strictly speaking, always belonged to the master and were revocable at any time. To live in slavery, accordingly, was to be utterly disempowered.[26]

Enslaved prisoners-of-war, moreover, were also degraded – demoted that is in a quite literal sense from a state of freedom to a state of servitude. The prevalent Roman attitude was that the downward move was shaming, so that socially low and morally low became one and the same. The degraded slave was the symbol therefore of all that was abject and without honour. In the formula of M. Brutus, the assassin of Julius Caesar, it was possible to live honourably at Rome without exercising authority over others but to be a slave to anyone was not to be alive at all. Merely to label someone or something servile or slavish was to project the disgrace of slavery, and the demeanour of the slave was to be avoided at all costs. Thus Quintilian, towards the end of the first century AD, warned the aspiring orator not to give himself a slavish aspect: 'It is, as a rule, unbecoming to raise or contract the shoulders. For it shortens the neck and produces a mean and servile gesture, which is even suggestive of dishonesty when men assume an attitude of flattery, admiration or fear' (*Institutio Oratoria* 11.3.83). True, not all Roman slaves began their lives in freedom. But as the descendants of those who had once been captured and enslaved they inherited, as a matter of course, their forebears' degradation.[27]

---

[26] Familial bonds: see Varro *L.* 9.59; in practice it was impossible to deny that they existed altogether; see *Dig.* 2.4.4.3; 40.4.24, with Bradley 1987a: 47–80. Nor could slaves be completely prevented from participating in religious activities; indeed, in some contexts they worshipped together with the free. For the suggestion that, although there was no such thing as a slave religion *per se*, slaves tended in the west to favour divinities such as Silvanus and the Lares, see Bömer (1957). *Peculium*: see Bradley 1987a: 108–9.

[27] M. Brutus: Quint. *Inst.* 9.3.95.

The rightlessness and degradation of the slave were made manifest in countless ways, but particularly through sexual exploitation and physical abuse. Quintilian (*Inst.* 5.11.34–35) took the following statements as examples of opposing rhetorical arguments:

If sexual intercourse with a male slave is shameful for a female slaveowner, so is sexual intercourse with a female slave for a male slaveowner.

It is not the same for a male slaveowner to have sexual intercourse with a female slave as it is for a female slaveowner to have sexual intercourse with a male slave.

Underlying the arguments is a preoccupation with the moral evaluation of male and female behaviour in a patriarchal society that from its upper-class male perspective betrays the slaveowner's fear of finding his wife or daughter seduced by his slave (a possibility that could never be discounted in a society where body-slaves were ubiquitous). But it is taken without question that slaves can and do become objects of sexual gratification for both the men and women who own them. It is one of the prerogatives of ownership and the servile response is scarcely worth considering. To the emperor Marcus Aurelius it was a source of spiritual satisfaction that he had not taken sexual advantage of two slaves he identifies (*Meditationes* 1.17) as Benedicta and Theodotus when it had clearly been in his power to do so; his attitude was remarkable but not the situation which prompted it.[28]

Likewise with physical maltreatment: in a treatise called 'On the Passions and Errors of the Soul', written in the late second century AD, the philosopher and doctor Galen gave advice against reacting in haste to the loss of temper. He told how as a young man he had taken a vow not to strike his slaves with his hand, and of how his father, similarly minded, had reproved people for bruising tendons when striking their slaves in the mouth in the heat of anger: 'They could have waited a little while, he said, and used a rod or whip to inflict as many blows as they wished and to accomplish the act with reflection.' There was nothing untoward in abusing a slave, only in doing so in an uncalculated and undisciplined fashion. Galen continued with remarks on how common it was for slaves to be punched with the fists, to be kicked, to have their eyes put out, on how he himself had once seen a man stab a slave in the eye with a

[28] A possibility: see Hopkins 1993. Sexual gratification: see in general, Kolendo 1981.

reed pen in a fit of anger, and on how his own mother had been so quick to lose her temper that it had been her habit to bite her maidservants. His remarks are disturbing but their accuracy is not in doubt, as all manner of evidence indicates. To Galen's contemporary Artemidorus, a specialist in explaining the meaning of dreams, it was natural for example to take a slave's dream of dancing as a sign that the slave would soon be flogged, because beating was so common a servile experience that no other interpretation of the image of a writhing body was possible (*Onirocriticus* 1.76). Again, Plutarch (*Moralia* 8F) could support his point that physical blows were more suitable for slaves than the free by appealing to the common fact that a beating reduced the slave to an abject state. Artemidorus, it can be noted, was prepared to allow slaves their own dreams, though this was a luxury that some slaveowners denied. Pliny once claimed (*Ep.* 7.27.12–14) that he had narrowly evaded persecution from the tyrannous emperor Domitian, but a sign that he would remain unharmed had been given in dreams that a slave and former slave of his had experienced: their hair had been cut during the night by mysterious intruders, the connection being that it was common for those accused of crime to let their hair grow. Pliny appropriated the slaves' dream to himself. It did not occur to him to ask if it could have meant anything for those who had actually dreamed it.[29]

Powerlessness and isolation, rightlessness and degradation were the hallmarks of servitude, permitting slaveowners to use their slave possessions for whatever purposes they chose. In everyday reality the management and manipulation of human property demanded recognition of the property's human character. But the right to enslave and to keep enslaved was taken as axiomatic in Roman society, and in a milieu in which civic freedom was not looked upon as naturally available to all, slaveowning served constantly to validate and enhance the status of those who were free. From a cultural point of view, therefore, slavery was at no time an incidental feature of Roman social organisation and at no time an inconsequential element of Roman mentality.

At the end of the first century BC the servile population of the

---

[29] Physical maltreatment: see in general, Bradley 1987a: 113–37; Saller 1991: 151–65. Galen: *de Animi Passionibus* 1.4; 1.8. Natural: see also Artem. *Onir.* 2.25. Hair: cf. Artem. *Onir.* 1.22; Sherwin-White 1966: 437.

Roman heartland lay, according to modern estimates, in the order of two to three millions, representing 33–40 per cent of the total population. Most slaves were probably involved in agriculture. Thus if the phrase 'slave society' or 'slave economy' is best reserved for those historical contexts in which slaves have played an extra-ordinarily prominent role in primary production, Roman Italy of the first century BC and first century AD was a genuine slave society – but to the exclusion of other time-periods and regions embraced by Roman history and culture since a comparable slave population never appeared elsewhere. It is difficult, however, to find any period or region affected by Rome in which slaveowning did not function as a means of demonstrating power and domination. The attitudes and habits of mind evident when the slave economy of Roman Italy was at its height long antedated and long outlasted that economy's chronological and territorial limits. The distinction, moreover, between a genuine slave society and a society in which some slaves have simply been present is a modern, not a Roman, distinction, and it is a construct that can result in a certain narrowness of vision. To the extent that owning slaves always served to express *potestas* in a society highly sensitive to gradations of status, esteem and authority, Rome was always a slave society.[30]

[30] Modern estimates: Brunt 1971: 124; Hopkins 1978: 102. Roman Italy: note Plin. *Nat.* 37.201: slaves still one of Italy's greatest resources in the first century AD.

CHAPTER 3

The Roman slave supply

When seeking an example of a lowly category of men whose failure to recognise and greet him the philosopher should bear with equanimity, the younger Seneca thought naturally (*de Constantia* 13.4) of the slavedealers who plied their trade near the Temple of Castor in the Roman Forum. The choice was appropriate enough, for as in later history slavedealers were notorious in antiquity for their sharp business practices and unscrupulous devotion to profiteering.[1]

But what especially catches the attention in Seneca's observation is the reference to a particular spot in the heart of the city that was known as the place for slaveowners to go when they wished to buy new slaves. It was not the only spot where slaves were available: if for example buyers had something exotic in mind the upscale shops of the Saepta Julia were the place to look. But the shops of the dealers in the Forum teemed with slaves – slaves of the meanest sort, the *pessimi*, Seneca called them – and his readers were clearly expected to be familiar with the fact. Men of Seneca's station of course would not always have had the time or inclination to scout the market themselves. Advice from friends acting as agents would then come into play. But where did the merchandise itself come from when slaveowners were ready to buy? In taking that question as a point of departure, I discuss in this chapter first the means by which the slave supply of Rome was maintained and secondly the impact made by the operations of supply on the lives of the slaves concerned. The lack of quantifiable evidence means that the starting question can only be answered impressionistically. But a sense of the scale of what was involved derives from the estimates that for

---

[1] Later history: Karasch 1987: 39. Notorious: *Dig.* 21.1.44.1; cf. Bradley 1987a: 115–16. Much of this chapter is derived from Bradley 1987b; see also Bradley 1989: 20–6; 68–71; 91.

the generation from about 65 B C to about 30 B C 100,000 new slaves were needed each year in Italy and that from about 50 B C to A D 150 more than 500,000 new slaves were needed every year for the empire as a whole. In contrast, in the three and a half centuries of New World slavery, the annual average of Africans transported to the Americas has been calculated at about 28,000, with an annual peak average of 60,000 when the African slave trade was at its height.[2]

The reduction to slavery of enemies defeated in warfare was one of the principal mechanisms by which Rome provided itself with slaves in the central period of its history. In the last two centuries of the Republic, fighting against external enemies was more or less continuous, and although Rome's armies met defeat from time to time the overall rate of success was so high that most of the Mediterranean fell subject to its control. The sheer efficiency of the Roman military machine cannot be denied. Under the Principate the militaristic ethos of Rome was no longer able to express itself in unlimited expansionist warfare because opportunities for conquest on the grand scale no longer existed without shifting the empire's Mediterranean focus or unduly straining resources. Even so, warfare was by no means completely absent in the second half of the central period, so that at all times outlying regions of the Roman world were producing captives who could become new slaves. Sometimes warfare produced slaves closer to home. In the Social War (91–88 B C) a certain M. Aurius of Larinum was captured at Asculum and soon found himself in the possession of the Roman senator, Q. Sergius; his family later learned that he was working as a slave in the *ager Gallicus* on the northern Adriatic coast.[3]

Much is heard in the sources of enslaving a vanquished enemy *en masse*, a habit the Romans probably acquired as their military and

[2] Saepta Julia: Martial 9.59. Agents: see Plin. *Ep.* 1.21.2, where Pliny writes to an associate, like himself a native of Comum, 'I think the slaves you advised me to buy look all right, but it remains to be seen if they are honest; and here one can't go by a slave's looks, but rather by what one hears of him.' Estimates: Crawford 1977: 123; Harris 1980: 118. New World: Curtin 1969: 265; Gwyn 1992: 152–3, summarising the revisions of Eltis 1987: 241–54: 'Between 1781 and 1867, some 4,486,700 slaves – about 40 per cent of the estimated overall number of slaves involved in the Atlantic slave trade – were imported from Africa into the Americas. This was an average of 51,600 every year, from a high of 81,400 a year in the 1780s to 77,000 in the 1790s, 60,900 in 1801–1810, 53,400 in 1811–1820, 59,500 in the 1820s, 55,200 in the 1830s, 43,300 in the 1840s, 14,100 in the 1850s, to less than 3,800 a year from 1861.'
[3] M. Aurius: Cic. *pro Cluentio* 21. Cf. Syme 1979: 288.

political influence spiralled throughout the Italian peninsula in the fourth and early third centuries BC. In the early fourth century the Romans are said to have reduced to slavery the entire population of the rival Etruscan city of Veii, an event whose historicity is open to debate but which may have produced as many as 10,000 slaves. For later periods, however, less contentious information is at hand, revealing that once acquired the habit of mass enslavement was never broken: thus in 256 BC during the first war against Carthage the siege of Aspis in Carthage's territory was followed by the enslavement of more than 20,000 captives; in 146 BC when Carthage was destroyed after a third war, 55,000 people were enslaved; in 25 BC after a ruthless campaign against the Salassi, an Alpine tribe, Rome sold 44,000 prisoners into slavery; and in AD 198 the emperor Septimius Severus took 100,000 prisoners after reducing the city of Ctesiphon in his war against the Parthians. The connection between warfare and slavery at Rome was never broken.[4]

It does not follow, however, that all war captives were automatically conveyed from the site of capture for disposal in the marketplaces of the Roman heartland. At times Roman commanders allowed prisoners to be ransomed, so freedom might be recovered fairly quickly if relatives or friends were available to pay the necessary price. Likewise captives were often sold off on the spot to itinerant dealers or distributed to the troops as a form of payment or bonus. Their ultimate destination might still have been Italy, but for the dealers there were many other markets in the Mediterranean, including local ones, in which to sell their property. Nevertheless, it remains true that warfare always provided numbers of new slaves – at times very substantial numbers – though in haphazard and spasmodic fashion.[5]

A second major means of supply was natural reproduction among the existing slave population. Slaves born of slave women took their status from their mother (that of the father was irrelevant) and were known as *vernae*. They had a certain *cachet* that distinguished them from enslaved prisoners and they often identified themselves as home-born as a result: so for instance the slave Abascantus described himself on a tombstone for his prematurely

---

[4] Veii: Liv. 5.22.1; see Harris 1990: 498. Aspis: Polybius 1.29.7. Carthage: Orosius 4.23. Salassi: Strabo 4.6.7; Cassius Dio 53.25.4. Ctesiphon: Dio 75.9.4.
[5] Ransomed: Liv. 34.50.3–7; Plut. *Flamininus* 13.3–6. Sold off: Liv. 39. 42.1; 41.11.7–8; Str. 7.7.3 = Polyb. 30.15(16). Distributed: Caesar, *de Bello Gallico* 7.89.

dead son (*ILS* 1537) as 'a home-born slave of the emperor', in contrast to his wife Carpine who simply gave her single name. Galen indeed noted the opinion (*de Sanitate Tuenda* 2.1) that only war captives were true slaves. To the slaveowner *vernae* may have seemed generally less intractable than other slaves, given that they were born and grew up in slavery and knew no other condition. Certainly they had to be maintained through infancy and childhood but the costs they imposed on owners may well have been worthwhile. Cicero's friend Atticus is said to have used only *vernae* for his domestic servants, but how typical his practice was it is impossible to tell.[6]

One indication of the prominence of natural reproduction as a method of supply is the frequency with which references appear in legal sources to the technical problems posed by the offspring of slave women (*partus ancillarum*). For example it was common for slaves to be left as legacies when their owners died, but was the unborn child of a pregnant woman to be included with her if she were bequeathed? The jurist Julian answered that question emphatically (*Dig.* 30.84.10): 'the offspring goes with the mother and belongs to the legacy', even in the case of a woman who had run away from her owner. Again, Papinian pointed out (*Dig.* 23.3.69.9) that because the offspring of slave women given as dowry formed part of the dowry too, 'a pact with the husband to the effect that such offspring are to be held in common between him and his wife is void'. In rendering judgements of this kind the jurists were responding to the complications of childbearing by women who were not supposed to exist as human beings. But having children could bring slaves certain benefits in real terms. Columella believed (*de Re Rustica* 1.8.19) that female slaves should be rewarded for bearing children and said that he himself had given a mother of three time off from work and a mother of more than three children her freedom as well. There are, however, no accurate figures for the female slave population in any particular place or time, so the rate of natural reproduction among Roman slaves cannot be measured.[7]

Vernae, nevertheless, were conspicuous in the slave population at large and from time to time some achieved real celebrity.

---

[6] *Vernae*: see in general, Rawson 1986: 186–95. Atticus: Cornelius Nepos, *Atticus* 13.4.

[7] Frequency: see for some other instances, *Dig.* 5.3.27 pr.; 18.1.8 pr.; 18.1.31; 18.2.4.1; 20.1.15 pr.; 33.8.8.8; 41.3.4.5.

Q. Remmius Palaemon was a home-born slave born into a household at Vicetia near Verona who was taught the craft of weaving, but who also gained a more academic education as a result of escorting his owner's son to and from school (he must have worked as a *paedagogus* too). He was set free and became in the early first century AD a distinguished professor of literature with a school of his own at Rome. He was included in a sequence of biographies of famous teachers written a century or so later by Suetonius who, however (*de Grammaticis* 23), considered him memorable for his personal extravagance as much as for his academic success.

Another professor of literature included in Suetonius' collection (*Gramm.* 21) who was also once a slave was C. Melissus, a teacher and author who flourished in the Augustan era and who once actually received a commission from Augustus himself. But Melissus was not a *verna*. He was born of free parents but was exposed as an infant and then bought up in slavery by the man who reclaimed him after his parents had abandoned him. At all levels of society, whether due to poverty or fears of overburdening a patrimony with too many heirs, infant exposure was a widespread fact of life in the Roman world. But because those who chose to rescue abandoned children were free to raise them as slaves if they wished, infant exposure was also another important (though again immeasurable) means of replenishing the slave supply. The Christian polemicist Tertullian (*Apol.* 9.7) condemned pagans for abandoning their children to certain death from cold, starvation or being eaten by dogs. Yet like Melissus many abandoned children survived because of their value as new slaves. When Pliny was governor of the province of Bithynia-Pontus he was compelled at one point (*Ep.* 10.65) to consult the emperor Trajan on how to go about establishing the true legal status of people who had been brought up as slaves but who claimed to have been born free and exposed as infants: it was a serious problem, he said, affecting the whole province and not simply an isolated case or two, and while there were earlier imperial pronouncements on the matter that applied to various regions of the eastern empire going all the way back to Augustus, there was nothing particularly relevant to Bithynia. Trajan's reply shows that Pliny was not exaggerating.[8]

---

[8] Exposure: see Harris 1980; Boswell 1988: 3–179. Pliny: cf. Sherwin-White 1966: 650–5. Trajan's reply: Plin. *Ep.* 10.66.

Long-distance trade with peoples and communities beyond the frontiers of the empire – trade, that is, independent of expansionist warfare – was a further supplier of new slaves to Rome, as various items indicate. In the east, the western regions of the Black Sea had been supplying the Mediterranean with slaves since the seventh century BC and from recent investigations it appears that areas to the east of the Black Sea, specifically the regions of the Caucasus, had long been involved as well. It can hardly be doubted therefore that Italy felt the impact of this activity once control of the eastern Mediterranean had been gained, and as late as the sixth century AD the historian Procopius (*de Bello Persico* 2.15.5) noted the practice of Roman traders of exchanging salt and grain for slaves from Colchis; the traders were actually Black Sea residents. Supplies could be drawn from very remote sources: thus a trader's handbook from the first century AD shows that the ports of Malao and Opone, centres in what is now northern Somalia, exported slaves, and from Egypt, where some of them were sent, further redistribution westwards was straightforward enough. Ammianus Marcellinus wrote of the eunuch Eutherius, who was born in Armenia: 'His parents were free, but at an early age he was captured by members of a neighbouring hostile tribe, who castrated him and sold him to some Roman merchants, by whom he was brought to Constantine's palace' (16.7.5). Such forced migration must have been a common servile experience in the east for centuries.[9]

In the west, the distribution of Italian wine-jars discovered in Gaul has led to the suggestion that in the first half of the central period Gallic slaves were regularly exchanged for Italian wine, perhaps to the number of 15,000 a year. It is of great interest consequently that in 83 BC Cicero could refer (*pro Quinctio* 24) to a dealer named L. Publicius bringing slaves to Italy from Gaul and that Varro in his agricultural manual (*R.* 2.10.4) could recommend Gauls for work as shepherds. It has also been proposed that hoards of late Republican coins found in the lower Danube basin were cash payments made for batches of slaves purchased in the sixties, forties and thirties of the first century BC, while on the middle Danube the luxury and everyday goods that were imported in the second half of the central period (bronzes, cooking-pots, jars, wine-

---

[9] Black Sea: Finley 1981:173. Caucasus: Braund and Tsetskhladze 1989. Trader's handbook: *Periplus Maris Erythraei* 8; 13.

ladles) may well have been payments for slaves made to the Germanic tribes of the Marcomanni and Quadi. It appears therefore that Roman merchants were constantly traversing the spiderweb of trading routes that crossed the Mediterranean in search of slaves from locally powerful, distant rulers who were willing to exchange captives, or even the weaker members of their own communities, for the material goods the merchants carried.[10]

Piracy within the sphere of Roman influence, finally, must be acknowledged as a major means of generating new slaves. At the beginning of Rome's central period the pirates of Cilicia were already notorious for the scale on which they conducted kidnapping and trafficking activities: the island of Delos, where they dumped their victims because they knew Roman merchants were waiting there to receive them, is said to have turned over tens of thousands of slaves daily in the early second century BC. What the pirates' activities involved, however, is graphically illustrated by a piece of evidence from late antiquity, one of the newly discovered letters of Augustine, which shows among other things that at the turn of the fifth century AD piracy was still a scourge in the Mediterranean. Augustine spoke in his letter (*Epistulae* 10*) of the formidable presence along the coasts of North Africa, and especially at Hippo Regius, of itinerant slavedealers (*mangones*), Galatians in particular, who were buying up as slaves freeborn people captured by independent marauders who made it their business to undertake forays from the coast into remote rural villages in order to hunt down and kidnap as many victims as possible. In one village, the rumour went, they had carried off all the women and children of the community after murdering all the men. Some local people, Augustine continued, were conniving with the invaders: there was a woman who had a clandestine business specialising in young girls from the interior; there was a man (a Christian at that) who had sold his wife into slavery because he preferred to have the cash; and there were indigent parents selling their children because they needed the cash. Augustine said that it was the practice of the Christian community to use its funds to redeem as many of the kidnapped victims as possible, and in one recent episode 120

---

[10] Wine-jars: Tchernia 1983, with especially Diodorus Siculus 5.26.3; cf. Tchernia 1986: 90–2. Coins: Crawford 1977; Crawford 1985: 226–35; 348. Middle Danube: Pitts 1989. Merchants: men perhaps like Cn. Naevius Diadumenus (*ILS* 7534) and L. Valerius Zabda (*CIL* 6.9632 = 33813). Spiderweb: cf. *Dig.* 17.1.57.

'slaves' whom the Galatians were boarding, or were preparing to board, onto their ships had been saved. But the trade itself was so lucrative that there were advocates on hand who wanted to try to recover the reclaimed victims for the slavedealers, so their safety was in real jeopardy. It was a desperate situation, and one that must have been far from uncommon throughout the whole of the central period.[11]

A specific case-history concerns a woman – her name is not known – who when already the slave of a Roman soldier in Britain was abducted by brigands and sold off by them to dealers. The woman belonged to the centurion M. Cocceius Firmus, who was stationed in Britain in the mid-second century AD. For reasons that cannot be determined, the woman was condemned to a period of hard labour in a saltworks. But while serving her sentence she was carried off by brigands who had attacked from beyond the borders of the province and was sold by them, it seems, to continue her life in slavery elsewhere. By a true stroke of fate, however, it turned out that Cocceius Firmus was ultimately able to buy the woman back himself, and afterwards he sought through litigation to recover the money he had spent for her from the imperial treasury (*fiscus*). The story sounds like a piece of fiction. But it derives from evidence in the *Digest*, hard evidence that is to say, that takes the reality of enslaving brigands for granted.[12]

It was not just the distant provinces, moreover, in which brigands operated. Even Italy was unsafe. In the turmoil of the first century BC it was perhaps inevitable that outlawry should have been virulent, so that Augustus later took measures to stamp it out. (Tiberius, for example, when quaestor in 23 BC was charged with investigating private slave-prisons (*ergastula*) in rural areas to ensure that kidnapped travellers were not being held in slavery.) But in the more tranquil Italy of Pliny's day dangers were still present. Pliny reported two cases (*Ep.* 6.25) of men who had simply vanished without trace while on journeys in Italy, one of whom had been no more than a day's distance from Rome.[13]

---

[11] Piracy: see Shaw 1984 for a theoretical study of banditry in the Roman empire, and Shaw 1990 for a case-study of Isauria-Cilicia. Delos: Str. 14.5.2. Augustine: see Lepelley 1981; Chadwick 1983.

[12] See *Dig.* 49.15.16, with Birley 1953: 87–103; for the date, see Birley 1980: 613; Garnsey 1970: 134 n.5, gives late first century.

[13] Italy: App. *Bella Civilia* 5.132. Augustus: Suetonius, *Augustus* 32.1. Tiberius: Suet. *Tiberius* 8.

The means by which the Romans obtained their slaves can then be identified with relative ease. Wars of conquest, natural reproduction in the existing slave population, infant exposure, trade and piracy – these mechanisms created large supplies of new slaves from all regions of the Mediterranean, resulting in a slave population that was always highly differentiated and complex. It had much in common in this respect with the heterogeneous slave population of Rio de Janeiro in the early nineteenth century. Is it possible, however, to assess the relative significance or variance of these means of supply over the four centuries of the central period? That is a more difficult question to answer and one bedevilled by the dearth of quantifiable evidence. But logic dictates that the rate of supply produced by the individual constituents should have fluctuated from time to time as changes occurred in Rome's political and military history. So, for example, it is likely that the numbers of slaves generated by piracy on the seas declined drastically after the extraordinary success of Cn. Pompeius in 67 B C in ridding the Mediterranean of what had become a very dangerous problem – as whole fleets of marauders attacked Roman shipping, interrupted the overseas shipments of grain to Rome, and seized captives from the cities of the Italian coastline – only to rebound afterwards, for a few years later Cicero had much to say (*pro Flacco* 29–33) of the dangers of new outbreaks of piracy when he defended in a court case a former governor of the province of Asia. The Greek historian Cassius Dio, writing in the Severan era, observed (36.20.1) that there had never been a time when piracy and brigandage had been completely absent from human affairs and never would be without a change in human nature.[14]

From a basis of this kind a standard view of the historical development of the Roman slave supply has arisen. It can be summarised as follows (to give one formulation of many):

In the late Roman Republic a series of foreign wars and civil wars provided an ample supply of cheap slaves for the Mediterranean slave markets ... It looks as if women and children were not widely used as slaves in Italy during the Republican period ... [But] after the end of the Republic the sex-ratio among slaves began to grow more equal, and ... slave-breeding played a much larger part in the economy ... [Thus] by

---

[14] Rio de Janeiro: Karasch 1987: 3–28. Cn. Pompeius: Cic. *pro Lege Manilia* 31–5; 53–5; Plut. *Pompeius* 24; Dio 36.20–3; App.*Mith.* 91–3. Absent: cf. Dio Chrysostom 15.25.

the second century of our era it was playing a much larger role than in the last century B C.

This view is based on the notion that in agriculture, which was the heart of the ancient economy, slave men were needed in far greater numbers than slave women, so that under the Republic only men, or at least predominantly men, were brought to Rome and Italy where they were replaced in due course by fresh supplies of male slaves acquired in the continuing sequence of wars, until under the peaceful conditions of the Principate, when warfare no longer provided slaves in sufficient numbers, owners were forced to turn to the systematic breeding of slaves to keep up supplies. The orthodox view is founded on the indisputable truth that continuous warfare on the grand scale was characteristic of the first half of the central period of Roman history but not of the second, and it may well be right. But as some of the evidence already seen suggests, the standard view is open to objections of various sorts and a more flexible alternative might therefore be preferable.[15]

First, although under the Principate much was and still is made of the 'imperial peace', Roman emperors continued to fight wars on a considerable scale and to enslave vast numbers of prisoners as a result. For the Jewish war of A D 66–70, for example, which concluded with the savage destruction of the city of Jerusalem, indicative details (which are impossible to confirm of course) are available in the exhaustive account of the contemporary historian Josephus: 2,130 women and children sold into slavery after the capture of Japha; 30,400 prisoners enslaved at Tiberias in Galilee by the future emperor Vespasian; 97,000 prisoners taken during the siege of Jerusalem; 700 captives sent to Rome by Vespasian's son Titus for display in his triumph. In the earlier triumph of Germanicus in A D 17 there were captives from the Cherusci, Chatti, Angrivarii and other Germanic tribes. The submission or capture of Numidians and Thracians is recorded under Tiberius as well, as too the handing over of women and children into slavery by the Frisii when they were unable to meet Rome's tax demands. In Nero's reign Cn. Domitius Corbulo sold Armenians into slavery, and Domitian's enslavement of Germans, Dacians and Sarmatians during his military campaigns is reflected in the poetry of Martial.

[15] Formulation: Ste Croix 1981: 228; 234–6. See similarly, Brunt 1971: 707; Hopkins 1978: 102; Dyson 1992: 131–2; 187.

Pictorial evidence of enslavement, furthermore, can be seen on the column that was erected to mark the successes of Trajan against the Dacians in the early second century A D, as men, women and children submitted to him, and the assumption could easily be made in that age that captive women and boys were regularly available for the prostitution industry. Exclusive reliance on natural reproduction for the maintenance of the Roman slave supply under the Principate seems, therefore, an inherently implausible proposition once the evidence of warfare is properly considered.[16]

Secondly, since there is ample evidence that it was common practice under the Republic for Rome to enslave female as well as male prisoners of war, and since there is ample evidence that female slaves, and their offspring, were well established in both urban and rural contexts in the same period, there is no good reason to believe that natural reproduction was unimportant in supplying slaves at Rome in the first half of the central period. The historian Appian, writing in the second century A D, wrote (*Bella Civilia* 1.7) of a great increase in the slave population of Italy of the second century B C that was attributable to natural causes, and the elder Cato, when composing his monograph on agriculture, took the presence of women and children on the type of farm about which he was writing for granted. In his own household, moreover, it was the practice of Cato's wife Licinia to nurse the offspring of their slave women.[17]

Thirdly, the standard view implies that one of the reasons why Rome went to war so frequently under the Republic was for the express purpose of acquiring new slaves, a notion that raises the very large question of the nature of Roman imperialism (and a question that is much too large to be treated here in detail). But while it can be readily admitted that Rome cannot have been unaware of the economic dividends that successful war against overseas enemies produced, there is no evidence to prove that

---

[16] Jewish war: Josephus, *Bellum Judaicum* 3.305; 3.540; 6.420; 7.118; 7.138. Germanicus: Tac. *Ann.* 2.41; cf. 1.56; 2.25; Ov. *Epistulae ex Ponto* 2.1. Numidians and Thracians: Tac. *Ann.* 3.74; 4.25; 4.50–1. Frisii: Tac. *Ann.* 4.72. Corbulo: Tac. *Ann.* 13.39. Martial: see Garrido-Hory 1981: 116. Trajan: see Rossi 1971: 146, 152, 208, 210. Prostitution: Dio Chrys. 7.133; cf. 7.138. See also Str. 17.1.54, 1,000 Ethiopian prisoners sent to Italy by the prefect of Egypt, P. Petronius, under Augustus.

[17] Common practice: Bradley 1987b: 50–1. Ample evidence: Bradley 1989: 23–6; 28–9; contrast Dyson 1992: 37–8. Cato: Bradley 1989: 25–6. Licinia: Plut. *Cato* 20.3.

economic aims generally outweighed political and strategic factors in the decisions made to embark upon war or to annex land. The growth of the Roman empire under the Republic may well have increased the numbers of slaves in Italy, but a policy to increase those numbers did not by itself cause the growth of empire. Moreover, it stands to reason that when a decision to go to war was being contemplated, success could never be guaranteed in advance no matter how attractive the prospects. Warfare could never therefore be counted on as an unfailing source of slaves. It should be kept in mind, in fact, that Roman generals did not always enslave defeated populations: mass butchery was at times a preferable alternative.[18]

Fourthly, the orthodox view neglects to pay sufficient attention to the independent slave trade as a prime mechanism of supply throughout the central period. The reasons are perhaps comprehensible. In such Republican sources as the historical narratives of Polybius or Livy, enslavement of captives receives a high profile in view of the connection between warfare and the growth of empire, the historians' main subject of interest. Then, given the disappearance of that theme in the historical writing of the Principate and the sudden visibility of *partus ancillarum* in legal sources and of *vernae* in inscriptions and literature (for which under the Republic there is almost nothing comparable), the substitution of slavebreeding on a large scale for acquiring slaves from war seems to make sense. In the general history of slavery, however, only one slave population, that of the United States, has ever been able to sustain itself through natural increase alone, which makes it the more surprising that few historians have drawn the obvious implication of texts such as the following, a passage from Ulpian (*Dig.* 21.1.31.21) on the rules governing the sales of slaves, which presuppose under the Principate a constant influx of new slaves to the Roman heartland that can have nothing to do with slavebreeding:

Those selling slaves should declare their nationality (*natio*) when making the sale; for the slave's nationality may often induce or deter a purchaser; therefore, we have an interest in knowing the nationality; for there is a presumption that some slaves are good, coming from a race with no bad repute, while others are thought bad, since they come from a notorious people. If, then, the slave's nationality be not declared, an action will be

---

[18] Policy: to my mind the best discussion of economic motives and Roman imperialism in the mid-Republic is Harris 1979: 54–104. See also, however, Gruen 1984.

given to the purchaser and to all interested parties whereby the purchaser may return the slave.

In his references to slaves at Rome from Egypt, Cappadocia and Syria, Spain and Greece, Arabia and Ethiopia, Martial again illustrates how dealers were constantly bringing slaves to the heartland from distant places within and without the empire late in the first century AD. In the second century the sophist Favorinus of Arelate bequeathed to his friend Herodes Atticus a slave from India (a region which was also sending eunuchs to the west), though even in the age of Augustus it had been possible to have an Indian slave as a special symbol of wealth and luxury. Also in the second century, the jurist Gaius (*Inst.* 3.148) assumed that partnerships for slave-trafficking purposes were routinely organised. The independent slave trade of the imperial age developed as a matter of course from that of the Republic. Similarly, infant exposure remained constant across the central period, and like trading was assumed to be a perennial source of new slaves by the Roman jurists.[19]

In the end, then, it is only a matter of common sense that Roman slaveowners who were anxious as time passed to find new slaves should have realised how foolish it was to rely on a single mode of procurement, for every method of supply was unpredictable as far as a guarantee of product was concerned. But the evidence shows that slaveowners in the central period were able to draw on several sources of supply that complemented one another and kept pace with demand, fluctuating from time to time in their relative standing one to another, but with no single source ever completely dominating the rest. The Roman slave supply was met from a combination of sources that commonly reinforced one another. It is unlikely, therefore, that there was a fundamental shift from reliance on warfare under the Republic to reliance on slavebreeding under the Principate.

What impact did replenishing the slave supply make on the lives of those who comprised the supply? In the absence of direct testimony

[19] General history: Fogel 1989: 116–17. Martial: see Garrido-Hory 1981: 75–6; 114–18. Favorinus: Philostratus, *Vitae Sophistarum* 1.8. Eunuchs: *Dig.* 39.4.16.7. Age of Augustus: Tibullus 2.3.59. Partnerships: cf. also *Dig.* 17.2.60.1; 17.2.65.5. Exposure: see the evidence compiled in Boswell 1988: 57–75. Jurists: e.g. *Dig.* 3.5.10 (Pomponius), assuming *novicii* always available for purchase; 21.1.65 (Venuleius); 39.4.16.3 (Marcian). Cf. Tac. *Ann.* 3.53: to Tiberius in AD 22 it seemed that Rome was full of foreign-born slaves.

from slaves themselves any answer to that question must be speculative. But speculation can be informed.

For those who found themselves the victims of war or abduction,
the sudden and abrupt shift from a state of freedom to a state
of servitude, from being able to exercise control to being utterly
powerless, must have been devastating. It was a situation certainly
whose consequences many were not prepared to face. In 22 BC two
Spanish tribes, the Astures and the Cantabri, rebelled against
Roman rule. They were quickly suppressed and reduced to slavery.
But in the event only a few of the Cantabri were actually enslaved,
for, so Cassius Dio (54.5.2–3) reported:

when they saw they had lost all hope of freedom, they lost all desire to
preserve their lives either. Some set fire to their forts and cut their own
throats, others willingly remained with their companions and died in the
flames, while others took poison in the sight of all.

This willingness to participate in mass suicide rather than suffer
the fate of enslavement is compelling evidence of how dreadful and
terrifying the consequences of falling into slavery were thought to
be. But the behaviour of the Cantabri was by no means an isolated
episode: self-inflicted death was often preferred to slavery in the
ancient world and not simply when enslavement by Rome was at
hand. The inhabitants of Xanthus in Lycia are reported to have
undertaken mass suicide on three occasions during their city's
history, once after capture by a general of Cyrus the Great, once
after capture by Alexander the Great, and once after capture by M.
Brutus. Even the Romans at times chose death over slavery: in
AD 28 a body of 400 troops killed themselves rather than risk capture by the Frisii. To stand on the threshold of enslavement was
clearly an horrific experience, and a sense of the terror it brought
can still be felt when observing monumental representations of
captives taking their own lives. The scenes on Trajan's Column of
Dacians killing themselves in preference to being enslaved by
Trajan and the Roman imperial army are riveting examples.[20]

What was involved? For many, enslavement must have meant
the rupturing of familial bonds that were never likely to be

[20] Astures and Cantabri: Dio 54.5.1–3. Xanthus: App. *BC* 4.80. Frisii: Tac. *Ann.* 4.73.
Dacians: see Rossi 1971: 196–7; 204–5; Lepper and Frere 1988: 168–9, with plates xc,
xci, cii. See in general, Grisé 1982: 61–3.

repaired. Indeed this was impossible in cases where Rome enslaved the women and children of a reduced city but killed the men, an option pursued for instance by C. Marius after the siege of Capsa in North Africa during the war against Jugurtha in the late second century BC and again by Cn. Domitius Corbulo in campaigns against the Parthians in the middle of the first century AD. It was also unlikely in such a situation as that at Tiberias in Galilee in AD 67 when the future emperor Vespasian not only sold over 30,000 captives into slavery, as noted above, but also executed (or murdered) 1,200 of the weak and infirm and deported 6,000 young men to work on the canal that Nero was building at the Isthmus of Corinth. There was after all no compulsion on the captors to respect or even to recognise the kin associations of the captured, and an orator portraying the fall of a city was expected as a matter of convention to rouse the emotions of his audience by describing a mother's efforts not to lose her child in the confusion and chaos of the scene – which brings to mind the pitiable representation on the Column of Marcus Aurelius of the captive German woman, surrounded by Roman troops, clinging desperately to her young son (see Frontispiece). Sale under any circumstances threatened to sever servile family connections. The following extract from the autobiography of an eighteenth-century African, Olaudah Equiano, describing his sale as part of a slave cargo in Barbados, may be taken to express something of the anguish felt by slaves in antiquity under comparable circumstances:

We were not many days in the merchants' custody before we were sold after the usual manner, which is this: – On a signal given, such as the beat of a drum, the buyers rush at once into the yard where the slaves are confined, and make choice of that parcel they like best. The noise and clamour with which this is attended, and the eagerness visible in the countenances of the buyers, serve not a little to increase the apprehensions of the terrified Africans, who may well be supposed to consider them the ministers of that destruction to which they think themselves devoted. In this manner, without scruple, are relations and friends separated, most of them never to see each other again. I remember in the vessel in which I was brought over, in the man's apartment, there were several brothers, who, in the sale, were sold in different lots; and it was very moving on this occasion to see their distress and hear their cries at parting. O, ye nominal Christians! might not an African ask you, 'learned you this from your God, who says unto you, Do unto all men as you would men should do unto you? Is it not enough that we are torn from our country and friends, to toil for your luxury and lust of gain? Must every tender feeling be likewise sacrificed to your avarice? Are the dearest friends and relations, now rendered more dear by their separation from the rest of their kindred, still to be parted from each other, and thus prevented from cheering the gloom of slavery, with the small comfort of being together, and mingling their sufferings and sorrows? Why are parents to lose their children, brothers their sisters, or husbands their wives? Surely this is a new refinement in cruelty, which, while it has no advantage to atone for it, thus aggravates distress, and adds fresh horrors even to the wretchedness of slavery.'[21]

Captives transported from outlying areas to Rome or other centres of the slave trade such as Aquileia at the head of the Adriatic must often have suffered the shock of cultural disorientation as the journey from a familiar to an alien environment took place, just as Roman troops sometimes found themselves terrified by remote, foreign quarters. Before the age of Augustus, Roman geographical knowledge, especially of the Celtic world, tended to be vague and rudimentary and although significant advances were made under the Principate it would be wrong to assume that authoritative geographical knowledge could ever exist at a popular level. Among many of the populations who bordered the Roman world the lack of understanding had to be greater still. Imagine therefore the experience of the captives taken to Rome from Britain in the wake of Julius Caesar's expeditions in 55 BC and 54 BC (Strabo saw British captives in the city). Against their will these people were removed from a tribally based and non-urbanised society, to be deposited eventually in a huge, densely populated city whose physical appearance alone, dominated as it was by temples, basilicas and colonnades, tenements and town houses, they would scarcely have been able to comprehend. Their forced journey, by sea to the Continent and then overland to Italy, would have taken them across a vast region of which they could previously have had hardly any detailed knowledge or awareness – they were, quite literally, travelling into the unknown, in a timeless and directionless way, with no prospect of ever returning – and along the route they would probably have been sold several times from dealer to dealer. They would also have become increasingly isolated from a

---

[21] C. Marius: Sallust, *Iugurtha* 91.7. Corbulo: Tac. *Ann.* 13.39.6–7. Vespasian: Jos. *BJ* 3.540. Orator: Quint. *Inst.* 8.3.69. Column of Marcus Aurelius: Ramage and Ramage 1991: 211 (plate 8.24). Olaudah Equiano: Gates 1987: 37–8.

linguistic point of view: newly imported slaves were expected to pick up the rudiments of Latin in the slave-market, but at first they would have been completely marooned and scarcely able to communicate in any normal way except with one another. As Cicero sardonically remarked (*Att.* 4.16.7.), one could hardly expect British captives 'to be highly qualified in literature or music!'[22]

Cultural and psychological dislocation of this kind must have been commonly endured by the great numbers of slaves brought from the fringes of the Roman world, those for instance procured from the regions that bordered on the Black Sea or from within the Asian interior. The results were not of course always permanently damaging, and it is possible to find success stories showing how the victimised were sometimes capable of adapting their new circumstances to their personal advantage. For example, the freedman Licinus, who came to hold a procuratorship in Gaul under Augustus and whose name became a byword for great wealth, had originally been captured in war in Gaul, where he was born, but fell into the ownership of Julius Caesar and was fortunate enough to be manumitted by him. Then there was Cleander, the notorious freedman who in the reign of Commodus held the high office of praetorian prefect and exercised enormous political influence; he was a Phrygian by birth who had been brought to Rome as a slave where he was sold on the block. At a more humble level one might notice a pair of freedmen who as slaves had originated from Cilicia and Paphlagonia respectively, the cloak dealers L. Arlenus Demetrius and L. Arlenus Artemidorus.[23]

How many of the newly enslaved showed the resourcefulness of Licinus and Cleander it is difficult to tell. But it is not difficult to believe that many, and perhaps most, slaves were overwhelmed by the experience of capture, sale and forced migration. A sense of the human tragedy the process created emerges from the romance *Chaereas & Callirhoe*, written probably in the middle of the first century AD by the Greek author Chariton, in which the heroine Callirhoe is taken as a captive from her home in Syracuse first to Miletus and then Syria and Cilicia. The disruption, Callirhoe says at one stage (5.1), had been tolerable as long as she had been able

---

[22] Roman troops: Tac. *Ann.* 2.24. Geographical knowledge: Nicolet 1991: 57–94. Britain: Str. 4.5.2–3; cf. Caes. *Gal.* 5.23. Rudiments of Latin: A. Gellius, *Noctes Atticae* 4.1.4–6; cf. Var. *L.* 8.6; *Dig.* 21.1.65.2.

[23] Licinus: *PIR²* I 381. Cleander: *PIR²* A 1481. Cloak dealers: *ILS* 7577.

to hear Greek spoken and to see the sea. But as her journey east-
wards continued and she faced the prospect of entering the domain
of the Persian King across the Euphrates, 'then longing for her
country and family welled up in her, and she despaired of ever
returning'. Her journey of course was a fiction but one can compare
with it, though the direction is different, the authentic journey in
the middle of the third century A D of the young woman Balsamea,
who began her life in Osrhoene in Mesopotamia, was sold as a
slave in Tripoli in Phoenicia, and at just about the age of seventeen
found herself living in Oxyrhynchus in Egypt.[24]

Furthermore, the material conditions under which slaves lived
during their travels can hardly have been enviable. The famous
stele of the Black Sea slavetrader A. Kapreilius Timotheus (of early
imperial date), depicts a file of eight slaves walking along in chains
and there is no reason to imagine that that was anything but a
normal mode of conveyance when slaves were being moved overland or by sea. Independent mobility will thus have been completely lacking, and privacy for eating, sleeping or personal hygiene
nonexistent. Before undertaking an expedition the provident slavedealer might have prepared some supplies for the slaves he hoped
to sell (food, bedding, firewood) and perhaps there could be pack-
animals to carry them – if not the slaves had to double as porters.
But in general changes of clothing must have been few and food no
more than enough to keep the merchandise alive. Altogether, therefore, malnutrition and disease were probably rife among the slaves
who were the objects of the long-distance slave trade, which makes
it hardly surprising that the law contained provisions for slaves
who, when travelling by sea, became sick or killed themselves by
jumping overboard.[25]

The trauma that accompanied enslavement in warfare or abduction cannot have been experienced by home-born slaves. Given
that owners tended to prize *vernae* highly, home-born slaves may
often have grown up in relatively stable and materially secure

---

[24] Balsamea: *P.Oxy.* 3053 (A D 252). Cf. Jos. *Antiquitates Judaicae* 18.39–42 on the Italian slave
Thesmusa, who was given as a gift by Augustus to Phraates IV of Parthia to be his
concubine and who must also have travelled vast distances under compulsion. Thesmusa,
however, was able to turn the infatuation Phraates felt for her to real advantage, as she
became his wife and queen. Her son both succeeded, and killed, his father.

[25] A. Kapreilius Timotheus: see Duchêne 1986. Provident slavedealer: *Vita Aesopi* 12, 17, 19.
Law: *Dig.* 14.2.2.5.

circumstances. It is in the production of *vernae*, however, that abuse, particularly sexual abuse of slave women, might be suspected.

A certain proportion of *vernae* must always have been the offspring of slave women who had been victimised by free males. The law recognised that slaves might be sexually assaulted by a third party and gave slaveowners several means by which to secure redress for any damage suffered by their property – the slaves themselves of course received no compensation. The law also said that a provincial governor investigating a case was to bring down a very severe penalty if a sexual attack on a slave threatened to cause commotion among the other slaves of the household. And when the sale of a slave was rescinded, if the value of the slave had been lowered because of sexual abuse on the purchaser's part, the seller was due to be compensated. Awareness of the sexual dangers to which slaves were exposed was thus very sharp. Even a slave overseer might be a threat. Yet because proprietary rights were absolute, there was nothing the law could do to prevent slaveowners themselves abusing their slaves if they wished to do so. A tension developed consequently between the need to uphold the rights of ownership on the one hand and a need to punish such obvious injustices as rape on the other. The dilemma is visible in a directive given by the emperor Antoninus Pius (*Dig.* 1.6.2) for cases of abuse, including sexual abuse, of slaves, in which sale of the slaves concerned to a new household was recommended: 'The power of masters over their slaves certainly ought not to be infringed and there must be no derogation from any of man's legal rights. But it is in the interest of masters that those who make just complaint be not denied relief against brutality or starvation or intolerable wrongdoing' – the latter to include *impudicitia*, sexual wrongdoing. The significant point here is that the owner's sexual access to slaves was regarded as conventional, a norm made explicit in Chariton's romance (2.6) when the servant Leonas says to his master Dionysius of the beautiful Callirhoe, who seems beyond his reach: 'Sir, don't *you* curse yourself! You're her master, you can make her do what you want whether she likes it or not – I bought her; I paid a talent for her!' And it was this norm that provided the basis for Martial's lampoon (1.84) of the Quirinalis who filled both his urban household and his country estates with *vernae* he had fathered himself on his *ancillae*. Not all sexual relationships between masters and slave women have to be judged abusive; but there was little to deter abuse.[26]

Under the law slaves could not marry. They could therefore produce no legitimate children. In reality, however, slaves did contract unions (*contubernia*) which they regarded as marriages and issue naturally resulted from them. Ironically in such cases slave-owners then expected slave families to conform to their own standards of moral comportment. From the slaveowner's vantage point of course it must often have been convenient to sanction slave marriages because of the new slaves that could be anticipated from them – so convenient that perhaps more than mere approval was involved. To judge from Columella's example owners were at least likely to encourage reproduction among their slaves by promising manumission or other rewards; and there is evidence of slave-owners' interest in rearing them, once born, by supplying infants with nurses and other attendants. There can therefore be no doubt of slaveowners' sensitivity to the potential economic gain to be derived from *ancillae*, even if people quibbled over comparing slave offspring with the young of animals. But to what lengths were they prepared to go to realise the potential? An incident in another Greek romance, the *Ephesian Tale* of Xenophon of Ephesus (2.9) from the second century AD, in which a jealous female slaveowner unilaterally assigns her slave to a slave goatherd to be his wife ('if she refuses, his instructions were to use force'), suggests that slave *contubernia* might well be contrived by owners, no matter what the inclinations of the 'marrying' couple. Likewise a passage in the *Digest* (40.4.59) refers to a slaveowner who had stated in her will that when she died all her female attendants (*pedisequae*) named in her account books were to be set free, but who before she died had given one of them to her bailiff to be his wife. The lawyers were interested in the question of whether this former attendant was still to be set free (she was), but they took the owner's action in marrying her off as inconsequential. Behaviour of this sort caused abolitionists of the nineteenth century to protest against 'the application of practices employed in animal husbandry to obtain the greatest number of slaves for sale on the market'. From the Roman

---

[26] Third party: *Dig.* 47.10.9.4; 47.10.25; 48.5.6 pr. Provincial governor: *Dig.* 1.18.21. Rescinded: *Dig.* 21.2.23 pr. Overseer: Col. 11.1.4. On the effects on Roman family life of slave exploitation, see Saller 1987.

evidence it cannot be proved that such manipulation was rampant, but the possibility must be allowed that some slaveowners were prepared to interfere in their slaves' sexual lives for the sake of breeding new slaves.[27]

No matter what the original means of acquisition, slaves might find themselves put up for sale by their owners in the local market-place at any time. References and allusions to the event are common in the historical record – a religious dedication to the Genius of the slave-market for instance or an observation that dealers could expect to do well at provincial assize centres because when the governor arrived the local economy boomed. To dwell on the details of the process, however, is to disclose something of the humiliation and indignity to which slaves were subjected when sales were transacted. Viewed as a single episode, sale in the marketplace stands as a symbol of the degradation associated with slavery in general and with maintaining the slave supply in particu-lar.[28]

At Rome itself, most probably from an early date in the central period, the sale of slaves was regulated by an edict issued by the aediles, the magistrates who supervised the marketplace. Since the aediles only held office for a year at time the edict had to be annually renewed if its provisions were to remain valid. But eventu-ally it assumed a fixed form and through the central period gradu-ally came to regulate sales of slaves throughout the empire. The sale of Abaskantis, seen earlier, is a case in point. The principal object of the edict was to protect the buyer against fraudulence on the part of the seller. The edict thus required the seller (*Dig.* 21.1.1.1) 'to apprise purchasers of any disease or defect in their wares and whether a given slave is a runaway, a loiterer on errands, or still subject to noxal liability' (i.e. subject to being handed over to a third party as compensation for wrongdoing). Likewise the buyer had to be informed of 'any capital offence committed by the slave; any attempt which he has made upon his own life; and whether he has been sent into the arena to fight wild animals'.

---

[27] Conform: Saller 1991: 149–50; note the use of the phrase 'nuptiae servulorum' (slave marriages) at Jerome, *Epistulae* 107.11. Attendants: Bradley 1987b: 55–8. Quibbled: *Dig.* 22.1.28.1; cf. 5.3.27 pr. Abolitionists: Fogel 1989: 119–20 (quoted). Cf. Goodman 1983: 200 n. 181; on slavery in Roman Galilee; 'R. Judah approves of taking a fee for lending one's slave as a stud for another man's slave girl.'

[28] Genius: *ILS* 3671; 3672; 3673; 3674 (all from Rome). Observation: Dio Chrys. 35.15–17.

Transactions were recorded by bills of sale, which could later be used as evidence as necessary. If the provisions had not been met the sale could subsequently be rescinded and the buyer of the slave could recover the purchase price. In time, it was also required that the seller declare the slave's nationality.[29]

The seriousness with which these requirements were taken is reflected in the body of legal discussion that grew up around them. How was 'disease' to be distinguished from 'defect'? What was the difference between a 'runaway' and a 'loiterer on errands'? How did specific, and perhaps unprecedented, circumstances fall within the general guidelines? The section of the *Digest* that deals with questions of this sort provides one of the most realistic collections of slave experiences available for classical antiquity. Consider just a brief sampling from Ulpian (*Dig.* 21.1.12.1–4):

Pedius writes that a man who has one eye or one jaw bigger than the other is healthy, so long as he can use both properly; for he says that a discrepancy between jaws, eyes or arms is no ground for rescission if it does not affect the slave's ability to perform his duties. But imbalance, or the fact that one leg is shorter than the other, can be a hindrance to such performance; and so a slave, thus affected, is for rescission. If a slave speak gutturally or have protruding eyes from birth, he is regarded as healthy. It should also be known that left-handedness is neither a defect nor a disease, unless the slave use his left hand by reason of the weakness of the right; such a slave is not left-handed but defective. It has been asked whether one whose breath smells is healthy. Trebatius says that it is not a disease that one's breath smells like that of a goatherd or scabrous person for this is an accident of exhalation. But if it be due to a bodily defect, such as liver- or lung-complaint or something similar, the slave is diseased.

The information on a given slave that the law required was written on a label that was hung from the slave's neck at the time the sale took place. The slave stood on a raised platform (*catasta*) to allow potential purchasers a good view, and if newly imported had his or her feet marked with chalk to signify the fact. The distinction between a new slave (*novicius*) and a veteran (*veterator*) was worth making because it was the general opinion that a new slave was more easily trained than an old one. Those with an interest in the merchandise, however, could do more than look: they could insist on having the slave undressed in case a dealer was trying to conceal

---

[29] Bills of sale: Seneca, *Controversiae* 7.6.22; cf. *Dig.* 32.1.92 pr.

a physical defect – fine clothes, conveniently available to entice buyers, could serve the purpose – and they could poke and prod the slave to see precisely what it was they were going to get if they made a purchase. The slave had to be inspected and tested for all manner of complaints. What if there were a fever or an inflammation of the eyes, tonsillitis, a slight toothache or earache? What if there were wounds, scars or sores to be seen? What if the slave were deformed, deaf, dumb, short-sighted, afflicted with a speech impediment? (An Egyptian slave, a girl aged sixteen, was described when about to be sold as 'squinting slightly with the right eye'.) What if the slave had lost a finger or a toe or had a limp or varicose veins, what if a woman were pregnant or had been sterilised or had a history of menstrual difficulties, what if the slave had a problem with wetting the bed? Perhaps furthermore the slave was an epileptic, in which case a stone called *gagates* could be burned and the slave's reaction observed to find out. Then there was the issue of the slave's character. Wishing to conclude the sale, the vendor might profess that the slave under consideration was of impeccable reputation – loyal, industrious, diligent, vigilant, thrifty, honest, reliable. But had the slave ever actually stolen anything or run away? Did he have a reputation for gambling? Had he ever absconded and taken refuge at a statue of the emperor?[30]

As all these questions and more were asked, the physical examination on the *catasta* reduced the slave to the level of an object, mute, passive and devoid of any human dignity. It was as though the slave were an animal – an ox, a cow or mule that had to be put through its paces before a deal could be made; indeed the aedilician edict that regulated the sale of slaves also regulated the sale of cattle and beasts of burden and required similar disclosure of diseases and defects. To the jurists there was no distinction between one object and the other (*Dig.* 21.1.38.2):

The reason for this edict (i.e. on livestock) is the same as that for the return of slaves. And in effect, the same applies as in respect of defects or

[30] Label: Gel. 4.2.1; cf. Propertius 4.5.51–2. *Catasta*: Mart. 6.29.1; Persius 6.77; cf. Cic. *in Pisonem* 35. Chalk: Plin. *Nat.* 35.199–201; cf. Tib. 2.3.63–4; Prop. 4.5.51–2; Ov. *Amores* 1.8.64; Juvenal 1.111. Distinction: *Dig.* 21.1.37; cf. 21.1.65.2. Undressed: Sen. *Epistulae* 80.9. Fine clothes: *Vita Aesopi* 21. Poke: Pers. 6.77. According to Plutarch (*Mor.* 520c), there were some at Rome who deliberately sought out the monstrous rather than the good-looking. Complaints: see *Dig.* 21.1.1.6–21.1.16; 21.1.50; cf. Gaius, *Inst.* 3.124, implying that a lame or one-eyed slave was not a rare sight. Egyptian slave: *P.Oxy.* 3477 (AD 270). *Gagates*: Ap. *Apol.* 45. Reputation: *Dig.* 21.1.18 pr.' 21.1.19 pr.

diseases of slaves, so that what we have said of them should be transferred to the present context.[31]

The sale of slaves was normally viewed then as a transaction equivalent to the sale of livestock. Slaves were simply merchandise (*merx*) and devoid of all pretensions to humanity if defective in any way. The attitude was detached and unemotional, and very much like that of the French doctor J. B. A. Imbert, who gave the following clinical description of what to look for when buying a slave in Brazil in the nineteenth century. A man was to be sought, he said, who had:

smooth black, odorless skin, genitals neither too large nor too small, a flat abdomen and small navel or hernias may develop, spacious lungs, no glandular tumors under the skin – signs of scrofulous infection leading to tuberculosis, well-developed muscles, firm flesh, and in countenance and general attitude eagerness and vivacity.

If these conditions were met, the doctor concluded, 'the Master will have a slave with guaranteed health, strength and intelligence'. It seems not to have occurred to Imbert, however, or to the Roman jurists who said so much about them, that what buyers perceived as imperfections in the merchandise might well have been physical manifestations of the inner burdens of life in slavery.[32]

It is impossible to bring forward a Roman slave's account of the psychological response or emotional reaction to being examined and sold on the auction block. But a hint of the dehumanisation involved can be gleaned from the contempt that representatives of the slaveowning classes felt for successful slaves who had once been sold in the marketplace. The elder Pliny noted when giving a catalogue (*Nat.* 35.199–201) of slaves who had been imported to Rome from overseas and had appeared on the *catasta* that some had gone on to high attainments in literature but that others, reprehensibly in Pliny's view, had used the confusion of the times in which

---

[31] Edict: *Dig.* 21.1.38.
[32] Normally: *Dig.* 14.3.17. pr. Merchandise: *Dig.* 32.1.73.4. Devoid: *Dig.* 17.1.50. Imbert: quoted in Karasch 1987: 43. Note that sale could be accompanied by restrictions that benefited the slave, namely that the slave be set free upon sale and that in the case of sale of a female slave, the slave not be prostituted; to this extent the humanity of the slave could be recognised. On the other hand, sale could be accompanied by a ban on the slave's future manumission and a requirement of relocation. For discussion especially of the prostitution clause, see McGinn 1990.

they lived to their own advantage and had prospered financially as a result; worse yet, within the recent past senatorial honours had been conferred on some – and at the instigation of the emperor's wife, no less. The transformation from passive object to human agent that their success implied was to Pliny's mind beyond reason: these men 'arrived with chalk on their feet, and virtually returned to the same places with a retinue of lictors bearing fasces wreathed with laurel'.

The slaves of Pliny's catalogue were people of considerable resili-ence, one must suppose, and certainly exceptional in one way or another. But for all slaves the experience of being sold from one owner to another must have been emotionally debilitating, an experience that reinforced the sheer powerlessness of the state of suspended death in which all slaves lived. According to Artemidorus (*Onir.* 4.15), it was a sign of impending good fortune if slaves who wanted a change in their lives dreamed of being sold, but for many such a dream must have been in fact a nightmare. Slaves could of course always turn to each other for comfort, like the Clarus and Urbanus between whom a deep friendship began when they met for the first time as slaves on the block, lasting through their manumission (in the same household) until Clarus' death. As an object of exchange, however, an investment to be disposed of at any time according to the fluctuations of the market, the individual slave was denied any sense of personal identity, a fact reflected not only in what the legal rules on sales contain but in what they omit as well. To identify oneself by reference to one's father, grandfather or even a more distant forebear was one of the staple features of social intercourse in classical antiquity, a conven-tion that gave validation much like the display in today's world of a driver's licence or credit card. But while the seller of a slave had to be frank about the condition and character of the slave he was selling and while he had to say where the slave came from, he was not required to name the slave's parents. Since slavery destroyed all kinship ties, there were no parents to be recognised in any formal manner. The contrast between free and slave was thus a contrast between person and non-person, and the contrast stands out strongly in documents like that recording the sale of Abaskan-tis: the man who sold the girl was Artemidoros, son of Aristokles, the man who bought her Pamphilos, otherwise known as Kanopos, son of Aegyptos. But she was merely 'the slave girl Abaskantis, or by whatever other name she may be known, a ten-year-old Galatian'.[33]

The Forum was the heart of the city of Rome, the site of the senate house, the courts of law, a variety of religious buildings and monuments to civic attainments. It was here at one time or another that citizens could hear politicians addressing the crowds, catch a glimpse of senators debating matters of high policy, listen to advocates pleading their cases before a jury, watch the passing of a triumphal procession, observe priests offering sacrifices to the gods. But because the Forum was also the main centre of commerce and exchange people could hear too the sounds of buying and selling. And near the Temple of Castor in the south-western corner there was a particular noise to be caught, that of 'the regular, daily traffic in slaves'. Amid the sounds of Rome's political and legal life, of its religious and commercial business, the voices of the slavedealers could often be heard ('Sardinians for sale!'), and for the objects on view the response to the dealers' cries determined the whole future course of their lives – to whom they belonged and for whom they worked, what jobs they did and where they lived, what social universe they built for themselves. Yet as they stood at this crossroads in their lives the objects themselves seem for the most part to have endured the proceedings in silence.[34]

---

[33] Debilitating: on the treatment of depression ('tristitia'), see Celsus 3.18.17–18 for the sort of understanding that most slaves would not normally expect. Clarus and Urbanus: *CIL* 6.22355a. Investment: *Dig.* 17.2.65.5; 24.1.31.10.

[34] Noise: Mart. 9.29.5–6. 'Sardinians': Festus 428 L.

CHAPTER 4

Slave labour

In the Egyptian town of Oxyrhynchus in A D 79, Herodes son of Apion sent word to local officials that two slaves named Amarontos and Diogenes, one a slave in the service of his brother, the other in that of his wife, had died. The papyrus document that records the news (*P.Oxy.* 3510) gives little information about the slaves. But because Herodes described them as slaves 'without a trade' it makes clear that while alive they had not been trained to perform specific jobs – say those of weavers or fullers or stenographers. An orator of the second century A D observed that in a poor household the same slaves did the cooking, kept the house and made the beds, and even a weaver who had been rented out might have to return at night to bake bread for her master. So perhaps Amarontos and Diogenes had been slaves, like Apuleius' Photis, who did anything and everything required of them – in Photis' case portering, stabling horses, carrying messages, preparing food, attending guests, waiting at table and putting her mistress to bed; Photis even knew something of her master's money-lending business. In wealthy, upper-class households, by contrast, it was conventional for slaves to be assigned very precise duties, a point that Tacitus emphasised (*Ger.* 25.1) when comparing Roman and German slaveowning practices. It was a habit reflecting the Roman's fixation with categorisation and hierarchy, a fixation that in the sphere of religion – to the cynical bewilderment of Augustine (*de Civitate Dei* 3.12) centuries later – assigned a protective divinity to every imaginable process of the natural world. Whether undertaken in wealthy or not so wealthy households, however, slave occupations covered an enormous range of activities. My purpose in this chapter therefore is to illustrate the diversity of slaves' work-roles in the Roman world and to draw some inferences from the evidence on slave labour about the nature of Roman slavery at large.[1]

For legal purposes the Romans divided slaves into two categories, those who belonged to the city household, the *familia urbana*, and those who belonged to the rural household, the *familia rustica*. The division was predicated on the assumption that the typical slave-owner maintained a residence or residences in the city stocked with slave domestics and owned landed property in the country that was worked, at least in part, with slave labour. Among the upper classes, if not slaveowners generally, this pattern was common. The classification, however, was sometimes taken to mark a distinction between domestics on the one hand and slaves who did agricultural work on the other, no matter where they lived; in other words it was not the place of employment but the type of work that determined how a slave was categorised. Thus a *dispensator* (steward) who kept the accounts of a rural estate and lived there was an urban slave regardless, as too the child of city slaves sent to the country to be reared. To some degree, therefore, the classification was artificial, and in practice much depended on the individual slaveowner's judgement of who was an urban and who was a rural slave.[2]

Within both categories the number of occupations discharged was virtually limitless. The range of jobs held by slaves who normally worked in the country can be illustrated from a section of the *Digest* (33.7) discussing what was included in the legacy of a rural estate (*fundus*) with its equipment (*instrumentum*), the equipment being not just the tools and machinery of the farm but also the human work force 'provided for the producing, gathering and preserving of the fruits (*fructus*)' (*Dig.* 33.7.8 pr.). This could comprise both the slaves who actually worked the land and those whose responsibility it was to cater to their, and their owner's, material needs. At times it became necessary to specify exactly which slaves

---

[1] 'Without a trade': see Montevecchi 1973: 180–1; Hübner 1978: 198–200. An orator: Aelius Aristides, *Eis Romen* 71. Rented out: *P. Wisc.* 16.5. Photis: Ap. *Met.* 1.22–4; 1.26; 2.7; 2.11; 3.13. For comparable situations in modest households in Rio de Janeiro, see Karasch 1987: 208. For Roman slaves or former slaves with double occupations, note *ILS* 7402: Flavianus, *notarius* (stenographer) and *actor* (manager); *ILS* 7672: P. Cornelius Philomusus, *pictor scaenarius* (stage-painter) and *redemptor* (contractor); *ILS* 7659; Julius Victor, *cuparius* (cooper) and *saccularius* (porter).

[2] *Dig.* 32.1.99 pr. – 5; 33.9.4.5; 33.10.12; 50.16.166 pr.; 50.16.210.

Table 1 *Rural slave jobs in* Digest *33.7 ('The legacy of* instructum *or* instrumentum*')*

1 auceps	: fowler	14 cellararius	: steward
2 bubulcus	: ploughman	15 diaetorius	: valet
3 fossor	: ditcher	16 figulus	: potter
4 ovilio	: shepherd	17 focaria	: kitchen maid
5 pastor	: herdsman	18 fullo	: fuller
6 putator	: pruner	19 molitor	: miller
7 saltuarius	: forester	20 mulio	: muleteer
8 venator	: hunter	21 ostiarius	: doorkeeper
9 vestigator	: tracker	22 paedagogium	: trainee waiter
10 vilicus/monitor	: overseer	23 scoparius	: sweeper
11 ancilla	: maidservant	24 suppellecticarius	: furniture
12 aquarius	: water-carrier		supervisor
13 atriensis	: majordomo	25 topiarius	: gardener
		26 vilica	: vilicus' wife

27 faber, qui villae reficiendae causa paratus sit :	mason intended to repair the villa
28 lanificae quae familiam rusticam vestiunt :	the woolmakers who make clothes for the rural household
29 mancipia ad cultum custodiamve villae et quae ut ipsi patri familias in ministerio ibi essent :	slaves intended to cultivate and guard the villa and to wait on the head of the household
30 mulier villae custos perpetua :	woman who is permanent custodian of a villa
31 mulieres quae panem coquant quaeque villam servent :	women who bake bread and look after the villa
32 quae pulmentaria rusticis coquant :	women who cook relishes for the rural slaves
33 pistor et tonsor, qui familiae	a baker and barber intended to serve
34 rusticae causa parati sunt :	the needs of the rural household
35 servus arte fabrica peritus :	a slave skilled in the craft of a smith

went with a legacy, and it is from such lawyers' rulings that Table 1 is compiled.[3]

The list is instructive on several counts. The combination of agricultural and domestic jobs suggests for example that many rural estates were largely self-sufficient enterprises (that was certainly the Roman ideal), while the inclusion of jobs for women, all within the domestic sphere, confirms that throughout the central period female slaves were normally to be found on farms. The list is most useful, however, as an introduction to the wide variety of

[3] Cf. also *Dig.* 19.2.19.2.

Table 2 *Some rural slave jobs from Columella*

1 actor	: bailiff	19 messor	: reaper
2 arator	: ploughman	20 monitor	: overseer
3 arborator	: tree-pruner	21 olearius	: oilpress
4 atriensis	: majordomo		worker
5 aviarius	: poultry-keeper	22 opilio	: shepherd
6 bubulcus	: ploughman	23 pampinator	: vine-trimmer
7 caprarius	: goatherd	24 pastinator	: trencher
8 capulator	: oil-drawer	25 pastor	: herdsman
9 cellarius	: storekeeper	26 pastor gallinarum	: poultry keeper
10 ergastularius	: jailer	27 porculator	: pig-breeder
11 faenisex	: mower	28 procurator	: agent
12 fartor	: poultry fattener	29 promus	: provisions keeper
13 fossor	: ditcher	30 putator	: pruner
14 holitor	: market-gardener	31 stabularius	: stable-keeper
		32 subulcus	: swineherd
15 iugarius	: stableman	33 veterinarius	: animal doctor
16 magister operum	: taskmaster	34 vilicus	: bailiff
17 magister pecoris	: head shepherd	35 vilica	: wife of vilicus
18 magister singulorum officiorum	: foreman	36 vindemiator	: vintager
		37 vinitor	: vine-dresser

Roman slave occupations and to the way slaves tended to be given precise positions. For instance it might have been thought that the jobs of the *ostiarius* and the *scoparius* were too light to require two slaves in one household for them, that perhaps both could have been done by the same person; but that is not the implication of the specialised job-titles. And again, while the *bubulcus* might have been 'one who ploughed with the oxen' or 'one who fed the plough-oxen', in neither case does it seem that he did anything that overlapped with any other functionary. For farm work in general that is also the impression conveyed by Table 2, a list of jobs compiled from the agricultural treatise of Columella, most if not all of which could be held by slaves.[4]

---

[4] *Bubulcus*: *Dig.* 33.7.18.6. Table 2: Columella's text frequently makes clear the slave status of the workers mentioned, but not always. But it is doubtful that any of the jobs listed in the table could not have been held by slaves: at Col. 10.228 the status of the *putator* is uncertain, but the appearance of the term in Table 1 is enough to show the possibility or likelihood of slave status.

Columella's handbook, it should be noted incidentally, is essentially Italocentric, as are the treatises on agriculture of Cato and Varro. What is said about slave labour, therefore, cannot automatically be taken to apply to the provinces or to give evidence of provincial conditions. Indeed the argument has been made that because rural slaves almost never appear in commemorative inscriptions, rural slavery in Rome's provinces was negligible under the Principate. The subject is contentious. Excavated provincial villas, however, have shown that farmsteads certainly had the capacity to house slave workers and further investigations may make the picture clearer. Meantime the presumption that the very poor ought to have been able to leave epigraphic traces of themselves for modern historians to see is not in itself self-evident, while the reality of mass rural slavery in Italy in Rome's central period, which is not in dispute, could scarcely be documented from the inscriptional record alone.[5]

In the urban domestic sphere both the range of slave jobs and the tendency to particularism can be seen from Table 3, a list of jobs filled by domestic servants from the household of Augustus' wife, Livia. They are known from the survival in a tomb used by Livia's household of inscriptions recording the names and functions of various members of her staff. They do not include the jobs of servants such as cooks, waiters or launderers, all of which were essential to any upper-class Roman household, nor those of very menial workers such as the servants who catered to their owners' most basic personal needs. (Note, for instance, the slaves who were required to brush the teeth of the decrepit consular, Cn. Domitius Tullus.) The list is impressively long nonetheless. Some jobs were held by servants who at the time their names were written on the inscriptions had been set free from slavery, but there is no indication that manumission was a requirement for any single occupation. Detailed study has revealed that Livia's domestic staff 'was relatively large; that the structure was highly organised, though not rigid; that there was a chain of command, and degree among the servants ... and a strong emphasis on specialisation'.[6]

---

[5] Argument: MacMullen 1987. Villas: Samson 1989.

[6] Personal needs: see Petr. *Sat.* 27.3 for a eunuch kept by Trimalchio to carry around a silver chamber-pot for him, and cf. Epictetus 1.2.8–11. Cn. Domitius Tullus: see Plin. *Ep.* 8.18.9. Detailed study: Treggiari 1975 (quotation, 60).

Table 3 *Slave jobs in the household of Livia*

1	aquarius	: water-carrier	30	paedagogus	: pedagogue
2	arcarius	: treasurer	31	a pedibus	: supervisor of footmen
3	argentarius	: silversmith			
4	ab argento	: servant in charge of the silver	32	pedisequus	: footman
			33	pedisequa	: female attendant
5	atriensis	: majordomo	34	pictor	: painter
6	aurifex	: goldsmith	35	pistor	: baker
7	calciator	: shoe-maker	36	ad possessiones	: financial administrator
8	capsarius	: clothes folder			
9	colorator	: furniture polisher	37	a purpuris	: servant in charge of purple garments
10	cubicularius	: chamberlain			
11	supra cubicularios	: supervisor of the chamberlains	38	rogator	: issuer of invitations?
12	delicium	: pet child	39	a sacrario	: servant in charge of shrine
13	dispensator	: steward			
14	faber	: craftsman			
15	insularius	: keeper of apartment block	40	sarcinatrix	: clothes mender
			41	a sede	: chair attendant?
16	lanipendus	: wool-weigher			
17	lector	: reader	42	strator	: saddler
18	libraria	: clerk	43	structor	: builder
19	a manu	: secretary	44	ab suppelectile	: servant in charge of furniture
20	margaritarius	: pearl setter			
21	medicus	: doctor			
22	supra medicos	: supervisor of the doctors	45	tabularius	: record keeper
			46	a tabulis	: servant in charge of pictures
23	mensor	: surveyor			
24	nutrix	: wetnurse			
25	opsonator	: caterer	47	unctrix	: masseuse
26	obstetrix	: midwife	48	ad unguenta	: servant in charge of perfumed oils
27	ab ornamentis	: servant in charge of ceremonial dress			
			49	ad valetudinarium	: sickbay orderly
28	ornatrix	: dresser	50	a veste	: servant in charge of clothes
29	ostiarius	: doorkeeper			

Source Treggiari 1975

Table 4 *Further slave jobs in elite roman households*

1	ab admissione	: servant in charge of screening guests?	20	ocularius	: oculist
			21	praegustator	: food-taster
			22	pumilio	: dwarf
2	asturconarius	: groom	23	quasillaria	: spinster
3	architectus	: architect	24	sarcinator	: clothes mender (m.)
4	caelator	: chaser			
5	cantor	: singer (m.)	25	specularius	: glazier
6	cantrix	: singer (f.)	26	a specularibus	: servant in charge of windows?
7	cellarius	: storeman			
8	chirurgus	: surgeon	27	a statuis	: servant in charge of statues
9	cocus	: cook			
10	comoedus	: comic actor	28	sumptuarius	: cashier
11	a cubiculo	: servant in charge of the bedroom	29	symphoniacus	: musician
			30	tabellarius	: courier
12	a cyatho	: cupbearer	31	textor	: weaver (m.)
13	diaetarchus	: room supervisor	32	textrix	: weaver (f.)
14	fullo	: fuller	33	tonsor	: barber (m.)
15	ad imagines	: servant in charge of pictures & busts	34	tonstrix	: barber (f.)
			35	topiarius	: gardener
			36	tricliniarcha	: dining-room supervisor
16	inaurator	: gilder			
17	librarius	: secretary (m.)	37	unctor	: masseur
18	marmorarius	: marble-cutter	38	vestificus	: tailor (m.)
19	ministrator	: waiter	39	vestifica	: tailor (f.)

Source Treggiari 1973

Since Livia was the wife of an emperor it is not surprising that her domestic entourage was large. But if her household was extraordinary, it was extraordinary only in degree not in kind. Investigation of elite households at Rome in the Julio-Claudian era has shown how complex the urban *familiae* of the wealthy generally were, with even more titles of jobs emerging to add to those known from Livia's staff (Table 4). Moreover, the domestic retinue was not restricted to the very rich nor confined to the capital. Apuleius' portrait of a leading provincial citizen in the *Metamorphoses* (8.30–9.2) comes complete with slave retinue including a cook (who had his own wife and son), a muleteer, a chamberlain and a doctor; and similarly a papyrus from the early second century A D (*P.Oxy.* 3197) detailing how the slaves of the prominent Alexandrian Ti. Julius Theon were to be divided among his descendants, shows that Theon had owned in his lifetime at least five stenographers, two amanuenses, one cook, a barber and a repairer (perhaps a clothes-mender). The retinue of Musicus Scurranus may also be recalled.[7]

Then there is the staff of the rich and boorish freedman
Trimalchio in Petronius' fictional work the *Satyricon*, a group of
domestic servants with functional titles just like those found in elite
households – the *ostiarius* and the *atriensis*, the *dispensator* and the
procurator, cooks and carvers, doctors and masseurs, messengers
(*cursores*), an *actuarius* (record-keeper) and a *nomenclator* (a slave to
announce the courses at dinner in this case). Trimalchio also had
troupes of entertainers on hand, musicians, acrobats and readers,
and any number of attractive boys from Alexandria and Ethiopia
to wait at table and catch the eye of his guests. Petronius assumed
in this picture that men of means, no matter how newly acquired,
would wish as a matter of course to ape the lifestyles of the rich
and famous and that a former slave like Trimalchio would show
no hesitation at all in submitting a host of underlings to the sorts
of indignities of which he had first-hand experience himself.
The elite set fashions that *arrivistes* valued far more highly than con-
science.[8]

It is evident from Tables 1–4 that slaves were often skilled artisans, so it is not surprising that slaves were also to be found in the
workshops that produced Arretine ware, the high-quality red-
glazed pottery that was widely used in the Roman world (and
beyond) during the central era. The slave contribution to this
industry, which was considerable, is known from the potters'
stamps displayed on the finished pottery products, where the
workers' names and those of their owners are given on the pattern
'Damas Ar(ri) Q(uinti) servus' or with ownership expressed by a
simple genitive case alone. At Arretium (Arezzo) itself, where in
the middle of the first century BC production of what was to be
called Arretine ware seems to have begun on a large scale, about
ninety workshops have been identified, employing up to as many as
sixty slaves. A certain Rasinius and a man named L. Titius are on
record at least as having owned sixty slaves each, though the slaves
were not necessarily all at work at the same time. Other owners had
much smaller numbers, many in the teens. Many slaves had names
that suggest eastern origins – Agatho, Cerdo, Hermia, Pamphilus
and the like – which may mean that they were imported to the west

---

[7] Investigation: Treggiari 1973.
[8] See Baldwin 1978.

because of their special expertise. But this can be no more proven than the common belief that slave and master worked alongside each other in the manufactories; nonetheless, the slave presence in the production of Arretine ware is beyond dispute.[9]

From the simple procedure of surveying slave jobs, it appears that no occupation in Roman society was closed to slaves. The only exception, as it happens, was military service, from which slaves were legally, and uniquely, barred. Yet this did not mean that there were any occupations that were formally reserved for members of the servile population alone. In practice domestic servants tended overwhelmingly to be slaves or ex-slaves as far as can be told, but job titles, especially those from the world of agricultural work, were used of slave and free alike. The free poor of Roman society had to provide themselves with income, which for many meant working as casual wage-labourers in jobs sometimes, and sometimes simultaneously, shared by slaves: at Rome itself under the Principate, for example, the construction of public works sponsored by emperors drew on casual wage-labour to a significant degree but without completely excluding slave labour. Many former slaves also continued after manumission to do the same jobs they had done previously as slaves. Nothing indicates therefore that there was a strict separation of slave labour from free labour, or indeed that there was necessarily any competition between the two. In a society where slaves were primarily a social, not an economic category, any such notion would have been alien to the prevailing mentality. In the famous discussion of occupations in Cicero's treatise *de Officiis* (1.150–1), Cicero makes clear the view that anyone who worked for wages, which of course slaves did not normally do, was living in a state of servitude. But while the Romans passed down from generation to generation a stereotyped portrait of the slave as an unscrupulous, lazy and criminous being, and while they thought of certain races, Asiatic Greeks, Syrians and Jews, as being born for slavery, and while they thought certain punishments like crucifixion and burning

---

[9] See Pucci 1973; Pucci 1981; Peacock 1982: 120–2; Dyson 1992: 115–16. Potters' stamps: Oxé and Comfort 1968.

alive were suitably servile, they never thought of any one form of work as being specifically appropriate just for slaves.[10]

The wide range of slave employments, whether functional (*officia*) or skilled (*artificia*), appears to have been well established in Roman society by the beginning of the central period. In the late Republic the elite tended to stock their residences with greater and greater numbers of domestic servants as a form of competitive ostentation, while in agriculture, particularly in regions of central and northern Italy, slaves tended to grow in numbers at the expense of the Italian peasantry (though not to the extent of ever eradicating the peasantry). A marked increase in slaves' work-roles could thus be expected in the first century BC, but such a development would only have intensified patterns already well in existence in the second century BC. When C. Sempronius Gracchus returned to Rome from Sardinia to stand for the tribunate in 124 BC, he deemed it prudent to inform the people that he had not surrounded himself while in his province with a retinue of handsome slaves, the implication being that it was already conventional for the Roman aristocrat to regale himself in this way. Earlier Cato took the use of slave labour by his peers as normative when writing his agricultural handbook, while in Plautus a multiplicity of slave occupational titles can be seen that closely resemble those visible in Tables 1–4, especially in the domestic sphere. Consequently the heterogeneous nature of slave work should be regarded as characteristic of Roman slavery throughout the central era.[11]

---

[10] Military service: to have allowed slaves to fight as troops, for which citizenship was required, would have been to promote the integration of the slave into established society, an object that in other respects Romans did promote, but at a certain risk. Unless in abnormal conditions such as civil strife, therefore, the arming of slaves was not sanctioned. (The Roman attitude anticipated that of the slaveowning states of the United States, but in Brazil necessity at times dictated the use of slave troops, see Degler 1971: 75–82; and on the more regular use of slave troops in Islamic society, see Lewis 1990: 62–71.) Roman slaves, however, regularly accompanied their owners on military service as batmen and animal caretakers, see Welwei 1988 with Vegetius 3.6; 3–7; cf. Dio 56.20.2. Reserved: see Joshel 1992: 176–82 for an extensive list of job-titles held by slaves and free workers. In practice: Finley 1973: 81. Public works: see Brunt 1980a. Discussion: see Finley 1973: 41–61. Stereotyped portrait: Bradley 1987a: 26–30. Certain races: Cic. *de Provinciis Consularibus* 10; Liv. 35.49.8; 36.17.5. Specifically appropriate: note, however, that according to Veget. 1.7, some jobs held by men (those of fishermen, fowlers, confectioners and linen-weavers) could be judged womanish in comparison with those of the blacksmith, carpenter, butcher and the hunter of stags and boars.

[11] *Officia, artificia*: *Dig.* 50.15.4.5; 32.65.1. C. Sempronius Gracchus: Gel. 15.12.2. Cato, Plautus: see Astin 1978: 245–6; Dumont 1987: 373–8; Bradley 1989: 26–30.

Table 5 *The hierarchy of slave jobs in elite households, Rio de Janeiro 1808–1850*

1 *Mucamas*:
    (a) ladies-in-waiting, personal maids
    (b) housekeepers and domestic slave managers of unmarried owners; wetnurses; sometimes owners' mistresses/common-law wives.

2 Slave children of masters:
    (a) playmates and babysitters for owners' legitimate children
    (b) later trained as *mucamas* (girls) and valets/pages (boys)

3 Domestic slaves:
    (a) coachmen, liveried footmen, stablemen, sedan chair carriers
    (b) cooks, food buyers
    (c) clothes makers, launderers
    (d) cleaners, water-carriers, waiters, kitchen workers, refuse workers

Source Karasch 1987, 208–10

The great diversity of slaves' work roles, however, was not unique to Roman slave society. Because the slave systems of the New World were principally concerned with the production of marketable crops, it is an easy assumption that, save for a few domestics, slaves were field hands and nothing more. But the assumption is false, for in the cities of the Americas slaves worked in all manner of service industries and in trades of every level of skill imaginable, from portering and quarrying, street-cleaning and milling to skilled manufacturing, commerce, slave management and personal service. The city of Rio de Janeiro in the early nineteenth century is an especially apposite example, for there, as at Rome, prosperous slaveowners kept sizeable entourages of specialised retainers in their urban residences both for the personal services provided and as symbols of wealth and status, arranged in carefully nuanced hierarchies (see Table 5). There too slave artisans working in manufactories made cigars and candles, hats and paper, soap, cotton and tiles. And there, in the city at large, slaves were ubiquitous, to quote a partial list, as 'printers, lithographers, painters, sculptors, orchestral musicians, nurses, midwives, barber-surgeons, seamstresses and tailors, goldworkers, gemcutters, butchers, bakers, sailors, ships' pilots, coachmen, stevedores, fishermen, hunters, naturalists and gardeners'. The correspondence with Rome is striking, despite the gulfs of time and distance.[12]

Slaves, of both sexes, were expected to work throughout their lives. On farms children were put to work at early ages tending animals, helping to prune vineyards, harvesting fodder for live-stock; and in the artisanal sphere it was common for the young to be trained in handicrafts such as weaving, shoe-making, jewellery-making and so on. In domestic service instruction of some sort might also be required – it could take two months for example to become an *ornatrix* – and at court even the cupbearer had to be taught his art. Slave boys sometimes worked as grooms in the imperial cavalry unit known as the *equites singulares Augusti*: thus a boy named Primitivus, a Cappadocian by birth, is known from an inscription set up by his master when he died, aged only thirteen. In later life slaves could again be assigned the simple tasks of childhood, henkeeping, gathering fodder, watering animals, or else be given jobs like that of a doorkeeper that cannot have been onerous. Others could continue to work as nurses or innkeepers, obstetricians or shepherds, but the concept of retirement did not exist.[13]

Because slaves worked from childhood into adulthood (or simply through the force of circumstance), it was possible to progress from one job to another of greater responsibility. Columella rec-ommended (1.8.1–3; 11.1.3) that although he should be prepared for the post from boyhood a slave should not be appointed as farm bailiff (*vilicus*) before the age of thirty-five, so great were the prior knowledge and experience needed for such an important position. The historian Timagenes of Alexandria, who once caused offence to Augustus, is said to have come to Rome as a captive in 55 BC and then to have advanced from the job of cook to that of litter-bearer before gaining the chance to pursue an intellectual interest (the jurists, however, saw the promotion of litter-bearer to cook as more

---

[12] Easy assumption: Dyson 1992: 34. Cities: see Wade 1964, on the United States. Rio: see Karasch 1987: 185–213.

[13] Children: see Bradley 1991: 103–24. *Ornatrix*: *Dig.* 32.65.3. Cupbearer: Heliodorus, *Ethiopica* 7.24; 7.27, which can be presumed relevant to the Roman *a cyatho* (Table 4, no. 12). Primitivus: see Speidel and Panciera 1989. Later life: Col. 8.2.7; Plin. *Nat.* 13.132; Ap. *Met.* 9.27; Plaut. *Curculio* 76; Sen. *Ep.* 12.3; Heliodorus, *Ethiopica* 7.14; Plaut. *Aulularia* 807; Ap. *Met.* 1.21; *Dig.* 37.10.3.5; Ap. *Met.* 8.19. Cf. Petr. *Sat.* 132.3 on the standing of the *quasillaria*; and *Dig.* 32.1.61 for the progression from *textor* to *ostiarius*, perhaps as a result of advancing years.

realistic – or else the two were jobs to be held in combination). The dream-interpreter Artemidorus knew of a domestic slave (*Onir.* 2.15; cf. 2.30) who was promoted to oversee the whole household to which he belonged, a move that of course had been presaged by a dream. Conversely, slaves thought to be in need of punishment could be demoted, the cook suddenly becoming just a messenger-boy, and the privileged urban domestic being sent off to manage a distant rural estate.[14]

Promotion is better understood, however, though still no more than imperfectly, in the case of the slaves of the imperial household who as clerks, record-keepers and financial agents served as low-level operatives in the administration of the Roman empire in the second half of Rome's central period. Their names and occupational titles are often known from sepulchral inscriptions – as with Felix, a *verna* who was *adiutor rationalium* (assistant keeper of accounts), or Hermas, a *dispensator a tributis* (tax-steward), or Rhodon, an *exactor hereditatium legatorum peculiorum* (collector of inheritances and bequeathed *peculia*), or Abascantus, also a *verna*, a *dispensator annonae* (steward of the grain supply), or Quintianus, another *verna*, and *vilicus et arcarius XX hereditatium* (supervisor and treasurer of the 5 per cent inheritance tax), or Alexander Pylaemenianus, *ab bybliothece Graeca templi Apollinis* (in charge of the Greek library in the Temple of Apollo), and so on. It was possible for such men, whether born into the imperial *familia* or recruited from outside, to advance through what loosely resembled a career structure, beginning with subordinate positions while still young and proceeding to positions of greater authority after manumission, which typically came when they were about thirty. For some, especially in the first century AD, the way was open to participate directly in the highest levels of Roman government.[15]

Few careers are known in detail. But one that is relatively full, and quite astonishing, is that of a man who can be identified not in his own right but only as the father of a son named Claudius Etruscus. Originally from Smyrna in Asia – he was born about AD 2/3 – this man served as a young administrator in the household

---

[14] Timagenes: Sen. *Con.* 10.5.22; Sen. *de Ira* 3.23.4–8; cf. Treggiari 1969: 223. Jurists: *Dig.* 32.65.1 (Marcian); 32.99.4 (Paul). Punishment: Petr. *Sat.* 47.13; 69.3.
[15] Felix: *ILS* 1480. Hermas: *ILS* 1512. Rhodon: *ILS* 1523. Abascantus: *ILS* 1537. Quintianus: *ILS* 1557. Alexander Pylaemenianus: *ILS* 1589. Career structure: see Weaver 1972: 199–281.

of the emperor Tiberius, by whom he was set free. He accompanied
Caligula when the emperor travelled north in AD 39 and was probably promoted to a provincial financial posting under Claudius and
Nero before eventually becoming *a rationibus*, secretary in charge of
the emperor's accounts, under Vespasian. Vespasian indeed conferred upon him the rank of *eques*, second only to that of senator,
and his marriage, under Claudius, to a woman of free birth produced two sons who also gained equestrian standing. Under
Domitian he fell into disfavour and was exiled, but he had been
reinstated by the time of his death, close to the age of ninety. His
overall advancement was spectacular.[16]

The slave career depended on the fact that within the individual
familia there was an occupational hierarchy in which, say, the *vilicus*
was acknowledged to be the superior of the *pastor*, the *cubicularius* of
the *ianitor*, and this in turn depended on the wide range of jobs to
which slaves were generally admitted. For slaves to quarrel over
who had the highest standing in the household was not unknown.
But in society as a whole there was also a *de facto* hierarchy of servile
statuses, positioning in which was determined by not only the type
of work done but also its context: so *rustici* were automatically
inferior to *urbani* (at least in a slaveowner's judgement), the size of
the *familia* to which the slave belonged was relevant and the social
standing of the owner as well. The situation was again very much
like that of Rio de Janeiro in later history, when slaves at the
bottom of the scale in wealthy households ranked higher than the
top slaves of less prosperous slaveowners, and mulattoes could even
have more social prestige than many free whites. At Rome the
slaves who enjoyed the most elevated rank in the hierarchy were
those like the father of Claudius Etruscus who belonged to the
greatest and most powerful slaveowner in the world and who
played a role in governing the Roman empire. Their standing was
such that they were commonly able to take as wives women of
superior juridical status, women that is who were freed or even
freeborn. Many of them lived in relatively secure material sur-
roundings, enjoying wealth and power which others could come to
resent. And often they were slaveowners themselves.[17]

---

[16] Weaver 1972: 284–94; cf. Millar 1977: 73–4; Evans 1978: 104–5.
[17] Quarrel: Dio Chrys. 34.51. *Rustici*: their 'inferiority' emerges, for example, from Quint.
Inst. 1 pr. 16; 1.11.16; 2.20.6; 2.21.16; 6.1.37; 6.3.13. Rio: Karasch 1987: 66–75. Wives:
Weaver 1972: 112–36. Resent: Plin. *Nat.* 18.7.

At the opposite extreme, however, there is the slave world evoked by Apuleius when describing the farm to which his hero Lucius was sent – transformed as he was into an ass – to sire mules. The property, owned by a woman of good standing but a provincial, supported a community of grooms, herdsmen and shepherds who with their wives and children lived in comparative isolation far from their owner's urban residence, working under the supervision of a *vilicus* and a *vilica*. They had little opportunity to acquire wealth or power or status. The *vilica* was resourceful enough to use the new ass to mill grain, some of which she sold to neighbours, and a slave child sold wood that he gathered on the mountainside to cottagers who needed fuel. But these were not sources of great income. The *vilicus* and his wife, the highest ranking slaves on the farm, lived in no more than a cottage (*casula*) and the hands' wives were their juridical peers, not their superiors. Life was so harsh in fact that the men had to be prepared to take justice into their own hands at any moment and to show little hesitation about physically assaulting travellers they suspected of stealing from them. And such was their lack of security that when their owner unexpectedly died, the slaves were compelled to flee, fearing that a new owner might disrupt their lives completely: the arrival of a slaveowner at a farm he seldom visited was a predictably disturbing experience that could split slave families in an instant. Having loaded up their few possessions on pack-animals and appropriated the livestock in their charge (chickens, geese, goats and dogs), the slaves made off under the *vilicus'* direction and travelled for several days before reaching a town they thought would be safe from pursuers, protecting themselves along the way with weapons with which they usually protected their animals. They were taken for a pack of brigands and driven off, however, and it was only after further travels that they were able to find a refuge in which to try to begin a new life.[18]

Most *rustici* – and most slaves were *rustici* – will have lived in circumstances like these, in relative seclusion, at subsistence or near-subsistence level, with a minimum of social and economic security and few prospects of betterment. As with other groups – the slaves who worked in the appalling conditions of the mines (the silver mines of Spain for example where at New Carthage alone in the second century BC there were 40,000 workers) or those who

[18] Ap. *Met.* 7.15–28; 8.1; 8.15–23. Cf. Longus, *D & C* 4.19.

were kept most of the time in chains – their circumstances were variations on a theme of desperation. They can have had little community of interest with the slaves of the emperor.[19]

The employments to which Roman slaves were admitted, then, required so many different levels of skill, expertise and education and were so great in number and so disparate in nature, context and social meaning that slaves in the Roman world could never come to comprise a single, homogeneous class. A prominent Marxist historian of antiquity has described a social class as 'a group of persons in a community identified by their position in the whole system of social production, defined above all according to their relationship ... to the conditions of production ... and to other classes'. Its concomitant, class struggle, he calls 'the fundamental relationship between classes ... involving essentially exploitation, or resistance to it'. It is indisputable of course that all Roman slaves shared a common juridical status and it is true that the fundamental distinction between slavery and freedom affected everyone; as Quintilian remarked (*Inst.* 5.10.26), it made a great difference whether one were free or a slave. Moreover Roman slaveowners exploited all their slaves, their elite slaves included, and exploitation was resisted in a variety of ways. Yet as far as can be told there never developed among the slave population a sense of common identity – or class consciousness – that led to an ideological impulse to produce radical change in society. The slave population was too fragmented for that to happen, one of the reasons being that the multiplicity of slave occupations, compounded by differences of origin and geographical location, utterly prevented the emergence of any idea of making common cause. The antagonism between farm hand and bailiff that popular literature assumed conventional illustrates the point. As the slaveowner's representative on the spot, the bailiff gave the slave orders for work, managed his daily routine, and disciplined him. In so doing he became the object of intense anger and defiance: he was after all only a slave himself. Accordingly a competition between the two for the favour and support of the master, fought out in an atmosphere of mutual antipathy, suspicion and fear, was not an obvious inducement to unity of cause and purpose. The diversity of

---

[19] Silver mines: Diod. Sic. 5.38.1; Str. 3.2.10 = Polyb. 34.9.9; the workers were probably slaves (though note the remarks of Edmondson 1987: 85–6; 1989: 95), but Polybius may have exaggerated their number: see Walbank 1979: 606; Richardson 1976: 142–3. Chains: Col. 1.7.1; 1.8.16–17.

slave jobs and slave statuses in Roman society served to disperse, not to unite, the slave population, which should never be conceived of as a solid, undifferentiated monolith.[20]

Why was so much stress put on particularism where slaves' jobs were concerned? The most revealing piece of evidence on this question is a passage from Columella (1.9.5–6) discussing slaves' work-roles ('opera familiae'). It refers obviously to agricultural slavery, but there is no reason to doubt that the principles it lays down applied in the domestic sphere too. According to Columella, jobs should not be shared because the individual slave would not work industriously if they were, and no one could be held accountable if it turned out that work had been done poorly. It was thus of great importance on this view to maintain a strong distinction between the *arator* (ploughman) and the *vinitor* (vine-dresser) and to keep both apart from the *mediastini*, the ordinary farm labourers. Columella was concerned with extracting high performance from a work force that had no inherent interest in either the quality or the rate of work being done, his object being to secure as substantial a revenue from the land as possible. He thus clearly recognised the need to create an incentive by which to induce efficiency from slave workers and appealed to their pride in urging that they be held responsible for specific tasks. It was a pragmatic response, one that both acknowledged the human character of the slave property and assumed a similarity of values between slave and master.[21]

The need to adopt a realistic strategy of this kind was present throughout the central period. In the last two centuries of the Republic the numbers of slaves involved in Italian agriculture increased dramatically as free peasants left the land under the impact of Rome's military requirements or in response to pressure from magnates seeking to extend and develop their landholdings with slave labour. Under the Principate, moreover, the profile of slave labour in agriculture remained high. An argument has been made that over time an increase in contiguous slave-staffed holdings necessitated more slave supervisors than was economically rational

---

[20] Historian: Ste Croix 1981: 43–4 (quoted). Class consciousness: not necessarily a requirement of class struggle, according to Ste Croix 1981: 44, which to my mind seems to be in the domain of M. Jourdain. Antagonism: *Vit. Aesop.* 9–11; cf. the remarks of Foxhall 1990: 103.
[21] Cf. Bradley 1987a: 21–2.

and that a labour crisis consequently developed by the second century AD; this, however, is a position that cannot be sustained by hard evidence. The maintenance of the agricultural slavery system over a period of four centuries or so – much longer than in any of the slave societies of the New World – implies on the contrary that slaveowners derived satisfactory and uninterrupted levels of profit from it, a view supported by the recent demonstration that slaves working in cereal production and viticulture (in particular) were kept fully occupied throughout the year by the demands of the production process and were not a wasteful form of labour as has sometimes been believed. But slaveowners were aware that lack of motivation (*inertia*) on the slave's part was a basic obstacle to labour efficiency, for while the free peasant had to work in order to feed himself and his family, the slave would always be fed by a master mindful of the need to protect his investment, whether he worked or not.

Not surprisingly, Italian landowners never relied exclusively on slave labour but preferred to use different methods of working the individual farms that made up their holdings. The younger Pliny, for instance, who owned a number of farms in two main units, one at Comum and one at Tifernum Tiberinum in Umbria, worked some of his lands with slaves and leased others to tenants, *coloni*, who might in fact have slaves of their own; likewise Columella (1.7.6) advocated free management of estates that the owner could not visit regularly. But when the decision to employ slaves had been taken the obstacle of *inertia* had to be overcome and specialisation was one solution. Another was to use a system of gang labour which, as cliometric studies of New World slavery have shown and as Columella again understood, increased efficiency not by making slaves work longer hours but by making them work faster. The two methods complemented each other. Columella described the gang system in this way (1.9.7–8):

You should . . . form groups of not more than ten men each – our ancestors called them *decuriae* and were very much in favour of them, since it is particularly easy to keep watch over this number of men, while a larger crowd can escape the control of the overseer as he leads the way. So if you have a large estate, you must assign these groups to different sections of it, and the work must be distributed in such a way that the men will not be on their own or in pairs, since they cannot be supervised properly if they are scattered all over the place; and conversely they must not be in groups of more than ten, since individuals will not consider that the work has anything to do with them personally if they are part of a large crowd. This system will induce them to compete with each other, and also identify those who are lazy.[22]

To emphasise the variety of slaves' work-roles is to emphasise how visible slaves were in every aspect of Roman economic life, both in primary production (agriculture, mining, manufacturing) and in the provision of services. In the cities, towns and countryside of the Roman world working slaves were a fixed element of reality that could not be missed, no matter what the local overall density of the slave population. In everyday commercial life – that is in activities such as shopkeeping, trading and banking – slaves were particularly noticeable, operating as their owners' managers and agents with a great degree of latitude and independence, a pattern clearly shown by a section of the *Digest* (14.3) that deals with the contractual liability of those who appointed agents to undertake business for them. The agent, who could be free or slave, a man or a woman, was called an *institor* and was appointed 'to buy or sell in a shop or in some other place or even without any place being specified' (*Dig.* 14.3.18). Any number of enterprises could thus be in the hands of slaves – managing a farm, buying houses, cattle or slaves, shopkeeping and innkeeping, banking and moneylending, trading and contracting of every kind. Slaves were to be found too as captains of the vessels that were sometimes needed for commercial activities – the ferries that crossed the Adriatic from Brundisium to Cassiopa or Dyrrachium, for example, and the freighters that carried cargoes of vegetables, hemp and marble. Keeping a shop or an inn was presumably a permanent occupation. But some commissions were short-term, going to slaves who already had more regular jobs, an *insularius* or a *stabularius* or a *mulio*. And the owners who appointed them were not just the very rich: the slaves of tailors and cloth merchants, of launderers and bakers were also appointed to hawk, deliver and sell their masters' products; even the slaves of undertakers conducted business for their masters.[23]

[22] Argument: see, for example, Carandini 1981. Satisfactory levels: Finley 1973: 84. Demonstration: Spurr 1986: 133–46. Lack of motivation: Var. *R*. 1.18.2 (see Spurr 1986: 134). Landowners: on the dispersed holdings of the very wealthy, see Garnsey and Saller 1987: 66–71. Pliny: *Ep.* 3.19.7; 9.37, with Duncan-Jones 1974: 19–20; 323. Cliometric studies: Fogel 1989: 72–80.

[23] Captains: *Dig.* 14.1. See in general, Kirschenbaum 1987: 89–121. Slave agents often had to be literate but they were the exception rather than the norm; see Harris 1989: 255–9.

One slave who can actually be seen at work, so to speak, is the financial agent Hesicus, a man known from a set of wax-tablets from Murecine on the Bay of Naples that give details of various money-lending transactions in which Hesicus was involved. In the summer of AD 37 Hesicus acted for his owner, the imperial freedman Ti. Julius Evenus Primianus, when a certain C. Novius Eunus, a dealer in foodstuffs, borrowed HS 10,000 from Evenus. The collateral for the loan was a volume of grain and other items of food that C. Novius Eunus had in storage at Puteoli. Beyond this, however, Hesicus also made a loan of HS 3,000 to the food merchant in his own right, using assets, that is to say, that were in effect his own. Thirteen months later the second loan had not been fully cleared and new terms were fixed for payment of the outstanding balance. Now, however, Hesicus was no longer the slave of Ti. Julius Evenus but of the emperor. He had changed hands, but his capacity to act as an independent financial broker had clearly not been affected.[24]

No commercial activities, it must be repeated, were the exclusive domain of slaves: 'If a master frees a slave whom he has appointed to manage a bank and then continues the business through him as a freedman, the change of status does not alter the incidence of risk' (so Papinian: *Dig.* 14.3.19.1). The freed banker was formally integrated into society in a way that was impossible for the slave banker. But from a strictly transactional point of view – at the very moment when money was being borrowed, or a house sold, or bread delivered – the status of the agent must often have been immaterial and the formal distinction between slave and free of little importance.

It is frequently said, however, that slaves were outsiders or marginal beings and that their marginality, continually reinforced by their rightlessness, contrasted very sharply with the centrality of those who were able to participate fully in human and civic affairs. 'The essence of slavery', on one formulation, 'is that the slave, in his social death, lives on the margin between community and chaos, life and death, the sacred and the secular.' This conceptualisation is very valuable, as seen earlier, for pointing up the extent of the slave's powerlessness and for emphasising that without the master the slave could not exist; and to recognise the slave's alien aspect makes it easier to understand why the slave, although a dominated being, was also an object of anxiety: for at Rome as in other major slave societies

---

[24] See Casson 1984: 104–7, with *A E* 1972.86, 87, 88; *A E* 1973.138, 143.

fear of revolt by those cut off from the mainstream was widespread and far more prevalent than the actual incidence of insurrection would suggest.[25]

Yet the social and economic intercourse between free and slave represented by the evidence on commercial life makes it impossible to describe Rome as a society simply comprising those on the inside and those on the outside. Full participation in the life of the civic community was in fact confined to wealthy, adult male citizens, a situation that by definition denied many social groups the full benefits of belonging. Under the Principate for example it was impossible until the time of Septimius Severus for Roman legionaries to marry and to produce legitimate offspring, but their incapacity did not generate a belief that Roman troops were in some way excluded from or did not belong to society. Slaves were a different category of course. But it is still probably better to think not so much in terms of all slaves being complete outsiders as in terms of degrees of relative incorporation into the mainstream of community life dependent on slaveowning interests; or, if the metaphor of marginality is kept at all, at least to acknowledge that the margins of society at Rome had to be very broad indeed. At the individual level, certainly, slaves were at times positively embraced by their masters and treated with personal regard.[26]

In Cicero's correspondence there is a sequence of recommendations (*commendationes*) in which Cicero typically solicits a favour from a well-placed addressee on behalf of a less privileged but deserving third party. The letters provide important evidence of how the benefits of authority were distributed in Roman society. In one example (*Fam.* 13.26) from 45 BC, Cicero wrote to the jurist and consul of 51 BC, Ser. Sulpicius Rufus, who was then governing the province of Greece, and asked him to intervene in a financial dispute on behalf of L. Mescinius, the man who had been Cicero's quaestor when he himself held the consulship in 63 BC. A problem had arisen in connection with the implementation of the will of Mescinius' brother, who had lived and conducted business in the Greek city of Elis. Cicero's request was evidently successful for later he wrote to Sulpicius again (*Fam.* 13.28) to thank him for his help, and to importune him further. He spoke of Mescinius thus:

[25] Frequently said: Lévy-Bruhl 1934: 15–33; Finley 1973: 70; Wiedemann 1987: 3–4. Formulation: Patterson 1982: 45–51 (quotation, 51).

[26] Legionaries: see Campbell 1984: 301–3.

I am clear that Mescinius himself will prove a source of great satisfaction to you. He is a man of fine, upright character, in the highest degree obliging and attentive, and he shares those literary pursuits which used to be our diversion and are now our life.[27]

On another occasion in 45 BC (*Fam.* 13.21) Cicero recommended to Sulpicius Rufus a resident of Sicyon, M. Aemilius Avianius, and, more arrestingly, this man's freedman, C. Avianius Hammonius. Clearly a person Cicero wished to advance did not have to be of the same social status, but the language of commendation Cicero used for the former slave was essentially the same as that used of the senator Mescinius:

I like him for his exceptional conscientiousness and fidelity towards his former master; moreover, he has rendered me personally important services, making himself available to me in the most difficult period of my life, with as much loyalty and good-will as if I had given him his freedom.

Then as now letters of recommendation were to some degree composed formulaically.[28]

That Cicero could speak so positively of an ex-slave is a fact that deserves attention (particularly when it is kept in mind how scathing he could otherwise be), as does Cicero's assumption that Sulpicius Rufus would not have been perturbed when he found a former slave warmly recommended to him. Yet this was not an isolated example. At other times Cicero spoke (*Fam.* 13.46) of the freedman L. Nostius Zoilus as a person 'of good character' and called him his friend, described (*Fam.* 13.23) the freedman L. Cossinius Anchialus as 'very highly thought of by his master and his former master's connections', among whom he counted himself, and called (*Fam.* 13.70) the freedman T. Ampius Menander 'a worthy, modest person' of whom he had 'an excellent opinion'. These remarks imply that it was perfectly possible at Rome for the socially inferior to win the esteem of their superiors and for the latter to draw the former firmly into society: 'So I do particularly ask you to take him under your wing

---

[27] *Fam.* 13.28.2: '... quod ex ipso Mescinio te video magnam capturum voluptatem; est enim in eo cum virtus et probitas et summum officium summaque observantia tum studia illa nostra, quibus antea delectabamur, nunc etiam vivimus'. See in general, Cotton 1986.

[28] *Fam.* 13.21.2: 'Nam cum propterea mihi est probatus, quod est in patronum suum officio et fide singulari, tum etiam in me ipsum magna officia contulit mihique molestissimis temporibus ita fideliter benevoleque praesto fuit, ut si a me manumissus esset.' I give the Latin here and in n. 27 to emphasise the similarity of language. Formulaically: see Saller 1982: 108.

and include him in your circle', Cicero said of the freedman C.
Curtius Mithres (*Fam.* 13.69), addressing himself this time to the
governor of Asia, P. Servilius Isauricus (cos. 48 BC). Patronage was
one mechanism by which the process of incorporation took place.[29]

These esteemed freedmen were not, of course, current but former
slaves, men whose movement from the far edges of the community
had already been greatly facilitated by having been set free. It must
be presumed, however, that their manumission had followed their
owners' perception in them of the very same personal qualities that
allowed Cicero to support them in his letters of recommendation, no
matter how conventionally those qualities were expressed. Thus it
was entirely appropriate for Cicero to recommend a man who was
still a slave if the situation called for such a step, as it did when he
wrote approvingly (*Fam.* 13.45) to a senatorial magistrate in Asia,
again in 46 BC, of the *eques* L. Egnatius and Egnatius' slave Anchialus: 'Of all Roman Knights, L. Egnatius stands on the most familiar
footing with me, and I recommend to you his slave Anchialus and his
business affairs in Asia as warmly as if I were writing of my personal
interests.'

The men Cicero commended were, like the entrepreneur Hesicus,
all dependants who in one way or another were occupied with
commerce or business matters (*negotia*). Hammonius was his
patron's *procurator*, an agent who transacted *negotia*; the slave Anchialus was associated with L. Egnatius' *negotia* in Asia, where again in
46 BC a group of three other freedmen recommended by Cicero,
Hilarus, Antigonus and Demonstratus, were also similarly active on
their patron's behalf (*Fam.* 13.33); Mithres needed help in a property
dispute. The pursuit of business was by law and tradition closed to
the Roman senatorial order, whose members throughout the central
period saw their primary function as directing the affairs of the civic
community through competitive careers in politics, law and government. Despite their high-minded devotion to statecraft, however, the
Roman elite were at the same time and without conflict equally
devoted to maintaining and increasing their private fortunes. Many
of them therefore were appetitively engaged in trade, banking,
moneylending and other business activities, but obliquely rather
than openly, working through intermediaries and agents who for the

---

[29] *Fam.* 13.69.2: 'Ut igitur eum recipias in fidem habeasque in numero tuorum te vehementer
etiam atque etiam rogo.'

most part were their slaves and former slaves. From an upper-class viewpoint procurators, shopkeepers and ships' captains were perhaps peripheral beings and without doubt contemptible as types, but the crucial part they played in managing their owners' affairs gave them a place that was firmly within society not outside of it. When Cicero spoke warmly of a friend's 'domestic circle, property and agents' (*Fam.* 13.38), the phraseology was integrative and inclusive.[30]

What slaves themselves thought of the particularistic work regime that slaveowners imposed upon them it is very difficult to tell. Many, it seems, estimated that their best prospects of survival and success lay in accepting their condition and in living within the confines of the social system around them. But in so doing they may have found in their work-roles the means by which to establish a sense of individuality and a sense of belonging to a community – the community of the *familia*. Many of the job-titles of Roman slaves, especially domestics, are known from commemorative inscriptions that were set up by or for men, women and children who had known the lived reality of slavery. Thus the fact that so many slaves and former slaves chose to leave records of the positions they had held and, if they belonged to the great *familiae* of the elite, where they had stood in the slave hierarchy may well reflect something of the values that they had created for themselves in slavery. The elite disdained physical labour and willingly demanded it of their slave dependants. But by taking the one commodity of which no one wished to deprive them, it may well have been possible for slaves to find some compensation for the human toll that slavery had taken of them.[31]

---

[30] *Procurator*: note the definition at *Dig.* 3.3.1 pr.: 'A procurator is one who transacts the business of another on a mandate from his principal' ('Procurator est qui aliena negotia mandatu domini administrat'). *Fam.* 13.38: 'domum eius et rem familiarem et procuratores'. For a letter recommending an imperial slave to a procurator in Egypt, see *CPL* 248, and on the conventional language it uses, see Cotton 1981: 28–33.

[31] See Joshel 1992.

CHAPTER 5

Quality of life

If slaves were able to find individual purpose and common support in the households in which they found themselves, the complaisant slaveowner who believed himself attentive to his slaves' needs would not have been surprised, for the household was like a miniature state, he would have said, and a sense of community was thus a natural expectation. But what did it mean to be attentive to slaves' needs? On the material plane Roman slaveowners were under a strong obligation to provide their slaves with the basic necessities of life – food, clothing and shelter (*cibaria, vestitus, habitatio*) – and the equation between good treatment and good performance was easily made. But material necessities were one thing, luxuries another, and as the law made clear it was only reasonable that there should be limits to what owners expended on maintaining their complements of slaves. What then were slaves' living conditions generally like at Rome? Under what sort of material regime did Roman slaves spend their lives? It is with these questions that this chapter is now concerned.[1]

To judge from conventional descriptions, the food rations (*cibaria*) that slaves were allotted were meant to be functional and little more. The term 'cibaria' meant most of all the lower-grade bread that seems to have constituted the principal element of the slave diet, or simply the grain from which the bread was made, if it was not alternatively converted to a form of porridge. But the term could also include other items, such as drinking-water, wine, oil, salt and grapes, as well as the *pulmentarium*, a sort of mash that was

---

[1] Miniature state: Plin. *Ep.* 8.16.2; cf. Sen. *Ep.* 47.14. Obligation: *Dig.* 15.1.25; 15.1.40; cf. 15.3.20 pr.; Tac. *Agricola* 31.2. Basic necessities: *Dig.* 34.1.6. Limits: *Dig.* 15.3.3.3; cf. 15.3.3.6; Sen. *Tranq.* 9.9.

eaten with bread as a relish and that could be made from any number of ingredients according to season and availability. Cato (*Agr.* 58) recommended the use of olives for the purpose, or allec and vinegar, and as a winter substitute Columella (12.14) recommended the use of dried apples and pears. In times of shortage the basic supply of bread could be replaced with dried figs.[2]

The prescriptive evidence of the agricultural writers indicates that slaveowners, even absentee landowners, had enough common sense to understand that their slaves – their rural slaves in particular – had to be adequately fuelled if they were to labour efficiently. So the *vilicus* was charged to ensure that the hands did not go hungry; the master must personally inspect and taste the rations the *vilicus* prepared to make sure they were edible; and from time to time the *vilica* was to inspect the kitchens and the workers who made up the slaves' food. In the domestic regimen, it was the custom for the *materfamilias* to supervise the provisioning of the slaves in the household. But the monthly allocations of grain or bread and the annual rations of wine, olives, oil and salt laid down by Cato (*Agr.* 56–8), the only agricultural author to go into detail on this topic, do not appear to have been overly generous. Any slaveowner who followed Cato's prescriptions was aware that he could not afford to be wasteful, and Varro's notion (*R.* 1.17.5) that good performance by slaves should be rewarded with additional amounts of food (among other things), with its touch of hard calculation, is rather sinister. A distinction could be drawn, it seems, between adequacy and generosity.[3]

A diet heavily dependent on cereals met basic energy requirements fairly well as long as sufficient supplies were available, but the mineral content of lower-grade breads was not easily absorbed and cereal alone could not supply some key vitamins. Dry legumes and vegetables could make up these deficiencies. But for this to happen, to increase their rations and to widen the range of foods they might consume, many slaves must often have had to use their

---

[2] *Cibaria*: Cato, *Agr.* 56–8; Var. *R.* 1.63; Col. 2.9.16; 12.52.18; 12.52.21; Plin. *Nat.* 14.35–6; 18.87; 18.90; Suet. *Galba* 7.2; Ap. *Met.* 6.11; 6.20; *Dig.* 15.3.3.1; 15.3.3.7; 33.7.12 pr.; 33.7.18.3. *Pulmentarium*: see Corbier 1989: 227–8; cf. Dionisotti 1982: 101. Figs: Col. 12.14.1; Plin. *Nat.* 15.82.

[3] Prescriptive evidence: Cato, *Agr.* 5; Col. 1.8.17–18; 12.3.8; cf. 1.8.12; 11.1.19. Custom: *Dig.* 15.3.21; 24.1.31.9. Monthly allocations: see Etienne 1981; cf. Bradley 1989: 51–2. See, in general, Foxhall and Forbes 1982.

own ingenuity and to fend for themselves. Domestic slaves in wealthy households, especially kitchen staff, were able to take whatever the master and his family did not want: thus Apuleius' pastry chef and cook (*Met.* 10.13–14) regularly brought back to their living quarters at night all sorts of things left over from their rich owner's dinner – meat, poultry, fish, desserts – much to the delight of Lucius the ass. A thoughtful slaveowner like Trimalchio's wife might even supervise distribution of the leftovers directly, if she were indecorous enough. Rural slaves, Varro suggests (*R.* 1.19.3), regularly kept livestock, more or less their own, from which to supplement their rations, and field hands who had only portions of bread and olives were able to gather as many wild greens as they wished to eat with them. Both in the city and the country, kitchen-gardens produced a wide range of vegetables – onions and lettuce, beets and artichokes, peas and beans – which not only gave extra food but allowed the chance of extra cash from sale of the surplus.[4]

A pattern that must be presumed typical emerges from the romance *Daphnis & Chloe*, where slaves working for an absentee landowner take what they need from the farm on which they work within the limits of restraint imposed by their accountability. Daphnis, trying to prove at one point (1. 16) that he is not impoverished, maintains that he has an abundance of 'cheese, bread baked on a spit and white wine', three food elements that recur in the story time and time again: thus cheese is often given as a gift, while wine can be drunk mixed with milk. In season, there are apples and pears, wild and cultivated, and in the autumn there is honey that can be used for honey-cakes. In the winter Daphnis hunts for birds to eat, but only once eats meat (boiled mutton) when he is a visitor in Chloe's house, not with his own slave family. The food available to Daphnis and his foster-parents does not seem particularly extensive in range, and the quality overall is far different from that served at the banquet at the end of the romance when a superior bread appears with waterfowl, sucking pigs and so on. Shortfalls are a real possibility. Yet there are no catastrophic shortages of

---

[4] Cereals: see Rickman 1980: 3–7, on grain as the dietary staple in antiquity. Energy requirements: Garnsey 1991: 70–7; 82–8 (pointing to the absence of vitamins A, B₂, C, D); cf. Evans 1980: 156. Leftovers: cf. Juvenal 11.142–3. Kitchen-gardens: Plin. *Nat.* 19.52–189; cf. Juv. 11.80; Jashemski 1979; see Karasch 1987: 89 on Brazilian slaves selling off surplus produce.

food in the world of *Daphnis & Chloe*. Initiative and self-reliance prevent crisis.[5]

The Roman domestic slave was usually housed in one of the many small rooms called cells (*cellae, cellulae*) that grand Roman houses and villas contained as a matter of course and that were often used for storage purposes. Most domestics, that is to say, lived under the same roof as their owners. Within the housing complex the wealthy owner, Pliny for instance (*Ep.* 7.27.12–14), was able to close himself off from the slave quarters when he wished to maintain his privacy, but it was thought odd nonetheless that the slave quarters should be absolutely separate from the owner's living space as among the tribes of Germany. The size and the furnishings of slaves' cells must have varied according to owners' resources and the abilities of slaves to improve and enhance what they were given. For Trimalchio it was a mark of great affluence (he thought) to be able to boast that the doorkeeper's cell in his house was very grandiose, and certainly some cells could easily house more than one person: the pastry chef and the cook in Apuleius (*Met.* 10.13; 10.15) – they were brothers – shared a cell large enough to accommodate Lucius as well, and it was an easy assumption that *servus* and *conserva* lived together in one of these rooms. But rather modest impressions tend to prevail in the literary record as a whole. Cicero for example (*Philippicae* 2.67) took it for granted that his social peers would be outraged by the notion of M. Antonius' slaves covering their beds with purple coverlets looted from the estate of Cn. Pompeius, and it was an enormous extravagance for a slave, even if an imperial slave, to have a perfumed bathroom. The bed in the cell where Nero slept when he fled to his freedman Phaon's villa in the crisis of AD 68 had just an ordinary mattress with an old cloak strewn across it for a blanket, far more appropriately. Both Horace (*Sermones* 1.8.8) and Seneca (*de Tranquillitate Animi* 8.6) envisaged the slave cell as tiny and cramped.[6]

Impressions of modesty also prevail in the evidence provided by Roman domestic architecture. Slave quarters in Roman houses are

---

[5] Longus, *D & C* 2.18; 3.7; 3.20; 1.15; 2.8; 3.18; 1.23; 2.38; 3.24; 3.33; 4.2; 3.5; 3.9; 3.7; 3.10–11; 4.26; 3.30. Cf. Musonius 18A (Lutz 113).
[6] Pliny: cf. *Ep.* 2.17.9; 5.6.41. Germany: Tac. *Ger.* 25. Trimalchio: Petr. *Sat.* 77. Assumption: Sen. *Con.* 7.6.8. Cicero: cf. Quint. *Inst.* 8.4.25. Bathroom: Plin. *Nat.* 13.22. Nero: Suet. *Nero* 48.4.

difficult to identify precisely and the subject seems not to have attracted a great deal of attention from archaeologists. But from the limited amount of information available a tendency is apparent for the service areas that would have accommodated slaves to have been marginalised in relation to the main residential areas, either by being secluded in some way or by being given inferior forms of construction and decoration, or both. In the very lavish House of the Menander at Pompeii, the area identified as the slave quarters was situated on a level below and beyond that of the main living area, in a sort of basement, and was accessible only by proceeding along and down long, narrow corridors. Nearby, in the equally opulent Villa of Oplontis (Torre Annunziata) slaves seem to have lived in rooms situated on two levels around a peristyle, all of inferior constructional quality, the rooms themselves painted with black and white diagonal stripes in a manner that has been termed simply 'crude'. In another wealthy house at Pompeii, the House of the Vettii, a service area was separated off from the main part of the house and focused on a secondary courtyard; here too the living space looks to have been poorly decorated and poorly lit as well. Even in a less prosperous house that had perhaps only a handful of slaves the same marginalising principles applied. So in the House of the Prince of Naples, also at Pompeii, the slave quarters were out of the way on an upper floor; access was controlled from the porter's lodge on the ground floor, a room which was completely without decoration – contrast Trimalchio's house – and which again had minimal lighting. Clearly therefore when domestics were no longer needed by their owners they could effectively be banished, though they were never far away. It was not only domestic slaves, however, who lived in houses such as these. The Villa of Oplontis, it has been suggested, like the Villa of the Mysteries at Pompeii, also accommodated slaves who worked the owner's lands (the Villa of Oplontis had a wine-press). Likewise the owners of the House of the Menander may have had slaves at work in vineyards and market-gardens kept nearby within the city walls. Domestic and farming slaves were not always rigidly segregated.[7]

A category of slaves who sometimes lived in relative freedom

[7] See Packer 1975: 136, 139; Wallace-Hadrill 1988: 78–81; 86; Clarke 1991: 14; 25–6; 128; 170; 208; Wallace-Hadrill 1991: 212–13; 214; 220–3.

were those who were involved with their owners' *negotia*. Ulpian
(*Dig.* 5.1.19.3) referred to a specific situation in which a provincial
had a slave *institor* selling merchandise for him in Rome, and Gaius
(*Dig.* 40.9.10) spoke generally of 'persons who carry on business
through slaves and freedmen beyond the sea or in regions where
they are not living themselves'. Such slaves could presumably enjoy
the benefits of independence, but they were also obliged to provide
for themselves in a way the members of a domestic entourage did
not.

In rural areas proper, farm slaves could also be housed in cells in
a villa, as the plans of excavated establishments in Italy suggest (at
Settefinestre for example) and the agricultural writers confirm. But
because of the kind of work they did some slaves could find themselves as an alternative inhabiting separate, more isolated structures. Columella (8.11.3; 8.14.1), giving instructions on how to
raise peafowl and geese, spoke of building cells for the keepers
within the enclosures that contained the birds, within the surrounding colonnades in the case of the geese keeper, while Varro
(*R.* 3.9.7) recommended a cell in the area of a farm that was
devoted to poultry-raising for the poultry keeper: it was in fact to
be a large unit, but not for the convenience or benefit of the *galli-
narius* so much as to provide lots of nesting space for the hens. Cells
of this type seem to have been intended for one person only. Living
units suitable for rural slave workforces but separate from the main
residential areas have also been detected at some provincial sites,
for instance at Warfusée-Abancourt in France and Köln-
Müngersdorf in Germany. In the latter case wooden partitions
may have been in use to create cells within a larger dormitory
structure.[8]

Many rural slaves, *pastores* in particular but arable workers and
fishermen too, lived in simple huts or cottages (*casae, casulae*) that
were very unpretentious in quality and aspect. They were thrown
up in makeshift fashion from whatever bits of lumber or other
materials might be available (reeds or turf, for instance) and had
roofs covered with thatch or leaves. They could accommodate families of husband, wife and children or just single individuals. Slaves
who followed the herds over vast areas of pasture would have to
build new huts frequently, in one spot after another, abandoning

---

[8] Plans: see Bradley 1989: 52–3. Provincial sites: Samson 1989: 103–6.

them when necessary like the *pastores* in Apuleius who undertook mass flight at the news of their owner's death. They were synonymous with poverty – not places where burglars were expected, only an inhabitant such as a poor market-gardener who 'could not even afford any straw mat or thin coverlet for himself . . . but had to live content with the leafy shelter of his *casula*'. It was in the *casa* that *cibarius panis*, the least nutritious of breads, belonged.[9]

What slaves wore was determined to a large extent by the jobs they did and, as in other matters, by the generosity of their owners. At one extreme rebellious *pastores* living in Sicily in the late second century BC are said by Diodorus Siculus (34/35.2.29), in a passage intended to stress slaves' ill-treatment and slaveowners' cruelty, to have used the hides of wolves and wild boars as clothing, presumably because they had been allocated nothing better. One Sicilian slaveowner in particular, Damophilus of Enna, instructed a number of naked domestics who dared to ask him for clothes to steal what they needed from passing travellers, a scenario that sounds quite implausible, though it was not unusual in modern Brazil to see slaves at work whose owners gave them nothing to wear at all. In a similarly pathetic context, Apuleius (*Met.* 9.12) describes slaves working in a mill wearing only threadbare rags, some no more than a loin-cloth. As long as they could survive and work, owners did not have to trouble themselves unduly about the material welfare of slaves like these.[10]

At the opposite extreme, however, domestic slaves who worked as *ministratores* and *pedisequi* had special liveries or uniforms, in addition to their everyday clothes, to wear on those occasions when their owners wanted to advertise their wealth and taste, including plentiful amounts of jewellery. So Byrrhaena, the type of the provincial aristocrat in Apuleius (*Met.* 2.19), had 'liveried waiters' and 'pretty curly-headed pages in handsome clothes' to put before her dinner guests, while Theagenes, the hero of Heliodorus' romance (*Ethiop.* 7.27), was given 'sumptuous Persian apparel' to

---

[9] Huts: Lucretius 6.1252–5; Var. *R.* 2.10.6; Liv. 5.53.8; Valerius Maximus 7.6.1; *Dig.* 1.8.5.1; Cic. *Scaur.* 25. See Frayn 1979: 117–22. Thrown up: Dion. Hal. 1.79.11; Liv. 25.39.3; 35.27.3; Tib. 1.10.39–42; Luc. 5.517, 522; Mart. 12.72.2. Accommodate: Tib. 1.10.39–42; Luc. 5.517; Juv. 14.166–71. Apuleius: cf. *Met.* 3.29. Herds: Var. *R.* 2.10.6. Poverty: Ap. *Met.* 9.32. *Cibarius panis*: Cic. *Tusculanae Disputationes* 5.97 (cf. Fronto, *ad Antoninum Imperatorem* 1.3.2); Celsus 2.18.4.

[10] Damophilus: Diod. Sic. 34/35.2.38; cf. Brazil: Karasch 1987: 130.

wear complete with 'bangles of gold and collars studded with precious gems', when serving as the cupbearer of Charikleia. In similar fashion Dom João VI was habitually carried in his sedan chair in Brazil by twelve black slaves dressed in red silk. Ostentation could reach outrageous limits, paradoxically so in the view of Damophilus: the Augustan senator Cestius Gallus is said to have made a habit of having himself waited upon by slave women wearing nothing at all. But perhaps more typical of the female domestic's dress was the simple linen tunic of Photis in Apuleius (*Met.* 2.7; 2.9), which she wore, attractively, with 'a dainty, bright red band tied up under her breasts'. For ordinary table servants Martial (14.158) thought the drab-coloured wool from Pollentia, near the Alps, good enough. Many of them worked barefoot, as did messengers – for the sake of swiftness, it was said, but pain and disease were more likely results.[11]

An identical degree of variety is visible in iconographic evidence. The servants depicted on the fourth-century AD toilet box known as the Projecta casket, for instance, recall the pampered servants of Byrrhaena: the women wear boots and mantles and either striped dalmatics with decorated cuffs and borders or long-sleeved tunics caught up under the breast, while the men have striped tunics with long, tight sleeves and ornamental discs. They are all well-dressed, but not as grandiosely as their bejewelled mistress. A similar situation obtains on a third-century AD relief from Neumagen where four female attendants are shown assisting their mistress in her toilet, none of them betraying any sign of material discomfort. Elsewhere, however, the look is altogether different. Shepherds in works of art typically wear just a short, sleeveless or half-sleeved tunic made of linen or sheepskin, especially the *exomis* exposing the right shoulder, with hide or sheepskin boots and sometimes leggings, while fishermen have only loincloths and bath attendants even less. In between these extremes fall the kitchen and table slaves shown preparing and serving food on a relief from Trier and mosaics from North Africa, and the smiths shown in their workshops on reliefs from Pompeii: all men, they wear various simple

---

[11] Liveries: *Dig.* 15.1.25. Jewellery: Sen. *Tranq.* 1.8. Dom João: Karasch 1987: 191; cf. 221–6 on the range of clothes given to slaves in Rio, very comparable to the Roman situation. Cestius Gallus: Suet. *Tib.* 42.2. Table servants: see D'Arms 1991: 173. Barefoot: Vitruvius 7.4.5. Messengers: Musonius 19 (Lutz 123). Pain and disease: cf. Karasch 1987: 130–1.

styles of tunic characterised by plain utility, not elaborate orna-
mentation.[12]

As with food allowances, practical slaveowners like Cato (*Agr.*
5.2) and Columella (11.1.21) knew that it was important to ensure
that their slaves were clothed reasonably well and that on the farm
the *vilicus* should regularly check that all was in order (twice a
month according to Columella). Slaveowners also knew that clothing allowances could be exploited to their own advantage, but
information on actual rations is minimal. In apprenticeship contracts the young apprentice, who may be slave or free, is sometimes
entitled to a new tunic every year. But Cato (*Agr.* 59) recommended new allocations to farm hands only every other year –
tunic, blanket/cloak, wooden shoes – and as far as possible the old
clothes were to be recycled. The clothes he gave out were probably
hard-wearing and longlasting, the kind Artemidorus (*Onir.* 2.3)
thought slaves might sometimes dream about, though this was a
bad sign, Artemidorus said, for slaves who were anxious to be set
free. There might of course always be a windfall: clothes for sex was
a not improbable exchange. Meantime mending clothes was a job
that could be done when heavy rain interrupted the slaves' normal
outdoor work.[13]

The material life of the slave in the Roman world, as in later slave
societies, was determined on the one hand by the slave's function,
standing and relationship with the master and on the other hand by
the degree of responsibility with which the master met his (or her)
material obligations to the slave. Generalisations about the 'typical' material environment of the slave in the central period of
Roman history must necessarily be cautious, therefore, yet the
evidence described so far implies on the face of things a fairly bleak
material regime for most Roman slaves. There were always exceptions. But in the hierarchical world view of elite Romans differing
material standards were supposed to reflect differences of status in

[12] Projecta: see Shelton 1981: 27–8; 72–4. Neumagen: see Wightman 1971: plate 14b.
Shepherds: see Frayn 1984: 84–7. Fishermen: see Veyne 1987: 135 (plate). Bath attendants: see Snowden 1976: 220 (plate); Desanges 1976: 256 (plate); Dunbabin 1989: 42.
Table slaves: see Gardner and Wiedemann 1991: plate 3; Dunbabin 1978: 123 and plates
114, 115. Smiths: see Stefanelli 1990: plates 2, 3, 5. On the contrast between the clothes of
house slaves and those of field hands in the United States, note McFeely 1991: 12.
[13] Exploited: Var. *R.* 1.17.7. Contracts: see for example *P. Oxy.* 725 (of a free apprentice),
with Bradley 1991:103–24. Clothes for sex: *Vita Aesopi* 75. Mending clothes: Cato, *Agr.* 2.3.

society at large and were to be deliberately maintained for that reason: it was, to many, perfectly logical and appropriate that the quality of food and wine served at dinner should match the varying 'quality' of the guests in attendance, and preposterous that a slave's clothing should be made of a finer fabric than the master's. It was the very hard cheese from Luna in Etruria that Martial (13.30) considered suitable for slaves. Comparison with the diet of troops in the Roman imperial army supports the point in matters of food. The basic military rations of grain, pork (in the form of bacon), cheese, vegetables and rough wine were not in themselves perhaps all that different from the rations allotted to many slaves. But it was conventional and acceptable for troops to increase their basic provisions in ways not usually available to slaves, by private purchase, for instance, or gifts from family members, or simple extortion. The result was a wide array of foods – meat, poultry, fish, seafood, fruits and nuts – that were probably not so easily available to the majority of the Roman slave population. And famine obviously enough could affect slaves as well as the free.[14]

It would be wrong, however, to claim that servile living conditions were uniformly and generically worse than those of all other groups in Roman society, as the *Moretum*, a poem written probably in the early first century A D but traditionally ascribed to Virgil, neatly illustrates. The poem describes how an impoverished farmer named Simulus rises at daybreak one winter's morning, rekindles the fire in his hearth and bakes bread and prepares an accompanying relish (*moretum*) to allow him enough for his daily need of food while ploughing his fields. Some help is given by the slave who lives with him, an African woman named Scyphale. The relish, made with pestle and mortar, is a concoction of garlic, parsley, rue and coriander, to which Simulus gradually adds some hard cheese, salt, olive oil and vinegar. He has grown the herbs in his own garden, to which in fact he devotes all his free time, producing a range of vegetables for sale in the nearby market, not for his own consumption. But it is the bread, about twelve or thirteen pounds' worth apparently, enough for Scyphale as well, that provides the basis of Simulus' food supply for the day, bread that he makes from flour he

---

[14] Dinner: Plin. *Ep.* 2.6; Lucian, *de Mercede Conductis* 26; Cic. *Att.* 13.52.3; cf. Sherwin-White 1966: 152–3. Clothing: Fronto, *de Nepote Amisso* 2.3. Diet of troops: Davies 1989. Famine: Tac. *Ann.* 3.54.

has milled and sieved himself from the store of grain he keeps in his cottage.[15]

Simulus lives in great poverty. His dwelling is a drafty *casula* that contains only a food cupboard, utensils for cooking on the hearth, and a truckle bed (where Scyphale sleeps is not clear). He cannot afford to keep a piece of pork in his house and fears hunger from his waking moment. Indoors he wears just a goatskin, with perhaps a tunic or cloak to cover his arms, adding leggings and a skin cap when he goes outside. The resemblances of detail in the *Moretum* to what has already been seen of servile conditions are striking, and even the poet's description of Scyphale as 'unica custos', though ironical, is realistic enough given Seneca's acknowledgement (*Ep.* 47.10) that a *casa* might well have a slave *custos*. It would be tempting therefore to believe that Simulus is a slave, yet the poem never clarifies his juridical status at all. It is convenient to call him a peasant, but is he freeborn, freed, or a slave? Is he working his own land or that of a patron or master? There is no way of telling. For present purposes, however, the ambiguity is important, because the authentic material situation the *Moretum* describes was at all times shared by the mass of the rural and urban population in Roman antiquity regardless of juridical rank: Simulus could just as easily represent the poor but free *colonus* as the rural slave worker in the quality of his material life.[16]

The *Moretum*, moreover, is not an isolated piece of evidence. Roman law makes clear (*Dig.* 32.1.41.3) that the material lives of former slaves cannot have improved significantly after manumission if they continued to live in the same cottages as before. Martial (9.73) quipped that a cell was a far more suitable place of residence for a free cobbler than the estate inherited from his patron. Apuleius (*Met.* 9.5) thought it realistic in one of the adultery tales in his novel to situate a poor builder and his wife in a *cellula*. Then there is Ovid's depiction (*Metamorphoses* 8.614–724) of the Italian peasant couple Baucis and Philemon: they live in a cramped *casa* (complete with thatched roof, earthen floor and kitchen-garden) that contains a minimum of humble furnishings – a rickety table has to be balanced with a piece of tile under one leg –

---

[15] On all aspects of the *Moretum*, see Kenney 1984. Scyphale: see Thompson 1989: 30–1.

[16] Peasant: Garnsey 1988: 56: 'Simulus, the peasant of the *Moretum*, is as close to an ordinary subsistence peasant as the literature of antiquity can take us.' Brunt 1990: 118 identifies peasants and slaves too closely.

and the food they eat reflects their penury: cheese and eggs, some
fruit and vegetables, pork to boil on special occasions, rough wine,
nuts, figs, dates and honey. But there is no indication that Ovid
thought of Baucis and Philemon as anything but a free peasant
couple: they are not slaves.[17]

In comparison with the free poor, therefore, slaves may often
have been at something of a material advantage: given that they
were to some degree provided for, they must in many cases have
enjoyed a security in their lives that the free poor could never have
known. The security came at a price, however, for to be protected
was to be dependent and to be dependent was to be without
control. Owners who looked to their own interests by ensuring, as
the agricultural writers advised, that their slaves were properly fed,
clothed and housed reminded their slaves of their subject status
and of slaveowners' authority and power every time material supplies were handed out. There was, after all, no guarantee that the
rations would always or consistently be made available. Those who
suffered the accident of sickness might, through no choice of their
own, suddenly find themselves on reduced amounts of food, and the
slave of a woman whose husband had provided the slave's clothing
might well be required to hand it back, still in pristine condition, if
the husband and wife divorced. Physical security was attended,
therefore, in uneasy equilibrium, by psychological insecurity. The
slave's perception of dependency cannot of course be seen directly
given the absence of slave evidence, but the records of later slaves,
to which attention may now briefly shift, provides sufficient
corroboration.[18]

In 1856 the American abolitionist Benjamin Drew published in
Boston a book of narrative accounts of life in slavery compiled from
interviews he had personally held with former slaves who had
escaped from the southern states of America to Canada. The book
was intended to win public opinion for the abolitionist cause, but it
remains an important indicator of what men and women who had
experienced slavery thought of the material environment under

---

[17] Baucis and Philemon: see Hollis 1970: 111; Frayn 1979: 121. Furnishings: cf. Quint. *Inst.*
2.4.21: conventional that the furniture of the poor should be shabby from long years of
use.
[18] Advantage: Brunt 1987: 706. Dependent: M. Aur. *Med.* 3.8. Sickness: Cato, *Agr.* 2.4; cf.
Musonius 18A (Lutz 114). Divorced: *Dig.* 24.3.66.1 ('within the year following').

which they had once lived. Many, like William Johnson, complained of the deprivation they believed they had endured: 'The man I belonged to did not give us enough to eat ... He never gave me a great coat in his life, – he said he knew he ought to do it, but that he couldn't get ahead far enough.' Francis Henderson, a former slave who escaped from Washington, D.C. in 1841 at the age of nineteen, went into much greater detail: he told of how the rain used to turn everything to dirt and mud in the log cabin in which he had lived with his aunt – the water just poured through the roof; of how he had had just a simple board for a bed and of how he had had to use his jacket as a pillow – he had never been given more than one blanket in his life; the food, 'a peck of sifted corn meal, a dozen and a half herrings, two and a half pounds of pork', had been rationed out to the hands once a week but had not gone far enough: many had had to make 'visits' to the granaries or animal pens to steal extra food; as for clothes: 'In the summer we had one pair of linen trousers given us – nothing else; every fall, one pair of woollen pantaloons, one woollen jacket, and two cotton shirts'.[19]

Identical complaints can be found in the interviews of former slaves conducted in the United States in the 1930s under the aegis of the Works Progress Administration. Jack Maddox, who had been a slave in Georgia, recalled that once he was old enough to be put to work his food ration was to some degree increased, 'but shoes, underwear, a bed was things I didn't know nothin' 'bout till I was sixteen years old'. That was a mild complaint. By contrast Jacob Manson told his interviewer:

We worked all day an' some of de night, an' a slave who make a week, even after doin' dat, wus lucky if he got off widout gettin' a beatin'. We had poor food, an' de young slaves wus fed outen troughs ... Our cabins wus built of poles an' had stick-an-dirt chimneys, one door, an' one little winder at de back end of de cabin. Some of de houses had dirt floors. Our clothin' was poor an' homemade.

Charlie Moses summed up his experience as follows: 'Hongry – hongry – we was so hongry!'[20]

[19] William Johnson: Drew 1856: 29–30. Francis Henderson: Drew 1856: 155–6.
[20] Interviews: on the problems involved in assessing the WPA evidence, see Blassingame 1975; and for the instructions the interviewers received, see Rawick 1972: 167–78. Cf. Fogel 1989: 177–8. Jack Maddox: Mellon 1988: 119. Jacob Manson: Mellon 1988: 219. Charlie Moses: Mellon 1988: 180.

At the same time many of the former American slaves knew that they had been better off than others. Benedict Duncan, a slave in Maryland for twenty-eight years, reported that he had not always had enough to eat and had had few clothes, which he wore night and day; he had had no bed, merely straw to sleep on. Nonetheless, 'The other hands were not so well used', he said, 'the truth is, I was rather ahead of them'. Thomas Cole, a slave as a child in Alabama, believed that he had always been well fed because of his mother's elevated standing in the slave hierarchy: 'We had lots ter eat dat de other slaves didn't have, as mah mother was a nurse and respectable – different from de other Negroes.' Other former slaves contrasted the hardships of life as free men and women with the relative abundance they had enjoyed in slavery. Clearly some American slaveowners were more generous than others in the way they provided for their slaves, and even on the same estate variations in material circumstances were to be expected.[21]

Given its subjective character the evidence of slave narratives is difficult to assess in absolute terms. Despite the complaints of hunger which the interviews contain, modern scholars have calculated that most American slaves actually enjoyed a varied diet that provided more nutrition than the diet of most nineteenth-century European workers. Likewise the diet of most Brazilian slaves in the nineteenth century was better than that of free poor Brazilians in the earlier twentieth century. Such generalisations have to be understood in context, however, because dietary deficiency was still an important contributory factor behind the very high mortality rates to which New World slaves were subject. But for immediate purposes, what needs to be stressed is that from their own perspec-

---

[21] Benedict Duncan: Drew 1856: 110. Thomas Cole: Mellon 1988: 56. Observe also the evidence of Georgia Baker, a woman born in Georgia who was fourteen when the Civil War in America ended; she spoke of her childhood almost with nostalgia (Mellon 1988: 5–6):

Oh yessum! Marse Alec had plenty of his slaves to eat. Dere was meat, bread, collard greens, snap beans, taters, peas, all sorts of dried fruit, and just lots of milk and butter ... Winter clothes were good and warm; dresses made of yarn cloth made up jus' lak dem summertime clothes, and petticoats and draw's made out of osnaburg ... Us had pretty white dresses for Sunday. Marse Alec wanted everybody on his place dressed up dat day (Mellon [1988], 5–6).

Such recollections may have been affected by fading memories when the WPA interviews were taken or by the contemporary conditions of the Depression. They were not common to all. Rose Williams, who had had two masters when a slave in Texas, contrasted the cruelty of the first with the generosity of the second (Mellon 1988: 128–9).

tive many slaves, whether well-fed, well-clothed, well-housed or not, were very much aware of the gulf that separated them from their owners and, more importantly, were equally aware of how their material dependence kept them anxiety-ridden and subject to their owners' control. 'I have known slaves to be hungry, but when their master asked them if they had enough, they would, through fear, say "Yes" ', observed David West, one of Drew's subjects. Edward Patterson, a fugitive from Maryland, expressed with eloquent indignation a slave's perception of good treatment:

I was well used, as it is called in the South, but I don't think my usage was human. For, what is *good* treatment? Look at the dress, – two pairs of pantaloons and two shirts in the summer; in the fall, one pair of shoes, one pair of pantaloons, and one pair of stockings. If they want more, they must buy them themselves if they can. No more till summer. Look at the eating, – a bushel of corn meal a month, sixteen pounds hog meat a month, rye coffee sweetened with molasses, and milk if they have any; for a rarity, wheat bread and butter. This is what I call good treatment. Look at the bedding, – sometimes they have a bed, sometimes not. If they have one, it is filled with straw or hay, and they have one blanket, and must get along as they can. Those who have no beds must sleep how they can – in the ashes, before the fire, in the barn or stable, or anywhere they can get . . . All this is good usage to the slave.

At all times the slave's material environment was a reflection and reinforcement of inferiority and submission to another's power.[22]

The Romans were very sensitive to distinctions of dress and the symbolic associations of costume. According to A. Gellius (6.12) it was a traditional sign of effeminacy for a man to wear a long-sleeved tunic and traditionally appropriate that a woman should conceal her arms and legs from view by wearing long, loose-fitting garments. Quintilian noted (*Inst.* 11.3.138–9) that a man's tunic was properly worn below the knee and a centurion's above, but a

---

[22] More nutrition: Fogel 1989: 140. Brazilian slaves: Queirós Mattoso 1986: 103. Context: Karasch 1987: 111–45. Gulf: Jacob Manson (Mellon 1988: 219–20):

Many of de slaves went bareheaded and barefooted. Some wore rags roun' deir heads and some wore bonnets. Marster lived in de greathouse. He did not do any work but drank a lot of whiskey, went dressed up all de time, an' had niggers to wash his feet an' comb his hair. He made me scratch his head when he lay down, so he could go to sleep.

Edward Patterson: Drew 1856: 121–2.

woman's tunic had to be well below the knee. Unadorned and simple dress, the kind that Marcus Aurelius (*Med.* 1.16) associated with his adoptive father Antoninus Pius, was the mark of a commendable frugality or even asceticism, in strong contrast to the reckless luxury of Caligula, who had a taste for silks and embroideries, gems and jewels. From time to time Caligula chose not merely to wear a long-sleeved tunic but offended all the proprieties by actually dressing as a woman. It was not quite so sensationalistic when the young Nero was displayed to the crowd in the circus in AD 51 wearing the costume of a triumphing general, but those who saw him can have had little doubt which of Claudius' sons, the adopted or the natural, was to succeed him: Britannicus, though not much younger than Nero, was wearing for the occasion only the red-bordered toga of the Roman child. The adult toga was the most distinctive item of all that Romans saw, a symbol of its wearer's citizenship and peaceful participation in the affairs of the civic community. Already in the second century BC Polybius (6.53) was aware of its immense communicative power: if purple-bordered it was the toga of a consul or praetor, if fully purple the toga of a censor, if gold the toga of a *triumphator*. Slaves could never officially wear it at all; hence the slavetrader's dodge to avoid duty on his merchandise by concealing the slave boy in a free child's toga.[23]

A correlation therefore between the clothes Roman slaves wore and the low esteem in which they were held is only to be expected. It is evidenced by the numerous anecdotes in literary sources that refer to the use of a slave disguise. Cicero for instance (*in Pisonem* 92) once accused an enemy, L. Calpurnius Piso, the consul of 58 BC, of having secretly taken ship from Dyrrachium to avoid paying his troops in Illyricum, as he had promised, wearing the clothes of a slave. After Caesar's assassination in 44 BC it was believed, so Plutarch says (*Antonius* 14.1), that M. Antonius had disguised himself as a slave as he went into hiding to protect himself. At a later date Nero is said by Tacitus (*Ann.* 13.25) to have dressed as a slave in order to wander through the streets of Rome unrecognised. For members of the Roman elite it was apparently

---

[23] Marcus Aurelius: cf. *Med.* 1.6; 6.30. Caligula: Suetonius, *Caligula* 52; cf. Seneca, *de Constantia* 18.3. Nero: Tac. *Ann.* 12.41. Toga: Luc. 7.267. Polybius: note his scorn for Prusias II of Bithynia, who to win Rome's favour is said to have dressed as a newly manumitted slave, wearing a toga, *pilleus* and *calcei*, and with shaven head (cf. Liv. 45.44.19). Dodge: Suet. *de Rhetoribus* 2; cf. Artem. *Onir.* 2.3

very easy to achieve the look of a slave – to assume what was
accepted as the stock image of a slave – and to sink thereby into
anonymity. Shaving the head to look like a prisoner-of-war or
counterfeiting the brand marks of a recaptured runaway were two
ruses that could be added to simply dressing down: slaves were
generally supposed to wear finery only at the time they were set
free.[24]

There were no clothes, however, that were uniquely associated
with slaves. Writing on the topic of legacies, Ulpian (*Dig.*
34.2.23.1–2) divided all clothing into the categories of clothing for
men, clothing for women, clothing that both men and women could
use, children's clothing and slaves' clothing; the last category comprised 'saga tunicae penulae lintea vestimenta stragula et consimi-
lia'. Strictly speaking the 'lintea vestimenta stragula', bed linens,
were not clothes at all. The *sagum* and the *paenula* were types of
cloak, the one a thick, loose-fitting woollen garment that was worn
pinned at the neck, the other a more tight-fitting cloak, heavy and
often hooded, made of wool or leather, that was intended to withstand rain and cold – a winter coat in effect. Both are associated
with slaves in the literary sources: Columella (1.89) recommended
a hooded form of the *sagum* for use by farm slaves, while Cicero (*pro
Sestio* 82) and Seneca (*de Beneficiis* 3.28.5) spoke in conventional
terms of the *paenula* worn respectively by the muleteer and the
litter-bearer. But the cloaks were worn throughout society, as was
of course the tunic, the most basic of all Roman items of dress: they
were not garments worn by slaves and slaves alone. Consequently
because the wearing of the toga by citizens was reserved for formal
occasions rather than worn everyday and particularly because
slavery was not identified with any specific racial characteristics,
the difference between slave and free was not always immediately
obvious from dress alone.[25]

The point of Ulpian's definition is that slave clothing was especially limited in comparison with that of the head of the household, his wife and his children. But it was for most slaves the
quality of what they wore, not the garments themselves, that

[24] Plutarch: cf. *Ant.* 5.5; 6.2; 10.4; 29.1. Stock image: *Dig.* 47.10.15.15. Ruses: Petr. *Sat.*
103.1–2. See Bradley 1988: 479 for other references to slave disguises; cf. Luc. 8.240.
Finery: Artem. *Onir.* 2.9.
[25] *Sagum* and *paenula*: see Wilson 1938: 104–9; 87–92. Difference: Sen. *Clem.* 1.24.1; App. *BC*
2.130; cf. *Dig.* 18.1.4–5.

allowed their appearance to be distinctive, a quality that emphasised the practical over the fashionable, the good value over the
costly. When recommending the hooded *paenula* and other items of
clothing for rural slaves Columella (1.8.9) spoke of the need to keep
off the wind, the cold and the rain, not of how the clothes looked,
and it was preferable if some clothes, perhaps those of the *vilicus*
and *vilica* and other ranking slaves, could be made on the estate
rather than be imported: it was cheaper that way. The *paenula* in
fact was commonly made from a drab, brownish but highly durable
wool from Canusium, particularly appropriate in Martial's view
(14.127) for Syrian litter-bearers. There was a lot of it to be seen in
the Rome of his day (14.129). Likewise the dingy-coloured wool
from Pollentia was suitable for slave waiters, but not the better
ones, only those who did not make the top grade. It was perfectly
correct, therefore, that when sold as a slave concubine in
Chariton's romance (*Chaereas & Callirhoe* 2.2) the heroine Callirhoe
should ask for a slave's tunic rather than put on the more opulent
clothes provided for her: in the Roman mentality clothing and
status were inseparably linked.[26]

The tie between subjection and abject appearance emerges again
in Achilles Tatius' portrait of his heroine Leucippe when she is sold
into rural slavery near Ephesus: the young woman is put into
shackles, has her head shaved, and is given only a short tunic of
cheap quality to wear; her hoe in her hand, she is a filthy and
pathetic sight (*Leucippe & Clitophon* 5.17). But the link remained
firm even in cases where the slave's dress might be of better
outward aspect as another illustration from romance indicates:
Xenophon of Ephesus' heroine Anthia is on one occasion (*Ephesiaca*
5.7) given beautiful clothes to wear by her owner, including jewels,
but not out of kindness on the owner's part: the man was a brothel
keeper in Tarentum and Anthia a prostitute working for him. As
with the liveried slaves seen earlier or, more relevantly, the Black
'Venuses' of Rio de Janeiro in a later era, the fine clothing Anthia
was compelled to wear at once advertised the owner's ostentation
and contributed to her own indignity. The dress of the *meretrix*,
(courtesan, prostitute), like that of the *ancilla* (slave woman, maidservant), was not supposed to be respectable like the dress of the
materfamilias (matron). To the extent that slaves' dress was dictated

[26] Pollentia: Mart. 14.158; cf. Plin. *Nat.* 8.191.

by the wishes and whims of their owners, the possibilities of expressing individuality and independence were automatically restricted.[27]

To judge from evidence in the *Digest* on arrangements owners made for their slaves' welfare once they – the owners – were dead, it must be inferred that many men and women took their material responsibilities very seriously. One owner for example imposed a testamentary charge on an heir for supporting slave temple guardians as follows: 'I request and impose on you a *fideicommissum* to give and supply in my memory each of my footmen (*pedisequi*) whom I have left to take care of the temple with monthly provisions and a fixed amount of clothing *per annum*' (*Dig.* 34.1.17). Another set free in his will the grandson of his nurse, provided him with an annual allowance of cash, and conferred ownership upon him of his own slave wife and children, together with 'the things he was accustomed to provide for them in his lifetime' (*Dig.* 34.1.20 pr.). Such liberality to slaves or former slaves was by no means extraordinary: alimentary arrangements, as they are called, appear in the well known Will of Dasumius, and the younger Pliny as seen earlier provided in his will for the maintenance after his death of one hundred of his freedmen.[28]

The material well-being of the slave, however, may not always have been uppermost in the owner's mind when alimentary arrangements were established. Generosity was often tempered in real life by conditions that continued to regulate the slave's existence well beyond the owner's death, thereby perpetuating the bonds of dependence that had existed during the owner's lifetime even if the slave were set free. The case of the slave Pamphilus (*Dig.* 34.1.20.3), who was manumitted by will and given an annual allowance of food and clothing on condition that he remain with the owner's son and heir, is typical. The temple slaves mentioned above would have lost their allowances had they ever abandoned their custodianship of their owner's temple. The heir, moreover, might prove to be a tyrant, prompting the beneficiaries to flee (*Dig.* 34.1.131.2). Benevolence was more apparent than real, therefore, the dispelling of uncertainty in the slave's life not a major preoccu-

---

[27] Black 'Venuses': Karasch 1987: 208. *Meretrix*: *Dig.* 47.10.15.15.
[28] Will of Dasumius: *ILS* 8379a; see the relevant restoration and translation of Gardner and Wiedemann 1991: 136. Pliny: *ILS* 2927.

pation of the slaveowner. In one case (*Dig.* 34.1.15.1) eight slaves bequeathed to their owner's concubine were to be maintained, according to the man's will, in the same manner after his death as before. But as rural slaves the eight had customarily been hired out at harvest and threshing time and during those periods the owner had had no material obligations towards them at all (the *custos praedii*, the farm bailiff, apart). Were, then, the owner's heirs obliged to give the slaves anything at those critical times of the year? The ruling, made in legal not humanitarian terms, was that nothing should change in the future unless the slaves concerned were transferred from rural to urban service, in which case the heirs were to fall under an obligation. From the servile point of view, however, the slaveowner's will did not necessarily alleviate anxiety about material subsistence despite the inclusion of alimentary clauses. At times, furthermore, controversy could arise over the precise meaning of what the will meant by 'aliment': was it just food, or clothing and housing as well? The jurists did not offer consistent replies.[29]

The suggestive fact remains that it was one of the functions of the city prefect, once the office of the prefect had been established by Augustus, to hear allegations from slaves that they were suffering from starvation caused by their owners. How common or successful such complaints were it is impossible to tell. But they cannot all have been without foundation. There were accidents after all as the jurists recognised: slaves might starve because grain that had been ordered for the *familia* never actually arrived in the household or because grain that had arrived was destroyed by fire or simply rotted (so too clothes bought for the *familia* could be lost before they ever reached their intended destination). And something more than accident might have intervened. Throughout antiquity communities lived with the omnipresent threat of famine and the recurring likelihood of shortages of food, and residents of rural communities at times of difficulty tended to feel the depredations of those who inhabited cities. All social categories were victimised, as noted earlier. But slaves were especially vulnerable in times of crisis: in A D 6 when Rome itself underwent a shortage of grain, slaves on the market, together with gladiators, were singled out, expelled from the city and driven a hundred miles away. Even when food was not

[29] Pamphilus: cf. *Dig.* 10.2.39.2; 34.1.18.5. Controversy: *Dig.* 34.1.6; 34.1.21.

in short supply it was axiomatic that slaves should eat the poorest and cheapest food in the household.[30]

Slaves who were unable to guarantee from day to day how or if they might adequately clothe and feed themselves might not always have shared the slaveowner's romantic view of the *familia* as a miniature state, a protective environment in which their wishes would be respected and implemented, particularly when at night many found little cause to thank their owners for providing them with a private living space. There were always some rural slaves who spent their nights not in the villa or the cottage but chained up in the prison-houses (*ergastula*) with which agricultural estates were provided as a matter of course, where opportunities for privacy and familial intimacy were nonexistent. Conditions for those unfortunate enough to work in mines were presumably even worse. When the domestic retinue was in transit, moreover, the cook or hairdresser could anticipate spending the night on a meagre issue of straw squeezed among the other servants, and personal attendants especially could expect to have to sleep in the owner's bedroom or outside the door on an improvised bed in case some service or other were required during the night: so a single *ancilla* attended Agrippina in her bedroom when Nero's assassin arrived to kill her. The importunate demands of owners must often have denied slaves whatever comforts and intimacy their cells might otherwise have given them, so that even to live in an opulent household brought no promise of material ease.[31]

How, then, did Roman slaves react to their material conditions? Were they sufficiently aware of the relative security in which they lived to tolerate the quality of life imposed upon them without demur, or did their material environment elicit other kinds of response? Many undoubtedly accommodated themselves to slavery and accepted their situation without question. Slavery was after all such a natural and accepted part of the social fabric in Roman antiquity that any serious questioning of it as an institution was

---

[30] City prefect: *Dig.* 1.12.1.8. Accidents: *Dig.* 19.1.21.3 (Paul); 15.3.3.7 (Ulpian); 15.3.3.10 (Ulpian). Famine: Garnsey 1988. Depredations: Ste Croix 1981: 13–14. AD 6: Dio 55.26.1. Axiomatic: Tert. *Apol.* 14.1: slaves receiving the same cuts of meat as dogs: heads and hoofs; cf. Musonius 18B (Lutz 119).

[31] *Ergastula*: Col. 1.8.16; Plin. *Nat.* 18.21; 18.36; Juv. 6.151. Mines: Diod. Sic. 5.38; Polyb. 34.9.9; Str. 12.40. Retinue: Lucian, *Merc. Cond.* 32. Personal attendants: *Dig.* 29.5.1.28; 29.5.14; Ap. *Met.* 2.15. No promise: cf. Karasch 1987: 126–7.

unthinkable, and in many real-life contexts there may equally have been little material incentive to protest. Imagine, for example, how slaves fared within a large domestic household such as that of Augustus' wife Livia. First the immense size of the *familia* was predicated on the fact that the slaveowner was a person of enormous wealth who was always able to control resources grand enough to maintain a household in a manner that continuously proclaimed the owner's renown and richness. To those comprising Rome's social and political elite, therefore, for whom slaveholdings were a mechanism of competitive display and a means of rivalry, it made little sense to allow the *familia* to deteriorate in any significantly noticeable way, which automatically meant that the slaves who made up such holdings – subject to the constraints that affected society at large – were never likely to find themselves hungry or without clothes and a roof over their heads. Secondly, Livia's household staff provided many services that were available not simply to the owner and her immediate family but to the slaves (and freedmen and freedwomen) who made up the *familia* as well: the cooks, caterers and bakers, fullers, wool-weighers, clothes-menders, weavers and shoe-makers, nurses, pedagogues, midwives and doctors – these were all functionaries whose labour contributed to the material well-being of the *familia* as a whole. In addition, thirdly, there were real prospects of manumission. Those within the household who were already freed indicated by their mere existence that slavery did not have to be a lifelong status, and those not yet freed had many opportunities for winning the owner's attention and favour from which their own freedom might result. Meantime, the relative stability of the large domestic household allowed slaves to form their own families and to enter into other social relationships under the benign supervision of a paternalistic, or maternalistic, aristocrat. For great numbers of Roman slaves, over time, there must have been every practical reason to display to their owners the unswerving loyalty and obedience that ideally all owners sought from those in their possession.[32]

Consider also how slaves fared in the context represented again by *Daphnis & Chloe*. For rural slaves of the type symbolised by the

---

[32] Accommodated: cf. the remarks of Thompson 1989: 154–5. Livia: see Treggiari 1975. Relationships: Flory 1978; Joshel 1992; cf. Bradley 1987a: 73–4. Loyalty: Bradley 1987a: 21–45.

farmer Lamon, his wife Myrtale and their foster-son Daphnis, life was in many respects severe, perhaps a perennial struggle for survival. Resourcefulness had to be displayed to ensure a sufficiency of food, as seen already, and yet if starvation were averted the quality of what there was to consume was still never as pleasing as the 'taste of urban cuisine' (4.15) that country dwellers might occasionally come to sample. The farm on which the family lived had of course to be worked and although the owner was an absentee seldom seen, Lamon and Myrtale were in the last resort responsible and accountable for the management of their master's property.

The anxiety that a visit of inspection from the slaveowner might induce among his slaves is brilliantly captured in *Daphnis & Chloe*. As the story nears its conclusion news is brought that the master Dionysophanes is soon to arrive from his home in Mytilene, and at once a burst of feverish preparations begins (4.1):

Lamon got his master's country house ready to please the eye in every way. He cleaned out the springs so that they could have clean water, carted the dung out of the farmyard so that it wouldn't annoy them with its smell, and worked on the enclosed garden so that it could be seen in all its beauty.

Beyond this Lamon instructs Daphnis 'to fatten up the goats as much as possible, saying that the master would certainly look at them' (4.4). Daphnis is confident enough of his accomplishments as a goatherd not to worry unduly about the state of the livestock, but he is very apprehensive about the way the inspection of his work could have an impact on his personal life, particularly his plan to marry Chloe: 'wanting his master to be more favourable to his marriage', he consequently gives the animals every attention (4.4). He is not the only one to feel alarm: Chloe herself, although not a slave, is well aware of how the master-slave relationship of Dionysophanes and Daphnis threatens disruption in her life too (4.6):

She was also very frightened. A young man who was used to looking at goats, a hill, farmers, and Chloe, was about to have his first sight of his master, when before he had only heard his name. She worried on his behalf, wondering how he would be when he met the master, and her feelings were agitated about the marriage, in case they were dreaming of something that would never happen.

A further problem arises. Discovering that their garden, with its

rich array of fruit trees, vines and flowers, has been vandalised by a
rival for Chloe's hand, Lamon, Myrtale and Daphnis are panic-
stricken as they imagine Dionysophanes' reaction to the damage:
they weep in terror, Lamon anticipates that he and Daphnis will be
hanged in punishment, Chloe foresees that her beloved Daphnis
will be scourged as well – again, note, it is Chloe who is especially
distressed by the fear that the very prospect of the slaveowner
produces in those whose lives he can confound at a moment's notice
(4.7–9). To allay their fears, Lamon, Myrtale and Daphnis are
forced to humble themselves before their owner's son, Astylus, who
arrives first, begging him to intercede with his father on their
behalf. More anguish still is generated when Daphnis learns that he
is the object of the amorous attentions of Gnathon, the parasite-
companion of Astylus, and that Astylus is intending to ask his
father to give him, Daphnis, to Gnathon as the latter's personal
slave, a request based on the slaveowner's, any slaveowner's, capacity to separate slave children from slave parents at will (4.10–
17). Daphnis is threatened with being forcibly taken from his home
to Mytilene and again tragedy appears to be about to overwhelm
his marriage plans. He is driven to desperate measures: 'Daphnis
was horrified and resolved to risk an attempt at running away with
Chloe or to take her as his companion in death' (4.18).

With Dionysophanes' fictional visit it is enough to compare the
authentic tours of inspection detailed at various points in his correspondence by the younger Pliny to illustrate how *Daphnis & Chloe* is
located in a world of social and psychological plausibility. Referring to his estates near Comum, Pliny speaks for instance (*Ep.*
5.14.8) of 'going the round of my few acres hearing the peasants'
many complaints and looking over the accounts'; on a visit to his
property near Tifernum Tiberinum for the grape harvest (so too
Dionysophanes) Pliny tells (*Ep.* 9.20.2) how he can 'pick an occasional grape, look at the press, taste the wine fermenting in the
vat' and so on. Longus (*D & C* 4.13) describes Dionysophanes'
inspection similarly: 'He saw the plains ploughed, the vine shoots
trimmed, and the garden looking beautiful . . . After that he went
down to the goat pasture to look at the goats and their herdsman.'
Pliny complains constantly of his workers' complaints but is
pleased by the excitement his appearances at Tifernum arouse
among the local people, as he perceives and reports the situation. It
is understandable that complaints and excitement should take on

the character of anxiety and distress when a literary artist is depicting a slaveowner's imminent arrival from a servile perception. *Daphnis & Chloe* is a story, but its slave psychology is drawn from contemporary reality.[33]

However, the arrival of the master at their farm was not an event rural slaves had to contend with every day. It had been so long since Dionysophanes' last personal inspection of Lamon's farm, it can be recalled, that Daphnis had never seen him before. So too Pliny remarked on one occasion at Tifernum (*Ep.* 7.30.3) that a long time had gone by since his last visit there, and when Q. Cicero visited his estate at Arcanum with his wife Pomponia in May 51 BC, it was only because the place was a convenient stopping-point on a journey through Italy he was making. In the slave world of *Daphnis & Chloe* there is enough to eat, and like Pliny's tenants Lamon and his family can always take more from the farm for themselves than they should if necessity demands. Who is there to prevent them? They eat and dress exactly like the family of Chloe, people who are free, do identical kinds of work, dwell in the same sort of dwelling. They do not talk of hopes of ever themselves being free. But their family life is reasonably secure, they have considerable independence of action and mobility, and they are free to make any decisions for themselves. It was the choice of Lamon and Myrtale after all to raise the foundling Daphnis: they did not first seek their owner's permission (though Lamon does inform Dryas, Chloe's foster-father, that his master must give his consent before Daphnis can marry Chloe). For many rural slaves in conditions such as these the slaveowner was, very literally, a remote figure whose direct impact upon their lives they experienced only spasmodically and intermittently, and with whom warmth and familiarity were impossible to expect. Unless extreme circumstances arose, there can hardly have seemed much cause to try to change patterns and rhythms of life that had always been the same and might, as far as they could tell, always remain so.[34]

Accommodation, therefore, was a strategy of survival that must easily have directed the course of many slaves' lives in Roman

[33] Pliny: see Sherwin-White 1966: 345–6; Duncan-Jones 1974: 19–24. Complaints: Plin. *Ep.* 7.30.3; 9.15.1; 9.36.6. Excitement: Plin. *Ep.* 4.1.4.

[34] Q. Cicero: Cic. *Att.* 5.1.3–4. Tenants: Plin. *Ep.* 9.37.2. Choice, consent: *D & C* 1.3; 3.31. Familiarity: Dyson 1992: 199–200 (cf. 115–6; 166) assumes many close relationships between slaves and masters.

antiquity regardless of the way individual situations varied across time and place. Dependence on the master could be turned to personal advantage, the constraints of servitude could be softened, and something close to security might be enjoyed. And yet the capacity of slaves to mould their own lives always came to founder on the immovable obstacle of knowing that absolute independence could never be realised unless they were set free, and the intervention of the unforeseen or unexpected could very quickly throw everything into confusion. A fragmentary wooden writing-tablet found in London some forty years ago contains part of a letter that its editor suggested was concerned with 'the realization of an estate'. Before the letter breaks off its author, a certain Rufus, son of Callisunus, instructs his addressee 'to see that you turn that slave girl into cash'. The slave girl in question is not named but she was obviously put up for sale, the eventuality that more than any other, time and time again, disrupted and destroyed whatever sense of self-direction slaves had previously experienced. The dangers of sale and other misfortunes could never be fully eradicated, and slaves may have been led as a result to think sometimes of responding to slavery in terms other than those of accommodation and acceptance. It may not always have taken drastic prospects to encourage them to do so. In AD 14 the Roman legions in Pannonia protested against their conditions of military service by mutinying. One of their grievances was that their pay was too low to provide, among other things, adequate clothing, the consequence being that the uniforms which they had were practically worn right through. Material deprivation, about which slaves knew a great deal, could become an incitement to rebellion.[35]

---

[35] Letter: Richmond 1953 (cf. *JRS* 44 [1954]: 108). Legions: Tac. *Ann.* 1.17–18

CHAPTER 6

Resisting slavery

In the reign of Caligula a slave named Androcles was set free at Rome in rather unusual circumstances. The story is told by A. Gellius (5.14). Having been sentenced to death by exposure to wild animals in the amphitheatre (a standard penalty for slaves guilty of capital offences), Androcles was one of a group of prisoners who appeared in the Circus Maximus on a day when the emperor himself happened to be in the audience. Expectations of a fine spectacle were high owing to the exceptional size and ferocity of one of the waiting lions, but instead of a bloody battle between man and beast, the crowd witnessed an altogether different sight: for the ferocious lion recognised Androcles as an old companion and to the amazement of all turned the slave's terror to joy by refusing to attack him. By popular demand Androcles was delivered from his punishment, set free and given custody of the lion.[1]

When summoned to account for the animal's extraordinary behaviour, Androcles informed the emperor that in Africa years before he had once removed a huge splinter from the lion's paw, having unwittingly taken refuge in the lion's lair while running away from his master, who was then serving as the province's governor. The grateful lion had subsequently shared his quarters with Androcles and helped him to survive, but Androcles was eventually captured by Roman troops and restored to his owner (now back in Rome), who had him condemned to death for having run away. Only in the Circus did Androcles discover that the lion too had been captured and brought to Rome – a discovery that meant his life was saved.

The liberation of Androcles is a marvellous tale, and perhaps no

---

[1] Androcles: cf. Sen. *Ben.* 2.19,1; Aelian, *de Natura Animalium* 7.48. Standard penalty: Garnsey 1970: 129.

more than that. But the story goes back to a writer who claimed to
have been an eyewitness of the event, Apion of Alexandria, and as
told by Gellius it is full of authentic details that lend the whole
episode a certain credibility. It is of particular interest, therefore,
that in Gellius' version (5.14.7) the story contains a very rare
example of a Roman slave's own explanation of his behaviour, for
Androcles accounted for his original act of flight in this way:

> When my owner was governor of Africa, I was driven to run away by the
> unjustified beatings I received from him every day ('iniquis eius et cotidia-
> nis verberibus ad fugam sum coactus'). And to make my hiding places all
> the more safe from him, the master of that whole region, I took refuge in
> isolated plains and deserts, intending if I should not find food somehow to
> kill myself . . .

From time to time statements of servile motivation appear, or are
implicit, in conventional Roman literary sources. Tacitus (*Ann.*
14.42.3), for example, attributes the murder of the city prefect L.
Pedanius Secundus in AD 61 to either Pedanius' reneging on a
manumission agreement made with the slave who killed him – and
presumably to outrage on the slave's part – or to the slave's in-
ability to tolerate his master in a homosexual liaison. And
Ammianus Marcellinus (28.1.49) tells of a slave named
Sapaudulus who in AD 369 informed against his mistress and the
lover she was concealing from prosecution because the slave's wife
had earlier been flogged: revenge was clearly at play in the act of
informing. It was possible, therefore, for proslavery writers sometimes to acknowledge that slaves were human beings with human
emotions, and to recognise that bruised feelings could lead to
violence and danger to themselves. But there could never be any
open encouragement or support of such reactions. Any injury by a
slave to a slaveowner was a crime, given the moral standards that
prevailed in Roman society, a transgression that as in the Pedanius
Secundus affair was attributable to some moral weakness such as
servile treachery; and as with Androcles, the offending slave had to
be punished, and punished in an appropriate manner.[2]

The personal evidence of Androcles, however, suggests that what
established society saw as crimes meriting punishment (in
Androcles' case, the 'crime' of flight) was perceived completely

---

[2] Acknowledge: cf. Cic. *Fam.* 11.28.3. Appropriate manner: cf. Galen, *de Placitis Hippocratis et Platonis* 6.8.82.

differently by the slave exposed to the grim realities of oppression. From his own point of view the flight of Androcles was not a crime at all but an act of self-preservation and survival that despite its attendant risks (which, paradoxically, included the risk of self-destruction) was preferable to a life of continued servitude. It was an act, that is to say, of resistance to slavery and to the power of the slaveowner based on the slave's standards of moral comportment, not on those of the master. What authors such as Tacitus and Ammianus report pejoratively as servile misbehaviour is in fact evidence of servile opposition to slavery, and it is to this subject of slave resistance at Rome at large that I now turn.

The likelihood that Roman slaves attempted from time to time to reduce the rigours of servitude or to extricate themselves permanently from their condition may be readily admitted in simple terms of human nature, especially in view of the already documented fact that prisoners-of-war in Roman antiquity often preferred to inflict death upon themselves than to submit to the horrors of capture. The evidence of revolt is decisive. Thus in 73 BC, to take the most celebrated instance, the gladiator Spartacus led a revolt of some seventy slaves from a gladiatorial training school in Capua and for almost two years roamed throughout Italy with an army formed from the tens of thousands of slaves who flocked to join him, defeating a series of Roman legionary forces in the process and at one point posing a grave threat to Rome the city. Spartacus was eventually defeated. But the insurrection he headed is enough in and of itself to demonstrate slaves' willingness to take positive action against their enslavement once conditions were conducive, as also to account for slaveowners' perpetual fears and suspicions of their slaves.[3]

Still, whether on the grand scale or at the less intensive level of a slave conspiracy organised in southern Italy in AD 24 by a former member of the praetorian guard, slave revolts were infrequent after Spartacus, and this has led some scholars to conclude consequently that there was little cause for slaves to offer resistance at all. The chief difficulty with this idea, however, is the false assumption that revolt was the only avenue of resistance available to slaves and that in its absence all was calm. In the New World slave revolts were

[3] See in general, Bradley 1989.

particularly virulent in the Caribbean, but in Brazil and the United States, just as at Rome, they were relatively infrequent. Indeed, an insurrection on the scale of that led by Spartacus did not occur again in the history of slavery until the turn of the nineteenth century when the modern state of Haiti emerged from the slave movement headed in St Domingue by Toussaint L'Ouverture. Once the difficulties of organising revolt, the risks of betrayal and detection, and slaves' fears of punishment and reprisal are brought to attention, this is comprehensible enough. But in spite of the low incidence of revolt in some regions, there was no lack of rebelliousness among New World slaves generally; rather, as historians of modern slavery have repeatedly shown, resistance to slavery was endemic but took forms less spectacular, and less obvious, than that of open revolt.[4]

Those forms ranged from violent acts, such as suicide or murderous assaults on slaveowners (often provoked by excessively brutal treatment), to the far less extreme actions of lying, cheating and stealing, of pretending to be sick or working at a calculatedly slow pace, of resorting in fact to any form of petty sabotage thinkable in order to indicate that slaves would not cooperate with their masters on a day to day basis, that they would cause their owners constant annoyance and frustration, and that they would take for themselves whatever relief from oppression was possible. In between was the ubiquitous practice of running away, either to gain temporary respite from slavery or in the hope of escaping servitude for ever, which New World slaves sometimes achieved, especially in Jamaica, Brazil and Surinam, through the formation of independent rebel communities in geographically remote locations. For the most part resistance was non-revolutionary, in the sense that most slaves most of the time were not impelled by ideological imperatives to effect radical political and social change, but were usually attempting only to protest against, and to diminish, their personal sufferings and to take a measure of revenge against their owners. (The Haitian revolution, which was not without antecedents or subsequent influence, was exceptional in that political aims were involved from the outset.) Generally speaking, slave resistance con-

---

[4] AD 24: Tac. *Ann.* 4.27, with *ILS* 961 and Alföldy 1969: 149–53. Some scholars: Alföldy 1988: 70; Dyson 1992: 38–40; see, however, Cartledge 1985, and cf. Brunt 1990: 112, on the lack of provincial uprisings against Roman rule.

cerned itself with individuals and small groups, not with global situations, and slaves knew very well what they were doing, for resistance was a term in their own vocabulary, serving as an anti-dote to the telling labels of 'rascality' and 'roguery' – the sheer troublesomeness – with which their masters constantly character-ised, or rather mischaracterised, their behaviour. From the servile perspective, therefore, the moral regime of the slaveowners did not apply. If for survival's sake slaves had to lie and deceive, then lies and deception were morally defensible. 'I always thought it right', said Thomas Hedgebeth, a fugitive from North Carolina, 'for a slave to take and eat as much as he wanted where he labored'. More eloquently, and emphatically, still, the runaway Harriet Jacobs declared in her autobiography that 'the condition of a slave confuses all principles of morality, and, in fact, renders the practice of them impossible'.[5]

The various forms of resistance behaviour other than revolt known from the history of modern slavery naturally invite the question of whether anything comparable is visible in the Roman record. Quite straightforwardly, the answer is yes.

The situation of war captives apart, there are several indications that Roman slaves were at times driven to a point of desperation from which the only relief was self-destruction. In 195 BC when the elder Cato was on campaign in Spain, one of his slave attendants, a man named Paccius, is said by Plutarch (*Cato* 10.5) to have rashly and improperly purchased from a batch of public prisoners three slave boys for his own use, and then to have killed himself rather than face his master, a strict disciplinarian and a model of personal restraint. It seems that Paccius was so afraid of Cato and his powers of correction that forestalling certain punishment by the act of suicide was all that he could do. The same is implied by an inscription from Moguntiacum (*CIL* 13.7070) which commemor-ates the freedman and *pecuarius* M. Terentius Jucundus, who was killed by one of his slaves whose name is unfortunately not

---

[5] Forms: see variously Bauer and Bauer 1942; Stampp 1956: 86–140; Genovese 1972: 585–660; Blassingame 1979: 192–222; Price 1979; Craton 1982; Gaspar 1985; Craton 1986; Quierós Mattoso 1986: 125–49; Karasch 1987: 302–34; Fogel 1989: 155–62. Trouble-someness: see the primary evidence, for example, of Col. Landon Carter of Sabine Hall, Virginia in 1770, in Rose 1976: 259–61; of the attorney Walter Tullideph in Antigua in 1748, in Gaspar 1985: 190; and of an Alabama slavedriver writing to his master in 1847, in Miller 1990: 157. Own vocabulary: Gates 1987: 380, 382 (Harriet Jacobs), with Yellin 1987. Thomas Hedgebeth: Drew 1856: 278. Harriet Jacobs: Gates 1987: 385.

recorded. After killing his master, however, the slave killed himself by jumping into a river and drowning, apparently because he too was so conscious of his powerlessness as a slave to defend what he had done that suicide was his sole recourse. Seneca (*Ep.* 4.4) acknowledged that excessive fear could drive slaves wishing to escape dyspeptic owners and runaways who could not stand the prospect of recapture to take their own lives; but in a passage remarkable for its utter failure to comprehend the world of the slave, Seneca calls such reasons for suicide frivolous, comparing the case of a lover who hangs himself in front of a girlfriend's door.[6]

Roman lawmakers regarded attempts at self-destruction on the part of slaves as commonplace to judge from information in the *Digest*. When a slave was sold the aedilician edict required the seller to declare whether the slave had ever tried to kill himself (*Dig.* 21.1.1.1), and like the requirements on disease and defect and place of origin, this suggests an objective reality of slave life that could be determined with some accuracy. According to Ulpian (*Dig.* 21.1.23.3), there were grounds for cancelling sale if the slave in question were disposed to suicide because of the 'badness' of character thus revealed. Moreover, when discussing the definition of a fugitive Vivianus (*Dig.* 21.1.17.4) said that a slave who threw himself from a height was not to be called a runaway if all he wished to do was to end his life, and Caelius (*Dig.* 21.1.17.6) said the same for a slave who threw himself into the Tiber or jumped from a bridge. The issue was clearly one of moral intent, and Paul (*Dig.* 21.1.43.4) could consequently define slave suicide as follows: 'A slave acts to commit suicide when he seeks death out of wickedness or evil ways or because of some crime that he has committed, but not when he is able no longer to bear his bodily pain.'[7]

It appears, therefore, that slaves always understood that they had the option of ending their enslavement by ending their own lives, and perhaps over time a considerable number – how many it is impossible to say – did so. They will have been slaves to whom the ultimate human sacrifice was preferable to the burdens of servitude.

Accounts of assault by Roman slaves against their owners are

[6] For further details, see Grisé 1982: 276–81; Bradley 1986a; van Hooff 1990: 171–2, 184–5. For comparable modern material, see especially Stampp 1956: 129; Genovese 1972: 639–41; Blassingame 1979: 7, 297; Conrad 1983: 59, 124; Karasch 1987: 316–20.
[7] Cf. also *Dig.* 14.2.2.5; 15.1.9.7; 47.2.36 pr.

rarely found, but two detailed episodes of murderous violence against prominent men are known from the reigns of Nero and Trajan. The first victim was L. Pedanius Secundus, the city prefect who was killed in A D 61 for reasons already noted, while the second was Larcius Macedo, a senator of praetorian rank who died in A D 108 because, according to Pliny (*Ep.* 3.14), he had been unusually cruel in his treatment of slaves. Another victim was Hostius Quadra, who was murdered when Augustus was emperor, perhaps for reasons that included sexual abuse. Not even a slave-owner who was himself a former slave was immune from attack, as the case of M. Terentius Jucundus shows.[8]

Assault against slaveowners was probably much more common than these specific instances suggest. In the record of Pedanius Secundus' murder, Tacitus (*Ann.* 14.42.2) alludes to an ancient Roman custom of torturing all the members of a murdered slave-owner's *familia*, that is, all the slaves 'under the same roof'. The rationale was that the slaves concerned had an obligation to come to the aid of their master at the time he was under assault and that they deserved to be executed had they not done so. The custom was the subject of legislation in the time of the dictator Sulla and on four other occasions from Augustus to Marcus Aurelius, knowledge of which depends chiefly on evidence from the *Digest* (29.5). Legislators regularly perceived a need, so it seems, to modify or re-implement the law because incidents of slaves attacking their masters also took place regularly. Assault at least was one of the obvious possibilities that occurred to Martial (*Spectacula* 7) when accounting for a slave's grisly execution.[9]

Whether investigation of the whole household occurred only when an owner had been killed by a slave, or in cases of murder by non-slaves as well, is not entirely clear. Ulpian (*Dig.* 29.5.1 pr.) refers to assaults both by *domestici*, household slaves (slaveowners' natural enemies in the view of Tertullian (*Apol.* 7.3)), and by *extranei*, outsiders, but not necessarily slaves. Tacitus, however,

---

[8] L. Pedanius Secundus: Tac. *Ann.* 14.42–5 (cf. *Vita Aesopi* 74, 79–80 for broken promises). Hostius Quadra: Sen. *Naturales Quaestiones* 1.16. See also Plin. *Ep.* 8.14 on Afranius Dexter, another senator who may have been killed by his slaves; and cf. Cic. *Brut.* 85; Artem. *Onir.* 5.25. For modern material, see especially Stampp 1956: 131; Genovese 1972: 616–17; Rose 1976: 193, 230; Conrad 1983: 251; Gaspar 1985: 193–5; McLaurin 1991.

[9] Rationale: *Dig.* 29.5.19. Evidence: see Buckland 1908: 94–5 for the minor sources. See in general, Griffin 1976: 271–3.

recording the passage of the *senatus consultum Claudianum* in AD 57 (*Ann.* 13.32.1), speaks unequivocally of slave murders. The jurists who are resumed in the *Digest* certainly anticipated some instances of assault by slaves, so the force of the simple word 'often' in Ulpian's discussion (*Dig.* 29.5.1.27) of the meaning of the phrase 'under the same roof' should not be underestimated for what it implies about the frequency of slave attacks:

Does this mean within the same walls, or, beyond that, within the same living room or bedroom or the same house or the same park or the whole country house? And Sextus says that it has *often* been decided by judges that whoever were in such a position that they could hear a cry are to be punished as having been under the same roof . . .

Callistratus (*Dig.* 48.19.28.11) similarly remarked that slaves who had conspired against the safety of their masters were generally ('plerumque') burned alive in punishment, implying again that conspiracy of this sort was not uncommon. The victims the jurists spoke of, whether real or putative, included adults and children, husbands and wives, people killed in the city or in the country or travelling from one to the other. They might have died from having had their throats cut, being strangled or thrown down, or because they had been struck with rocks or clubs or stones.[10]

The emperor Hadrian once wrote in a rescript that a slave woman (*ancilla*) who had not cried out for help when her mistress was being attacked, even though the assailant had threatened to kill her if she raised the alarm, ought in any case to be put to death, 'so that all other slaves may not think that when their masters are in danger each should look after himself' (*Dig.* 29.5.1.28). Reasoning of this kind imposed impossible demands on slaves, both male and female, and must presumably have fostered divisions among them. The severe dictates of the law, moreover, were certainly met, for in the sequel to Pedanius Secundus' murder some four hundred slaves were executed even though most could have had nothing to do with the killing. L. Trebius Germanus, moreover, the consul of AD 125, put to death, in his capacity as provincial governor, a slave boy who had been sleeping at his master's feet but who had not cried out when the master was attacked and killed. Despite the

---

[10] Anticipated: *Dig.* 29.5.16; 29.5.21; 29.5.22; 29.5.25. Victims: *Dig.* 29.5.1.7; 29.5.1.14–17; 29.5.1.27; 29.5.1.30–1. Poisoning was regarded as a separate type of killing: *Dig.* 29.5.1.18; cf. 29.5.1.22.

unprivileged legal circumstances in which they found themselves, however, slaves were evidently prepared at times to respond to the violence inherent in slavery as an institution by using violence directly against their owners.[11]

Roman slaveowners were very sensitive to what they perceived as the frittering away of time or resources on the part of their slaves, as the legal definition of the truant slave (*erro*) at once makes clear: 'one who ... frequently indulges in aimless roving and, after wasting time on trivialities, returns home at a late hour' (*Dig.* 21.1.17.4). Complaints from proslavery writers imply that owners had to contend with a constant undercurrent of day to day difficulties and harassment. Thus, in a notorious passage, Columella (1.7.6–7) cited a long list of the kinds of damage agricultural slaves could cause on the farm: hiring out the oxen without permission, improperly pasturing the cattle or ploughing, claiming to have sown more seed than was really the case, neglecting what had been sown, diminishing the yield of the harvest through theft or incompetence, and failing to keep proper records. He also recommended (12.3.7) that the *vilica* should make a daily check for malingerers who were trying to avoid work, as if the problem were widely familiar to his readers.[12]

Columella's evidence is far from unique. Cato (*Agr.* 67) knew that oil was likely to disappear from the pressing-room or the storeroom. Cicero (*in Verrem* 3.119) found the image of the fraudulent *vilicus* selling off his master's livestock and farm equipment realistic enough to exploit for rhetorical effect in an important trial. Seneca (*Tranq.* 8.8) numbered among the bugbears of slaveowning the fact that owners had to rely on people who were always breaking down in tears. The elder Pliny (*Nat.* 33.26) pontificated about pilfering slaves – hordes of them, there were – while Juvenal (11.191–2) thought it natural to associate domestic slaves with destruction and loss of property. Lucian observed (*Merc. Cond.* 23) that the newly enslaved slave, in contrast to the slave born into slavery, was not such a good investment because the memory of freedom encouraged poor performance from him at work; but there was also the opposite view, known to Tacitus (*Ann* 1.31), that it was

---

[11] Sequel: Tac. *Ann.* 14.44–5. L. Trebius Germanus: *Dig.* 29.5.14; see Syme 1988: 472, 557, 593.

[12] Definition: the *erro* was not thought culpable to the same degree as the runaway proper: *Dig.* 49.16.4.4.

homeborn slaves who were the poor workers – and they were insolent at that. Tertullian (*Apol.* 27.5) asserted that slaves generally took pleasure in offsetting their fears of their owners by deliberately causing them harm, while a bandit in Apuleius (*Met.* 4.8) reproached his less adventurous colleagues for being able to steal only on the miserable level of slaves with the words, 'But you, honest robbers, with your petty, slavish pilferings ['inter furta parva atque servilia'], are just junk-dealers creeping timidly through baths and old ladies' apartments.'

The jurists took it as given that slaves stole in all manner of circumstances. A slave leased to work in a shop could be expected to steal from the person hiring him; a slave working on board ship or in an inn would rob the passengers or guests; a slave undertaker could be expected to steal from the corpse he was preparing for burial. The objects stolen were on the small scale: cash, silver, plate, furniture, clothing, perishables – household items in the main that could be disposed of quickly. The jurists, recalling Apuleius' brigand, used the phrase 'domestic thefts' ('domestica furta') to refer to this sort of pilfering, misdeeds that were too trivial to justify prosecution, but which must have been deleterious to slaveowners in their overall effects.[13]

As for damage and destruction: breaking into storehouses and ransacking the contents, cutting down trees on a rural estate without permission, deliberately setting fire to property (the lavishly appointed Tusculan villa of M. Aemilius Scaurus, stepson of Sulla and praetor in 56 BC, for example) – the catalogue of slave crimes known to the jurists was endless. Slaves even caused physical damage to themselves, inflicting wounds for instance to make it seem that they had helped a slaveowner under assault in case they should be punished under the terms of the *senatus consultum Silanianum*. Literate slaves were able to falsify records and documents to the disadvantage of their owners. The late Republican jurist Alfenus Varus wrote (*Dig.* 11.3.16) of a slave accountant (*dispensa-*

---

[13] Jurists: *Dig.* 19.2.45 pr.–1; 47.5.1.5; 4.9.3.3; 14.3.5.8. Objects: *Dig.* 19.1.30 pr.; 47.2.57.5; 41.1.37.2; 30.48 pr.; 40.12.43; 46.3.19; 13.6.21.1; 40.4.22; 47.2.52.9; 40.7.40 pr. Cf. the list of items stolen by the slaves of Rio de Janeiro, subsumed under the heading of 'petty thievery': 'all articles of clothing, a French church history, parrots, oxen, horses, other slaves, watches, purses, clocks, weapons, bottles, glasses, a door, objects from churches, and so on' (Karasch 1987: 330). 'Domestic thefts': *Dig.* 48.19.11.1. See for further details, Bradley 1990: 141–2.

tor) who was found, when his accounts were examined upon manumission, to have spent his master's money on a disreputable woman ('apud quandam mulierculam'); another 'had not entered in the accounts certain moneys collected from [the owners'] tenants' (*Dig.* 40.7.40 pr). Tampering with records could become habitual, a 'consuetudo peccandi' (*Dig.* 11.3.11.1), so that the slave who drew up his owner's will could be expected to insert a clause guaranteeing, in due course, his own manumission (*Dig.* 48.10.22.9).[14]

As for shamming sickness, an episode from Xenophon of Ephesus' story (*Ephes.* 5.7) illustrates what was possible, when Anthia is sold as a prostitute to a brothel-keeper in Tarentum. Put on display, she attracts a host of clients, but to safeguard her chastity she collapses, pretending to be epileptic, and subsequently concocts a tale to explain to her owner how she became ill. The episode is not all fancy: doctors in antiquity were not always able to tell whether their patients were sick or simply pretending to be sick when they examined them.[15]

Truancy, dilatoriness, lying, dissembling, stealing, causing damage, feigning sickness – at the strictly factual level these types of slave behaviour are all well in evidence. The sources report them in a prejudiced way, however, constantly speaking of slaves' misdeeds, but seen from the servile point of view they are better understood as ways by which slaves could deliberately cause their owners vexation and thereby provide themselves with a measure of relief from their position of subordination and inferiority.

To secure relief from adversity by physically separating oneself from its cause is a universal human strategy of survival. Thus before Constantine, Christians regularly evaded persecution by running away from their tormentors, taking refuge either in cities where they could literally lose themselves in a crowd, or else in remote rural areas, woods and deserts, for instance, where they could avoid detection. The tactic was so common that theologians

---

[14] Damage and destruction: *Dig.* 19.2.55 pr.; 47.7.7.5; 18.6.12; 9.2.27.9;19.2.30.4; 9.2.27.11; 19.2.11.4. M. Aemilius Scaurus: Plin. *Nat.* 36.115. Wounds: *Dig.* 29.5.1.37; cf. 15.1.9.7. See Drew 1856: 178 for evidence of an American slave who cut off the fingers of his left hand with an axe to prevent being sold away. Falsify records: cf. *Dig.* 9.2.23.4; 10.2.18 pr.; 30.67 pr., and see Drew 1856: 185 for an American slave who in 1854 wrote himself three passes to aid his escape from Mississippi to Canada. *Dig.* 11.3.16: quoted in chapter 2.
[15] Quint. *Inst.* 2.17.39.

contrived a spiritual justification for it based on Jesus' withdrawal to Gethsemane before the Passion. For Christians, consequently, flight was a commendable act of self-preservation which allowed individuals to deliver themselves to the providence of God, not an act of weakness or cowardice. Likewise in Roman Egypt, peasants, and men of higher status too, frequently abandoned their homes when unable to satisfy the demands of the tax-collectors or to meet the liturgical obligations imposed upon them, preferring again to immerse themselves in large cities like Alexandria or to take up with itinerant bands of outlaws. It is not surprising, therefore, to find that Roman slaves ran away from their owners. What is surprising is the amount of attention flight by slaves receives in the ancient record.[16]

From Roman Egypt documentary papyri give very vivid impressions of what running away involved – of where fugitives made for and the means their owners used to recover them. A letter (*P. Turner* 41) from the late third century shows a woman named Aurelia Sarapias seeking the help of a district governor (*strategos*) in tracking down her runaway slave Sarapion. The slave had once belonged to her father; both for that reason and because Sarapion had held a position of responsibility in her household, Sarapias had never expected trouble from him; but now, she said, under the influence of an unknown party he had abandoned his duties and, forsaking the material comfort of the household, had secretly run away. Worse yet, he had taken clothing and other items at his disposal with him. Sarapias seems from her letter to have had some idea of where her trusted slave was, but whether she ever recovered him is unknown. Another document (*P. Oxy.* 1643), of the same period, shows a certain Aurelius Sarapammon, a citizen of both Oxyrhynchus and Athens, appointing an agent to go to Alexandria to find a runaway for him, a thirty-five-year-old man; 'and when you find him', Sarapammon wrote sternly, 'you are to deliver him up, having the same powers as I should have myself, if I were present, to ... imprison him, chastise him, and to make an accusation before the proper authorities against those who harboured him, and demand satisfaction'. Similarly one Flavius Ammonas, an official on the staff of a fourth-century prefect of Egypt, wrote to a

---

[16] Christians: Nicholson 1989. Egypt: Lewis 1983: 163–5, 183–4. Flight by slaves: see in general, Bellen 1971.

colleague authorising him to arrest his slave Magnus (*P. Oxy.* 1423): the man was a runaway and a thief and was understood to be living in Hermopolis.[17]

The fugitives in these examples were slaves who ran away by themselves, but the papyri also provide cases of men and women running away in small groups of three or four or five. They show too that even at the village level lists of runaways might be kept, and that the fugitives, as in Sarapammon's case, could sometimes count on the support of third parties in their flight: in one example from Oxyrhynchus (*P. Oxy.* 1422) a person accused of harbouring a runaway is said to have disappeared himself. The papyri also attest the practice slaveowners adopted of advertising for their runaways in public places such as temples by posting notices of their slaves' physical appearance and offering a reward for their return. One document (*P. Oxy.* 3616) refers to a runaway named Philippus, who was about fourteen years old, had pale skin and spoke badly, and who, when he ran away, was 'wearing a thick (?) woollen tunic and a used shoulder belt'; the owner promised his finder a reward. Another example (*P. Oxy.* 3617) concerns an anonymous Egyptian slave, a thirty-two year old man who was a weaver by trade and who could speak no Greek; he was 'tall, lean (?), smooth-shorn, with a slight (?) wound on the left side of his head, honey-complexioned, somewhat pale, with a scanty beard – (or rather) with no hair at all to his beard, smooth-skinned, narrow in the jaws, long-nosed'. The owner's indignation at his loss seems to emerge in the final details: 'he walks around as if he were somebody important, chattering in a shrill voice'.[18]

The hard record of papyri is not available of course for the Roman world at large, but the evidence of literature and the law indicates that the patterns of behaviour visible in Egypt were in fact visible everywhere. Advertising for runaways, for instance, emerges as a widespread convention from Ulpian (*Dig.* 11.4.18a), as also from the parody in Lucian's dialogue, *The Runaway Slaves*, where the

[17] Sarapias: cf. the similar experience of the Alabama slaveowner Sarah Gayle (Fox-Genovese 1988: 23–4), who owned a slave, Hampton, who had previously belonged to her father and who had known his mistress since her childhood; despite the long association, she found herself constantly complaining of his 'insolence and contrary disposition'.
[18] Groups: Biëzuńska-Małowist 1977: 141–2. Lists: Biëzuńska-Małowist 1977: 140. Practice: this was also the habit of New World slaveowners, who placed similarly detailed descriptions of runaways, and offered rewards for them, in newspapers; see for examples, Rose 1976: 57–8; Conrad 1983: 362–6.

action proceeds from the story line that Hermes, Philosophy and
various other deities are assisting three slaveowners in their quest
for three fugitive slaves in Philippopolis in Thrace on the express
orders of Zeus, who had received a complaint from Philosophy that
runaways impersonating itinerant philosophers are bringing her
into disrepute. To facilitate the search, Hermes at one juncture
issues the following proclamation (*Fugitivi* 27) – the advertisement
is oral rather than written – which is remarkably similar in form
and content to the genuine notices from Egypt:

> If anyone has seen a Paphlagonian slave, one of those barbarians from
> Sinope, with a name of the kind that has 'rich' in it, sallow, close-cropped,
> wearing a long beard, with a wallet slung from his shoulder and a short
> cloak about him, quick-tempered, uneducated, harsh-voiced, and abusive,
> let him give information for the stipulated reward.

As a literary device, the description of the runaway slave can be
traced to the Hellenistic poets Moschus and Meleager; but in Latin
literature it appears in Apuleius' story of Psyche and Cupid (*Met.*
6.8), where the informant, directed to proceed to the temple of
Mercury close to the Circus at Rome, is promised as a reward for
information on the runaway Psyche 'seven delicious kisses plus one
more, deeply sweetened by the touch of her caressing tongue' from
Venus.[19]

Runaway slaves, or slaves about to run away, are indeed ubiquitous in imaginative literature. In Petronius' *Satyricon* (107.4),
Encolpius at one point offers the plausible view that repentance
might lead runaways back to their owners; Photis in Apuleius'
Metamorphoses (3.16), afraid of being beaten by her mistress, tells
Lucius that only her desire to be with him has prevented her from
absconding; Daphnis in Longus' romance, afraid, it may be
recalled, of being handed over to a favourite of his master, sees
flight with Chloe as a preferable fate; and in Apuleius once more
there is the whole community of *pastores* who flee together when
they learn of their owner's death, alarmed apparently at the prospect of a change of ownership. In Chariton's novel (4.2), the
wrongfully enslaved Chaereas is seen at one stage working on a
chaingang in Caria: one night sixteen of his fellow slaves break out

---

[19] Poets: see Gow 1953: 126–7; Gow and Page 1965: 2.628–9; LeGrand 1967: 134–6.
Temple: cf. Robertson and Vallette 1965: 2.77 n.3. See also Petr. *Sat.* 97.2, where a herald
gives a description of the 'runaway' Giton. The herald's job was disreputable according to
Dio Chrys. 7.123.

of their chains, kill the overseer, and try to escape, but they are caught almost at once and crucified the next day.[20]

In legal sources references to runaway slaves are also abundant, and one section of the *Digest* (11.4), though relatively brief, is devoted entirely to them. It suggests that fugitive slaves, like fugitive Christians, might often make for secluded rural areas in which to hide, or that they could commonly be found in ports, presumably trying to board ship. It confirms, too, that fugitives were often given help while on the run or in hiding, by farm bailiffs among others, men who were frequently slaves or ex-slaves themselves but whose chief loyalties were supposed to lie with their owners. The law at least speaks of harbourers acting out of 'humanity or compassion' towards runaways.[21]

The law recognised that it was largely the owner's responsibility to effect recovery of his property (as seen in reality in the Egyptian evidence and fictionally in Lucian), but the owner could usually count on certain mechanisms of support, troops or civic officials or the provincial governor, as appropriate; the geographical scope of the phenomenon was obviously global. Callistratus wrote (*Dig.* 11.4.2) that captured runaways should normally be returned to their owners but that they should be punished 'more severely' if they had tried to pass as free while on the loose. His opinion is a reminder that, unlike New World slavery, Roman slavery had no association with skin colour (it was available to all), and it is likely therefore that 'passing' was a tactic fugitives commonly attempted. In defining what constituted a runaway, the jurists emphasised intent. If a slave ran away from a brigand or a fire or a collapsing building and was clearly trying to save his life from danger, he was not considered a fugitive; it was only if he planned to escape from his master that he became a runaway. Ulpian's view (*Dig.* 11.4.1.5) that the offspring of a runaway female was not a fugitive is a further indication that women as well as men were likely to abscond if they could.[22]

---

[20] *Pastores* (Ap. *Met.* 8.15–23): note the parallel with accounts from eighteenth-century Russia (Kolchin 1987: 279–81), of whole communities of serfs abandoning their farms and villages in resisting absentee landlords. See also *Vita Aesopi* 26: natural for a potential purchaser to ask the slave on the block if he intends to run away.

[21] Rural areas: *Dig.* 11.4.1.1; 11.4.1.2; 11.4.1.3; cf. 21.1.17.8. Ports: *Dig.* 11.4.4. Help: *Dig.* 11.4.1.1; 11.4.3; cf. 11.3.1 pr.; 11.3.1.2; 11.3.5 pr. 'Humanity': *Dig.* 11.3.5 pr.

[22] Responsibility: *Dig.* 11.4.1.2; 11.4.1.4; 11.4.3; cf. 18.1.35.3; 21.1.17.9. Mechanisms: *Dig.* 11.4.1–2; 11.4.4. 'Passing': e.g. *Dig.* 47.2.52.15; 47.10.15.45. Intent: *Dig.* 21.1.17 pr.–3.

The ways in which slaves in the Roman world responded to slavery seem to bear a striking resemblance, then, to the ways in which slaves in the New World resisted their servitude. Modern resistance strategies can be paralleled in almost every respect, making plausible the conclusion that the behaviour of Roman slaves illustrated so far represents not simply a set of reactions to slavery, but a determined and at times very conscious demonstration of defiance of oppression. This conclusion is incapable of proof, however, because it depends on evidence that offers no statements of motivation deriving directly from slaves themselves; but to reject its inherent probability is to be unduly sceptical.

Admittedly, in some circumstances slaves' behaviour, while in theory fitting the resistance pattern, might have had nothing at all to do with opposition to slavery. Evidence from the Roman jurists shows that slaves sometimes committed misdeeds because they were coerced by criminous slaveowners – they colluded with their masters, that is, in acts of theft, piracy and even murder. And with the strategy of suicide a variety of motives might have obtained, because like any free person a slave could commit suicide to put an end to the suffering of sickness, or else the demands of loyalty to the master might again come into play: in Alexandria in 30 BC the defeated triumvir M. Antonius ordered a faithful slave named Eros, specially trained for the task, to draw a sword and strike him down. Eros, however, appears to have been so devoted to his master that he thought it better to take his own life than to serve as the instrument of Antonius' death, for at the critical moment he turned his sword on himself and so inspired his owner, according to Plutarch (*Ant.* 76), to a similarly heroic end. Again, some instances of suicide may have had no rational explanation at all: on the first day of AD 38, a slave named Machaon entered the temple of Jupiter Capitolinus at Rome and began to utter strange prophecies; he next killed a dog which he had brought with him and then killed himself. Whether he was demented, a religious fanatic, both or neither, is unknown.[23]

The reasons why slaves behaved as they did can seldom have been uncomplicated. Yet the manner in which slaveowners judged

---

[23] Coerced: *Dig.* 44.7.20; 48.18.1.5; 47.2.52.23; 25.2.21.1–2; 47.2.35.1. Eros: cf. Dio 51.10.7, and see also Dio 69.22.2, on Hadrian and Mastor. Machaon: Dio 59.9.3 (cf. van Hooff 1990: 97).

both them and their actions was very narrow indeed, consisting of a bland moralistic division into good and bad. Pilfering could be forgiven if a slave had special gifts which endeared him to an owner, but the slave's tendency to commit wicked deeds was regarded, by Cicero (*Att.* 7.2.8) among others, as normal, so that when a newly manumitted slave betrayed the trust set in him, abandoned an important assignment and absconded, that was the unpardonable but typical behaviour of a reprobate that left Cicero no alternative but to revoke the grant of freedom. For Quintilian (*Inst.* 4.2.69), it was a given that slaves should always be trying to explain their shortcomings ('peccata'), an attitude like that of Cicero and countless others that was predicated on standards of undeviating obedience which slaveowners insisted upon from their slaves. When the standards were met, slaves were good; when not, they were bad.[24]

In the minds of the Roman lawyers all slaves were corruptible beings, capable of being persuaded to undertake criminal acts or to behave in other morally reprehensible ways. According to Ulpian (*Dig.* 11.3.1.5), any slave might be led to steal, to damage property, falsify accounts, mismanage his *peculium*, run away and waste time at the public shows, to cause sedition, behave promiscuously, be insolent to his owner, corrupt other slaves. The lawyers believed that gambling, drunkenness, truancy, excessive attention to the games or to works of art were 'defects of the mind' ('animi vitia') in slaves, and that their misbehaviour was attributable to the generic characteristics of cunning and effrontery (*calliditas, protervitas*). According to Gaius (*Dig.* 21.1.18 pr.), the good slave was loyal, industrious, diligent and thrifty, while the bad slave was fickle, wanton, slothful, sluggish, idle, tardy, a wastrel. The language is reminiscent of the 'rascality' and 'roguery' that New World slave-owners saw in their slaves, and it is scarcely surprising that Ulpian (*Dig.* 17.1.18.4) should have described the recalcitrant Roman slave as a 'servus onerosus', a· troublesome property.[25]

However, when representatives of the Roman slaveowning establishment referred to good and bad slaves – when, recall, they wrote of slaves killing themselves out of 'wickedness' or because of 'evil

---

[24] Standards: see Bradley 1987a: 21–45.
[25] *Dig.* 11.3.1.5: quoted in chapter 2.'Defects': *Dig.* 2.1.25.6; 21.1.65 pr. Characteristics: *Dig.* 15.3.3.9; 47.4.1 pr.–1. See further, Bradley 1990: 144–6.

ways' – it did not occur to them to question the appropriateness of their moral categories or to imagine that slaves might not have shared their values. Yet when slaves committed suicide because they were afraid of their owners, or assaulted them because of broken promises or cruel punishment, or ran away to avoid being beaten, or procrastinated at work to gain revenge, they were responding to conditions that for them made the morality of the established order meaningless and unacceptable, just as it was for New World slaves like Thomas Hedgebeth and Harriet Jacobs. 'Who can blame slaves for being cunning?' asked Jacobs; 'They are constantly compelled to resort to it. It is the only weapon of the weak and oppressed against the strength of their tyrants.' Slave behaviour could only be construed as misbehaviour by those it inconvenienced. Slaves themselves, Roman as much as any other, had to find every means possible to cope with adversity and they constructed in the process a morality that could be diametrically opposed to that of their owners.[26]

Roman slaveowners acknowledged from time to time that their slaves behaved 'badly' because of the way they were treated and not because of inherent character flaws. It was conceded that the master's threatening words could force the slave to run away, that the *dispensator* might embezzle because he needed food, that the slave might lie to avoid torture, that apparent greed might have something to do with the slave's hunger. Cruelty, fear, deprivation – these are recurring elements in the record of master-slave relations in the Roman world, and practical slaveowners could see that injustice caused resentment. Yet owners could never condone their slaves' misdeeds. The common sense argument was understood, as seen earlier, that a slave who ran away from a collapsing building or a fire in order to save his life was not strictly speaking a fugitive. But the next logical step was not taken: that slaves who ran away to save themselves from physical abuse or some other harsh consequence of slavery were acting in appropriate and defensible ways as victimised human beings. It was this failure to comprehend and to sympathise with the slave mentality that controls the moralistic and often pejorative presentation of slave

---

[26] Harriet Jacobs: Gates 1987: 426. On stealing as a cause of moral dilemma, see McFeeley 1991: 43–4.

behaviour in the historical record. It also necessarily obscures the true purpose and meaning of that behaviour.[27]

Once the moralistic camouflage is stripped away, however, the plain record of fact remains that Roman slaves reacted to slavery with a variety of strategies that can only be regarded as strategies of resistance intended, to one degree or another, to ameliorate their lives and to reduce the hardships of servitude. As in the slave societies of Brazil, the Caribbean and the American South, acts that slaveowners regarded as crimes were in reality acts that gave 'outward expression to inward rebelliousness' in slaves. The owner's power was absolute; but when power was exercised to the limit of human endurance, slaves responded with assertions of their human capacity that gave rise to struggles of the will and mind that their owners did not always win. Representatives of the slave-owning order wrote prescriptively of the ideal relations they thought should exist between masters and slaves, enjoining upon the latter the obligation to endure their condition with loyalty and obedience. Read uncritically, those writings suggest a willing acquiescence in their lot on the part of slaves and an uninterrupted stability in their dealings with their owners. Beneath the surface calm which elitist writings evince, however, there was a constant ferment of defiant activity as slaves, of every description, ran away, stole, cheated, damaged property and shirked work, or as they directed violence against themselves or their owners, all in an effort to withstand the cruelty and deprivation slavery heaped upon them. At no point in the central period of Roman history can it be said that passive acceptance of subjection was characteristic of the entire slave population.[28]

To stress the extent of resistance which Roman slaves displayed, across time and place, is to provide a better appreciation of what it was like to live in slavery, since attention has then to be forced on the risks and costs resistance naturally entailed. Any act which questioned the established order exposed the slave to potential

---

[27] Conceded: Plut. *Mor.* 459A; cf. Sen. *de Ira* 3.5.4; Quint. *Inst.* 6.3.93; Salvian, *de Gubernatione Dei* 4.3.16; cf. Philo, *de Fuga et Inventione* 1.3, and for the jurists' recognition that flight could be a response to cruelty (*saevitia*), see *Dig.* 21.1.23.1; 21.1.17.3; 21.1.17.4; 21.1.17.12. Resentment: Gel. 10.3.17, on the elder Cato.

[28] Quotation: Queirós Mattoso 1986: 133.

danger and so demanded a certain determination, if not courage, before it could be attempted. To consider the hazards involved in flight, in particular, makes the point.

Think first of travelling in Italy in safety, taking as a control Horace's account (*Serm.* 1.5) of the journey he made, with various companions, from Rome through Campania and Apulia to the port of Brundisium in 37 BC. The distance covered was about three hundred and fifty miles, the time spent on the trip some two weeks, the usual mode of operations to travel leisurely by day from one town to another, with nights spent in lodgings easily paid for, or, better, in the villas of friends. Carriages and carts were available for transportation, mules for carrying luggage. The open road (the Via Appia to begin with) took the party from stage to stage of the route. There was always enough to eat, the journey was comfortable and convivial, and the travellers could stay up late into the night to carouse if the fancy took them. There were some discomforts. At an early point Horace took the evening barge from Forum Appii to Terracina and was kept awake all night by biting mosquitoes and croaking frogs. In the marshlands his eyes suffered, a problem later aggravated by smoke from damp firewood in one of the places he stayed. And the food was not always ideal: the local bread was sometimes inedible and the water, if drinkable at all, could upset the stomach. Once a heavy rain washed the road completely away, and the hills of Apulia, scorched by the sirocco, Horace found debilitating.[29]

Given the company he was keeping – his patron, the rich and powerful C. Maecenas was with him part of the way – Horace was about as safe and secure as anyone could be in antiquity while making his journey. But how would a small group of fugitive slaves, intending to run away, say, from Rome to Brundisium to board ship for an eastern destination, have fared along the same route? How would they have managed to evade detection, to find their way, to feed themselves, to find shelter? Like soldiers on the march, they will have had to make sure that they steered clear of pestilential stopping-places and contaminated water that might poison them, and they will have had to protect themselves from fatigue and sickness caused by the sun, if travelling in the summer, or from frosts and snows if in winter. But worse than this, they will have

[29] Horace's account: see Fraenkel 1957: 105–12; Rudd 1966: 54–64.

known that efforts would be made to track them down as soon as they were missed: their owner might pursue them himself, he might send professional slavecatchers after them, he might contact friends or relatives and give instructions to use any means possible to apprehend them. He would certainly circulate their description, and perhaps even resort to magic to prevent them leaving the city limits in the first place.[30]

Runaways, therefore, will always have had to move swiftly and clandestinely, perhaps travelling by night under the cover of darkness, avoiding all figures of authority, perhaps using a disguise and pretending to be free, taking refuge for sleep in isolated spots away from populous centres. They may have taken some provisions with them at the moment of departure, but after a few days the risks of procuring new rations will have had to be run, exposing them further to the possibility of discovery if they chanced to steal from the farms and villages they passed through. If they put their trust in harbourers, there was always the danger of betrayal once rewards for information were announced. As the fugitives coped with the exigencies of weather, terrain and sheer survival, therefore, every moment must have been filled with tension and uncertainty, in utter contrast to the ease with which Horace made his journey. And if in the end the port was safely reached, there was still the obstacle of boarding a ship with which to contend.[31]

All of this after the fugitives had first resolved to try to escape, had devised some ruse to conceal their departure (in the way the cuttle fish disappeared in a discharge of thick, inklike fluid, Artemidorus said (*Onir.* 2.14)), after they had made some sort of plan, had chosen a time to put it into effect, and had perhaps made decisions about leaving behind family members and close friends. All of this, too, in the certain knowledge that failure would be followed by punishment and might result in the disgrace of being chained and having to wear iron collars on which their names and addresses were inscribed in case they should ever try to escape again. The following story, though only a fable (Phaedrus, *Appendix* 20), reveals dramatically and depressingly the deterrent effect upon the slave of the prospect of punishment, and captures the dilemma

---

[30] Soldiers: Veget. 3.2. Slavecatchers: see Daube 1952. Magic: Plin. *Nat.* 28.13.

[31] The practical hazards faced by runaways are best appreciated from the accounts of escape given by slaves fleeing from the United States to Canada; see especially Drew 1856: 69, 75, 260–1, with Silverman 1985; Ripley 1986: 3–46.

in which many slaves must have found themselves as they hesitated
between remaining in slavery and making a bid for freedom:

A slave running away from a master of cruel disposition met Aesop, to
whom he was known as a neighbour. 'What are you excited about?' asked
Aesop. 'I will tell you frankly, father – and you deserve to be called by that
name – since my complaint can be safely entrusted to your keeping. I get a
surplus of blows and a shortage of rations. Every now and then I am sent
out to my master's farm without any provisions for the journey. Whenever
he dines at home I stand by in attendance all night long; if he is invited
out I lie in the street until daybreak. I have earned my liberty, but I am
still a slave though grey-headed. If I were aware of any fault on my part, I
should bear this with patience. I have never yet had my belly full, and
besides that I have the bad luck to suffer tyranny exercised by a cruel
master. For these reasons, and others which it would be too long to
recount, I have decided to go away wherever my feet shall take me'. 'Now
then, listen', said Aesop, 'these are the hardships that you suffer, according to your account, when you have done no wrong; what if you commit
an offence? What do you think you will suffer then?' By such advice the
man was deterred from running away.[32]

Running away, then, was an enterprise requiring enormous
courage and resourcefulness, an experience overladen with danger
and emotional strain, a response to slavery demanding great
resources of inner strength. In the ancient record it is often trivial-
ised, and it is thus tempting for the historian, even now, to brand
flight a form of irresponsibility on the part of the slave. Assessing
what running away actually involved, however, reveals how almost
insuperable odds had to be confronted by those who undertook it,
which in itself is a straightforward measure of the simple horror of
slavery. Yet those odds were repeatedly faced by great numbers of
Roman slaves, and to understand why, the motivating power of the
desire to be free must of course be brought to the fore; for in the last
analysis, flight, as Ulpian said (*Dig.* 21.1.17.10), was 'a form of
liberty' for the slave, that at once brought relief from the power of
the master.

The risks slaves ran and the costs they paid in resisting slavery

[32] Punishment: Polyb. 1.69.4: already in the middle of the third century BC the slave
Spendius, a Campanian who ran away and joined the Carthaginians, was afraid of being
recovered by his owner, beaten or put to death. Collars: e.g. *ILS* 8726. On the emotional
elements of flight, see the modern evidence in Drew 1856: 71–2, 211, 282. Unlike American slaves who fled from the South to the North and to Canada, Roman slaves could never
know the experience of living in a slaveless society.

must obviously have varied according to the mode of resistance undertaken. An owner might insist that the slave maintain silence while at work, but such a dictate could not be permanently enforced and the level of personal danger involved in wilful disobedience was thus presumably minimal. Yet every time a slave stole an item of clothing or food, or failed to tell the whole truth or sabotaged property, the degree of risk increased considerably. Moreover, plans to assault an owner, if they backfired, could bring severe reprisals for innocent as well as guilty slaves, a factor that dissidents must always have had to consider in their preparations. Plans, in any event, could easily spread within the *familia* and, failing through betrayal, bring destruction upon their sponsors. In antiquity, the reality of these risks was not a subject that commanded the interest of elitist commentators, but it should not for that reason be glossed over: the fact is that behind almost every record or anecdote of theft, deceit, flight, suicide and so on, there lies a human story, even if now only dimly perceptible, of enormous struggle.[33]

Incontrovertible generalisations about which forms of resistance were the more prevalent cannot be made. Revolt seems to have been very uncommon, which can be explained by the argument that slaves could successfully express their protests in many other ways that were far less threatening to themselves. At the same time, however, a comprehensive record of slave behaviour is not available and it may be that there were many revolts about which nothing is now known. Similarly, sensationalistic episodes of suicide and attacks on owners found their way into the historical record precisely because they were sensationalistic, and how many other episodes went unrecorded it is impossible to say. No one can prove, therefore, that suicide was more common than assault, assault than theft, and so on.

At the impressionistic level, however, running away and petty sabotage seem to have been the most widely deployed means of resistance: the interest in fugitives and 'troublesome' slaves dis-

---

[33] Plans: *Dig.* 29.5.1.26; 29.5.1.30. In the modern evidence, the least dangerous mode of resistance was the transmission from one generation to another of subversive trickster stories, those for instance of Anansi the spider, Brer Rabbit, and John and Old Marster; see Levine 1977; Roberts 1989. In antiquity, Aesopic fables may have served a similar subversive purpose among slaves: see Bradley 1987a: 150–3. On Aesop himself as a trickster figure, see Hopkins 1993, and cf. Winkler 1985: 279–86.

played by those who created the historical record borders, after all, on the obsessive. Allowing slaves to challenge the existing order, to cause disruption, to prevent the owner from exploiting his property to the full, to reduce the owner's standing before his peers when an absence of discipline within the household was achieved, flight and day to day resistance were effective and relatively safe strategies for slaves to pursue. Over time the general pattern may well have been affected by changing historical conditions, because New World studies indicate that rates of running away, for instance, increased at times of political weakness or upheaval in the dominant regime. Possibly, therefore, at times of crisis in Roman politics – say in the revolutionary era of the first century BC or in the era of disintegration in the third century AD – there were surges in the numbers of runaway slaves. But there seems to have been no time in the central era at large when Roman society was utterly free from the impact of slave rebelliousness.[34]

Rebelliousness, however, must not be confused with notions of class solidarity among slaves, and there is no indication that resistance was fuelled by ideological programmes rooted in the desire to secure radical alteration to the structure of society. There was certainly never anything at Rome comparable to the movement that led in St Domingue to the creation of the state of Haiti. Rather, those who made up the Roman slave population, in all its diversity, were concerned with improving their lives as individuals or as members of small groups through whatever means of self-help they could find, so that it was personal, not collective, independence that was their object.[35]

It has been said that 'resistance not acquiescence is the core of history', a view that those who regard history as a ceaseless process of struggle between the forces of exploitation and the forces of opposition to exploitation would readily endorse. This is a view, however, that is based neither on a series of propositions that can be empirically verified or refuted nor on a set of conclusions drawn from a dispassionate analysis of evidence; and its implication that

---

[34] Obsessive: Finley 1980: 111, on fugitives. New World studies: e.g. Lovejoy 1986: 74.
[35] See the interesting parallel provided by the Islamic slave society of the Sokoto Caliphate in nineteenth-century West Africa, as described in Lovejoy 1986, and cf. Karasch 1987: 325–6, explaining the absence of slave revolts in Rio de Janeiro by the absence of slave class cohesion.

all the historically downtrodden have always consciously devoted themselves to resistance fails to allow for variations of individual strength and capability. Yet it is undeniably true that throughout history there have been many slaves who have withstood the oppression inherent in their condition. The proof lies in the combination of their words and actions, which leave the issue beyond doubt. Harriet Jacobs wrote that she was just fourteen when she first felt the conviction of having to fight slavery: 'The war of my life had begun', she said, 'and though one of God's most powerless creatures, I resolved never to be conquered'. William Troy, an American slave who took refuge in Canada, similarly told Benjamin Drew: 'I intend to be a terror to the system while I live.' For Roman slavery, statements of that kind do not exist. In all fundamentals, however, in terms of authority, control and the manipulation of power, the social relationship between slaveowner and slave was precisely the same at Rome as in the slave societies of the New World; and an objective assessment of the deeds and actions of Roman slaves shows that they fall into precisely the same categories of resistance behaviour associated with slaves in those same societies. It follows that resistance had a structural, and elemental, place in the history of slavery at Rome.[36]

[36] Quotation: Herbert Aptheker in Craton 1986: 96 (cf. 113 n.1). Harriet Jacobs: Gates 1987: 353. William Troy: Drew: 1856: 355.

CHAPTER 7

Change and continuity

When travelling on the river Ohio in 1841, Abraham Lincoln was struck by the sight of twelve shackled slaves who were being taken down river to be sold. 'A small iron clevis', he later wrote in a letter describing his experience, 'was around the wrist of each, and this fastened to the main chain by a shorter one at a convenient distance from the others: so that the negroes were strung together precisely like so many fish upon a trot-line.' He thought of the way the slaves had been uprooted from their homes, of the families and friends they had left behind, of the cruelty they would endure from their new owners, finding himself at a loss as he did so to understand how the slaves could continue in such a plight to seem so cheerful. Lincoln was long disturbed by the episode, and as he recalled the sight to a fellow traveller in another letter fourteen years later he remarked what 'a continual torment' the image of the shackled slaves had been to him ever since.[1]

In the Americas slavery was destroyed with astonishing speed. From 1807, when Britain placed a ban on the transatlantic slave trade, to 1888, when the last slaveowning state in the New World, Brazil, abolished slavery, less than a century was required to eradicate an institution that for hundreds, even thousands, of years had gone unchallenged until early in the eighteenth century philosophers and religious thinkers began to raise questions about the moral legitimacy and acceptability of slavery. Against the background of the rise of capitalism there followed from these beginnings a revolution in social consciousness – of which Lincoln's torment is symptomatic – that eventually led to historical change

---

[1] Quotations: Basler 1953: 1.260; 2.320. The respective dates of the letters are 27 September 1841, and 24 August 1855.

of a very dramatic and, most would surely say, very progressive kind.[2]

At Rome, in contrast, abolition never occurred. But the demise of slavery in the New World raises the question nonetheless of whether significant progressive change ever affected Roman slavery at all over the course of its long history. Scholars commonly maintain that through the central period of Roman history, and particularly under the Principate, a new spirit of humanity gradually came to permeate society, resulting in expressions of sympathy for slaves from philosophers and other intellectuals, and, more practically, a series of positive improvements to slaves' lives made at the public level. Claudius' famous grant of freedom in AD 47 to sick slaves who recovered after being abandoned on the island of Aesculapius in the Tiber is often taken as a case in point. But is the view of a general softening of slavery at Rome historically accurate? To find an answer a twofold approach is necessary. First, representative thought on the subject of slavery needs to be examined to see in what sense it was humane and how it developed; and secondly a practical test is required, to see whether significant signs of change emerge at the institutional level. Accordingly this chapter considers Roman thought, including early Christian thought, on slavery, and the next chapter deals with two features of the Roman slavery system well-suited to a discussion of slavery and humanity, manumission and torture.[3]

Late in life Cicero set out to instruct the educated elite at Rome in the tenets of the major schools of Greek philosophy by composing a series of dialogues modelled on those of Plato. The undertaking at once reflected and reinforced the cultural presence of Greek philosophy that had first begun to manifest itself in Rome a century earlier and that had been growing ever since. (Already in the era of Scipio Aemilianus it had become almost fashionable for the Roman aristocrat to have a Greek philosopher among his intimate friends and counsellors.) Philosophy, as it happened, was never to rouse the greatest enthusiasm at Rome. But educated members of society in the central period could scarcely avoid exposure to the philo-

---

[2] On the history of modern abolitionism see in general, Davis 1966; Davis 1975; Drescher 1986; Fogel 1989.
[3] Scholars: see the resumé in Manning 1989: 1519; 1533–4. Claudius: Levick 1990: 123–4. Note also MacMullen 1990: 5.

sophical achievements of the Greeks, both classical and Hellenistic. They knew, therefore, the doctrine of natural slavery that Aristotle, building on foundations laid by Plato, had established centuries earlier, according to which the slave was a unique being, an inanimate tool who could not possess or exercise reason but who could perceive it. The slave fulfilled his natural role by performing tasks for an owner who, with his superior intellect, made decisions for the slave which the slave could not make for himself, with the result that a mutually beneficial relationship between master and slave came into being. Aristotle's conclusion consequently (*Politica* 1.2.15) was that 'by nature some are free, others slaves, and ... for these it is both right and expedient that they should serve as slaves'.[4]

Reflective Romans were also aware that the theory of natural slavery had been articulated to counter a rival view that slavery was unnatural, a matter of convention only and unjust. The sophist Alcidamas, a pupil of Gorgias, is known for example to have claimed that freedom was common to all and that no one was born to be a slave, though his remarks were made in the context of the Theban liberation of the Messenians from Spartan control early in the fourth century BC and so may have referred to helots (that is, native-born Greeks) rather than to slaves in a strict sense. The sentiment was echoed later in the century, however, in a play by the comic writer Philemon, who said that slave and free had the same flesh, that no one was a slave by nature, and that it was simply chance that enslaved the body. Both men would presumably have applauded the sympathy for slaves evident in Euripides towards the end of the previous century.[5]

At Rome itself the controversy between natural and unnatural found expression in the legal view (*Dig.* 1.5.4.1) that slavery was 'an institution of the law of nations, whereby someone is against nature made subject to the ownership of another'; freedom on the other hand was a condition of natural law, according to which all men were equal and equally free from birth. Such ideas, and the

---

[4] Cultural presence: see Rawson 1985: 282–97; Rutherford 1989: 66–70. Aristotle and Plato: see Schlaifer 1936; Vlastos 1941; (cf. Calvert 1987); Ste Croix 1981: 416–18; Brunt 1993. Cicero may have believed Theophrastus to be the author of the *Politics*: Rawson 1985: 290.

[5] Rival view: see Schlaifer 1936: 199–201; Guthrie 1969: 155–60; and especially Cambiano 1987.

tradition on which they depended, imply that slavery was always regarded at Rome as an ambiguous, perhaps even vulnerable, institution, which means in turn that in theory there must always have been a certain potential for improving change from which the slave population might have benefited. Yet nothing suggests that it was natural for Romans to think in terms of reform simply because an institution could be categorised as contrary to nature. Indeed the legal phraseology might just as well be taken to represent a final Roman ossification of the original Greek debate completely devoid of any practical importance. For those, moreover, who responded to the attractions of Stoicism, the most popular brand of Greek philosophy at Rome, the debate was irrelevant.[6]

The Stoics were prepared to acknowledge the humanity of the slave, believing that the distinction between slave and free, or any other distinction for that matter, was of far less philosophical significance than that between the wise and the foolish. Their ideal was to achieve wisdom by living in accordance with nature, that is by harmonising the reason they saw in every human being with the rational principle that underlay the whole structure of the universe. Each individual was a necessary part of the universal order and to live in harmony with nature was the individual's destiny. But because choices between good and evil constantly had to be confronted and made, to live in harmony with nature was a difficult goal to attain and the pursuit of wisdom a lifelong struggle. The emphasis here clearly fell on the inner life of the human being as wisdom was sought through the cultivation of personal virtue. External realities, such as slavery, could not be controlled in the way that personal decisions could be controlled, and so they were matters of indifference. But the Stoics believed that it was possible for both slave and free to cultivate virtue: social status was no impediment to living in accord with nature because the only freedom that mattered was freedom of the spirit and that was available to all.[7]

The idea that the slave was part of a common humanity had probably made its presence felt at Rome by the first century BC at latest through the work of the Stoic philosopher Posidonius of

---

[6] Legal view: cf. *Dig.* 1.1.4. (Ulpian); 12.6.64 (Tryphoninus); 50.17.32 (Ulpian); *Inst.* 1.2.2.

[7] See Manning 1989; Brunt 1993.

Apamea, who was an associate of Cicero and Cn. Pompeius, among others. In a universal history Posidonius wrote accounts of the major slave uprisings in Sicily of the late second century BC. The narratives are no longer extant, but Posidonius' sympathies for the slave rebels have been detected in other writers who subsequently drew on him and it has always seemed logical to associate this concern with Posidonius' Stoic cosmopolitanism.[8]

It is in the writings of Seneca, however, from the middle of the first century AD, that a real sensitivity to the degradations and humiliations of slavery is particularly visible in a Stoic philosopher, together with a powerful argument for esteeming the slave's moral worth over his social standing. Seneca was emphatic that slaves should be recognised as human beings just like the free: they were born in exactly the same way, breathed the same air, and were subject to the same mortality as the free; simply because they were slaves, a matter of accident that was not their fault, they were not to be treated with cruelty and arrogance (of a sort he could vividly illustrate), but because they were human beings they were to be treated with consideration and courtesy. Their moral development, moreover, was to be given far more attention than the kind of work they did when judgements were made about them. Slaves displayed their humanity in voluntarily and self-effacingly catering to their masters' interests, not as a result of compulsion alone, and because they were human they were able to pursue the path of virtue. Slavery was a condition of the body, not of the mind, Seneca maintained, and slaves could transcend their physical bondage by exercising for good that freedom of the spirit that knew no subjection.[9]

These views continued to find favour in later generations. Following the common Stoic doctrine that only the wise man could be truly free, the Greek orator Dio Chrysostom (14.18) offered the variation in the age of Trajan that freedom consisted of knowing what was permissible and what was forbidden, while slavery was the opposite. Then, if the slave understood the real meaning of freedom it did not matter that he had been sold as a slave countless times or that he lived his life in shackles: he could, in fact, be a freer

[8] See Strasburger 1965; cf. Bradley 1989: 133–6; Sacks 1990: 142–4.
[9] The crucial texts are *Ep.* 47 and *Ben.* 3.18–28, on which see Bradley 1986b. Comprehensively, see Griffin 1976: 256–85.

man than a king as long as he realised that philosophy was the key to being set free – the metaphor of course being far more important than the reality. Similarly in a work lampooning philosophy of all descriptions, Lucian (*Vitarum Auctio* 21) had his Stoic representative contend that he did not mind being sold as a slave because the sale was a circumstance he was powerless to control and what he could not control was of no bearing on his spiritual progress. Lucian's intent was to draw a smile, but the Stoic's argument was expected at the same time to strike a chord of recognition. Towards the turn of the third century the emperor Marcus Aurelius (*Med.* 6.24) took for granted the common humanity of slave and free when meditating on the philosophical commonplace that death brought an equal end to all, Alexander and his stable boy alike.

Throughout the central period of Rome's history Greek and Roman intellectuals took pleasure in debating the meaning of slavery and freedom, and their ideas added to the philosophical inheritance that in every generation informed the lives of those of any education. Slavery was not ignored. But in spite of the stress the Stoics gave to the notion of spiritual equality, neither they nor anyone else ever seriously questioned the place of slavery in society. It might have happened that in their everyday relationships with their slaves some slaveowners were moved to treat their slaves moderately because of their Stoic piety, as a result that is of the injunctions given by Seneca and others like him. It is impossible to tell. But as long as philosophy could regard the slavery of everyday life as an issue of indifference, reformist fervour could never emerge from philosophers' disputations because there was no point to proposing or agitating for change. Thus when Seneca had the opportunity in the principate of Nero to influence legislation, both in the senate and with the emperor, he took no steps at all to effect any public relief of the abuses he knew slaves suffered as a matter of course. The fact is that philosophical disputes were purely abstract, cerebral affairs, utterly divorced from the world of lived reality, and to the extent that they were ever heard by the vast majority of slaves, even those who were educated, they can have meant very little: 'To me', remarks a character in Dio Chrysostom (14.19), 'it appears exceeding strange that one who wears fetters or has been branded or who grinds in a mill will be more free than the great king.' Stoicism was oriented to the practical goal of improving the individual's spiritual well-being. But because it was the individual, and especially the slaveowning individual, who was the focus, there could be no mental linkage between cosmopolitanism and social action.[10]

The point is exemplified further by Musonius Rufus, another Stoic of the first century AD, who in many ways entertained notions that by contemporary Roman standards were very liberal. Musonius for example favoured equal opportunity in education for both boys and girls; he saw no barrier to women studying philosophy as well as men; and rather unconventionally he regarded marriage as a truly companionate relationship. However, when he counselled against the sexual exploitation of slave women by their masters, it did not occur to Musonius to impugn the institution that gave rise to such behaviour in the first place or to wonder about the effects of sexual abuse on those abused. To the master who felt no shame in taking sexual advantage of a slave woman ('particularly if she happens to be unmarried'), Musonius' only retort was to ask how the master would feel himself if he discovered his wife had had an affair with a male slave, meaning that the master ought to feel the same sense of shame he would consider the due of his wife in such a circumstance. To that question, as seen in an earlier chapter, there was a standard response, or rather a double standard response, that has considerable significance for the attitudes it embodies: it was by no means as serious a matter for a master to have sex with a slave woman as it was for a mistress to have sex with a slave man. But in both question and response it was the slaveowner, not the slave, who was the object of concern.[11]

When philosophers, therefore, had any qualms at all about the manner in which slaves were ill-used, they were not in the first instance interested in the victims of immoderation, so much as in the immoderation itself and those slaveowners who exhibited it. The philosophers' purpose was to eliminate excessive behaviour by slaveowners for the sake of the owners' moral health, as one step on the long path of Stoic virtue. Accordingly Musonius declaimed against sexual abuse because it was philosophically desirable that the owners of slave women should learn how to control their baser instincts if they were to become wise. Protection for the victimised,

---

[10] No steps: Griffin 1976: 275–85.
[11] Musonius on sexual exploitation: 12 (Lutz 87–9). Standard response: Quint. *Inst.* 5.11.34–5 (quoted in chapter 2).

however, was given no thought. Similarly with Seneca: in his view of society, luxury and excess reduced men to slavery of all sorts – some were enslaved by wealth, others by social rank, others by sex and so on. But philosophy demanded that these forms of self-indulgence be abandoned if the enslaved were to be set free and to find spiritual redemption. To avoid cruelty in the way the owner dealt with his slaves was thus again a step in the right direction towards the Stoic goal, but the cruelty itself was not at issue – any more than wealth, rank and sex. Whatever benefits accrued to slaves as a result of what the philosophers taught, consequently, were incidental and secondary benefits. Slavery itself was beyond dispute.[12]

Despite the theory that virtue was available to all, it must be understood, Roman philosophers and moralists did not address themselves to audiences of slaves but to their social peers, men of status, wealth and education. Epictetus, the former slave and once pupil of Musonius who achieved fame as a Stoic teacher in the late first century AD, is proof enough that knowledge could not be confined by boundaries of status. But the majority of slaves, whether domestics or rural workers, can seldom have had the chance to listen to philosophers trumpeting lofty ideals of spiritual equality, let alone to devote themselves wholly to them. What for example would Seneca's slave Felicio, a man grown old in service, have thought of the Stoic virtue his master preached? When Seneca once visited the estate where the decrepit, toothless old man had been reduced to working as a doorkeeper, he failed to recognise the person who in childhood had been his playmate. Presumably therefore he had not recently given Felicio any assuaging words on the meaninglessness of servitude. Epictetus or Felicio: who was more representative of the typical slave? Seneca perceived, like the writers on agriculture, that if slaves were treated compassionately they would become more compliant to their owners' wishes. In improving his moral character the slaveowner could easily acquire a practical dividend. But compliance was not sought directly from slaves, in the manner of Varro and Columella (and even they never spoke of slaves more than they had to). The well-being of slave-owners consumed the interests of the moralists to such an extent

[12] Bradley 1986b; cf. Manning 1989: 1523.

that slaves themselves were utterly ignored, and this was a reality
that showed no change over time at all.[13]

From time to time the philosophers acknowledged the humanity of
the slaves in their midst, but they did not encourage slaves to
develop their human character in any independent, self-fulfilling
fashion. From time to time they found it instructive to catalogue the
atrocities to which slaves were routinely subjected, but they were
not constrained to eliminate those atrocities or to confront their
underlying cause. The philosophers established no intellectual
foundation on which reform could be built, and so slavery remained from this vantage point an unchanged and unchangeable
institution, regardless of arguments about its 'naturalness' or otherwise. Where Lincoln saw misery that led to inner torment and
abolition, the Roman philosophers, proceeding from a much nar-
rower vision of humanity, saw only the opportunity for personal
self-betterment.

What of attitudes at a less elevated level? One rare, though still
oblique, point of entry to non-elite thinking is offered by the *Dream
Book* of Artemidorus, the compendium of dreams and interpretations of dreams written late in the second century AD as a guide to
the future for those who consulted it, a sober, almost scientific
manual based on wide empirical research by an author of considerable learning who had travelled extensively in the Mediterranean
world. But for present purposes the book's most interesting feature
is that it does not restrict itself to interpreting the dreams of the
socially prominent but embraces representatives of all social levels.
When travelling in Asia Minor, Greece and Italy, Artemidorus had
collected dreams from all kinds of dreamers – men and women, rich
and poor, ambassadors and tax-gatherers, athletes and farmers,
priests and shipowners. He also collected the dreams of slaves.[14]

In the world of the *Dream Book* slaveowning is ubiquitous and the
patterns of slave life evoked are entirely conventional. Slaves are
variously bought and sold, hired out and given away as gifts,

[13] Social peers: on Seneca's friend Lucilius Junior, the addressee of the *Moral Epistles*, see
Griffin 1976: 91, 94; and on Aebutius Liberalis, the addressee of *de Beneficiis*, see Griffin
1976: 455–6. Majority of slaves: note the popular, and meaningless, Stoic platitudes at
Petr. *Sat.* 39.4; 57.5; 71.1. Felicio: Sen. *Ep.* 12. Varro and Columella: Spurr 1990: 80.
[14] On Artemidorus see in general, Price 1986; Lane Fox 1987: 155–8. On dreams, cf.
Rutherford 1989: 195–200.

flogged and put to the torture, promoted from one occupation to another and set free. Fugitives are everywhere, slavedealers common. The relationship between slave and master is one in which the slave is expected to obey and to please, standing in fear of the punishment an omnipotent owner can administer at any time. But the master has a responsibility to maintain the slave, he can hold the trustworthy slave in high esteem, and mutual affection between the two is possible. In terms that are virtually Aristotelian, Artemidorus speaks of the slave having the same relationship to the master as the body to the soul.[15]

In Artemidorus' method of dream interpretation the social status of the dreamer is a crucial variable: the same dream can mean different things to different people. For example (*Onir.* 2.3):

Wearing a soft, costly garment is auspicious for both the rich and the poor. For the rich, it is a sign that their present prosperity will continue. For the poor, it signifies that their affairs will be brighter. But for slaves and those who are financially embarrassed, it means sickness.

Among slaves themselves the significance of a dream may vary because of the position held in the household (*Onir.* 2.49):

To dream that one is dead, that one is being carried out for burial, or that one is buried foretells freedom for a slave who is not entrusted with the care of the house. For a dead man has no master and is free from toil and service. But for a slave who has been entrusted with the care of the house, it signifies that death will rob him of his trusteeship.

Yet Artemidorus assumes throughout that the interpretations he gives will be credible to all dreamers, no matter where they stand in the social hierarchy, which means that he takes for granted a set of normative attitudes that to one degree or another all ranks in society shared. The validity of his interpretations rests indeed on his understanding that his view of society was essentially held by everyone else, and from this point of view the connotations of slavery in the *Dream Book* take on special importance.[16]

Images in dreams are often symbolic and have to be properly understood. Thus while the head will indicate a father and knees will indicate freedmen, the feet, or even ankles and toes, will rep-

---

[15] See *Onir.* 1.35; 1.50; 2.68; 3.54; 3.41; 4.38; 1.76; 2.25; 1.70; 1.77; 2.28; 2.15; 2.30; 1.79; 2.31; 1.26; 2.14; 2.20; 2.19; 2.68; 3.17; 4.13; 1.24; 2.33; 2.19; 1.31; 1.13; 4.30 (cf. Arist. *Pol.* 1.2.13).
[16] Attitudes: Price 1986: 13.

resent slaves. Different parts of a bed will refer to different members
of the household, the upper parts indicating the master, his wife
and children, the legs his slaves. Functional objects – scrapers and
towels, oil flasks and the boxes that contain scrapers, baskets and
dishes, millstones – will symbolise slaves because of the tasks associated with them. A range of servile statuses is evident in the
equation of small jars to ordinary domestics, amphoras to attendants, and elaborate tables to domestic stewards. The correspon-
dences are very matter-of-fact: 'covers and sacks for the deposit of
bedclothes signify concubines and emancipated female slaves'
(*Onir.* 1.74). Furthermore, Artemidorus is undeviating in categoris-
ing slaves with 'all those in a subordinate position' (*Onir.* 1.56) or
'in any bad situation whatsoever' (*Onir.* 3.13), with those who are
poor and sick, those in debt or in jail, those in any way detained
against their will. Slavery is a condition characterised by misery,
hardship, struggle, outrage and danger, from all of which release is
sought, so that the freeborn slave fugitive will naturally try to
return to his original home when he makes his bid for freedom.[17]

The associations raised by slavery in Artemidorus are uniformly
negative, precisely the same as those seen in elite literary sources.
In a late treatise (*de Officiis* 1.41) Cicero stated baldly that slaves
constituted the lowest element in society, and 'lowness' in the
Roman mind meant every kind of inferiority imaginable, physical,
intellectual, moral. It was this way of thinking that justified the
practices of feeding slaves inferior grades of food and of allotting
them inferior types of clothing. It showed no significant variation
over time or place.[18]

Recall for example how at the physical level Quintilian (*Inst.*
11.3.83) advised the apprentice orator not to adopt a servile pos-
ture when performing. The point is that while utterly illogical the
assumption of a physical difference between slave and free was part
of the process by which slaves were visualised in the Roman mind:
not a difference of race or colour as in New World slave cultures
(where the differences were of course very real), but one that simply
distinguished between ugliness and beauty, between what was
seemly and what was not. Thus the slave ran – he was under

---

[17] See *Onir.* 1.2; 1.47; 1.48; 1.64; 2.24; 3.30; 2.42; 2.10; 1.14; 1.45; 1.50; 1.80; 2.3; 2.8; 2.12;
    4.15; 2.28; 1.20; 1.37; 1.73; 2.23; 4.56.
[18] Cicero: cf. Dio Chrys. 14.1: 'slavery is the most shameful and wretched of states' (see on
    Dio in general, Brunt 1973).

compulsion – when the free man, just because he was free, could walk leisurely. Quintilian tells (*Inst.* 6.3.32) how an orator who was rather ugly once argued in a court case concerned with the issue of a man's freedom that the man in question looked like a slave: he did not have the face of a free man at all. The inevitable riposte was made: 'Is every ugly man a slave then?', to which presumably there was no rejoinder. But this is not just a silly story; it illustrates a way of thinking in Roman society that never changed. In *Daphnis & Chloe* (4.17) the parasite Gnathon, when smitten by Daphnis, rhapsodises about the young man's looks: 'Don't you see how his hair is like a hyacinth, his eyes shine under his brows like a jewel in a golden setting, his face is very rosy, while his mouth is full of white teeth like ivory?' Yet he begins this paean by declaring that he loves someone 'who has the body of a slave but the beauty of a free man'. Once Daphnis' true identity is revealed, Dionysophanes makes the comment (4.20) that it was preposterous ever to imagine that Daphnis was the son of the slave couple who had raised him. The absolute stereotype of the ugly slave was Aesop, a veritable monstrosity: 'potbellied, misshapen of head, snub-nosed, swarthy, dwarfish, bandy-legged, short-armed, squint-eyed, liver-lipped' (*Vita Aesopi* 1).[19]

In matters of the intellect Quintilian is again instructive. Lumping together all slaves and all barbarians as uneducated, and recognising that representatives of each group might occasionally display a natural flair for rhetoric, Quintilian believed nonetheless (*Inst.* 2.11.7; 2.17.6) that slaves, simply by virtue of being slaves, could not normally be expected to become accomplished orators: because slaves were naturally inferior, certain areas of human endeavour were closed off to them. No great works of art had ever been produced by slaves, the elder Pliny said; painting was the preserve of the free (*Nat.* 35.77). The fact that many slaves had jobs that required knowledge and skills of a highly sophisticated nature did not seem to be an obstacle to articles of faith such as these.

As for morality, enough has been seen already to appreciate that the slave's moral character was evaluated by the degree of subservience shown to the slaveowner and that this criterion did allow for the emergence of good slaves. At the most fundamental level, however, slaveowners believed that the slave's natural disposition was

---

[19] Ran: Plaut. *Poenulus* 522–3, with Graf 1992.

to vice and that slavery itself was, in Cicero's phrase (*Phil.* 2.113), 'the worst of all evils'. By definition slavery was stigmatic, a disgrace if it befell even one's kin, and for a free man the ultimate shaming experience was to fall under the rule of his own slave. (For Claudius in Seneca's *Apocolocyntosis* (15), it was the height of indignity to be claimed as a slave by Caligula, to be given away as a gift and to become the slave of a freedman.) From the beginning of the central era, slavery was synonymous with insult and humiliation and it is not surprising, consequently, that slavery could become such a resonant political metaphor. Caesar's tyranny brought servitude to Rome in the view of Cicero, while for Tacitus the servility of the Julio-Claudian senate was a painful, and paining, fact of history. In a society where no one was immune from slavery's influence, these were not idle words.[20]

The negative associations of slavery glimpsed in Artemidorus were, then, widespread in Roman society and long-enduring. Slaves were in all senses a naturally inferior species, at least as far as the socially elite were concerned. But because of the assumptions Artemidorus makes about how to interpret dreams and about the way his interpretations will be credible to people from all walks of life, including slave dreamers, it must be presumed that the elite way of thinking about slaves was in fact shared throughout much of society as a whole, by the petty civic officials and peasant farmers, the artisans, traders, athletes and everyone else inhabiting the world of the *Dream Book*, slaves included. (The only possible objection that could be raised is the inherently implausible notion that Artemidorus is a completely unreliable witness to Roman imperial society in the second century.) In turn this implies that there can have been little likelihood of social improvement for slaves arising from the non-elite sectors of society, because slavery's stigmatic connotations were too pervasive to allow any realisable vision of a new or a different social order to manifest itself. A better world in which slaves knew no hardships or from which slavery had been

---

[20] Stigmatic: *Dig.* 40.12.2; Plin. *Nat.* 28.56. Cf. Petr. *Sat.* 54.5: Trimalchio, apparently injured by a falling acrobat, prefers to set the offending slave free rather than carry the scar of having been physically hurt, and so morally outraged, by one so beneath his station; Petr. *Sat.* 126.11: *superbia* marked the *matrona*, *humilitas* the *ancilla*; Quint. *Inst.* 1.11.2: *vernilitas*, the insolence of the *verna*, was not appropriate for the free youth. Beginning of central era: Gel. 10.3.17 (on the elder Cato). Cicero: e.g. *Fam.* 11.8.2; 12.1.1; 12.3.2. Tacitus: e.g. *Ann.* 1.2; 1.7; 14.49.

removed altogether was not what Artemidorus' dreamers dreamed of. In the real world many slaves experienced torments in ways that slaveowners could not and did not. Many slaves wished to be free from slavery, and many resisted it as best as they were able, rejecting established values for the sake of self-survival in the process as they saw fit. But the ideology of servile inferiority was too deeply embedded in the collective consciousness for a radical, large-scale change in moral perspective ever to emerge from below, and without that necessary pre-condition progressive change was impossible. The point is exemplified by the history of a free man who was enslaved by brigands in Britain in the early fifth century AD: carried off to Ireland, the man was forced to work as a slave shepherd until after six years of servitude he one day successfully escaped, first making his way overland to a port in which he could find a ship and then undertaking a sea voyage to the Continent – at great risk to his life from the ship's crew – before eventually returning to his family home in Britain. He later reported that he found slavery a humiliation; but his experience did not launch St Patrick on a career of social reform.[21]

From the outset Christianity offered its adherents an equality of religious opportunity that had previously been unknown. It gave access not only to spiritual fulfilment and contentment in the present world but also to salvation in the next. No one was denied, eschatologically speaking: 'There is neither Jew nor Greek, there is neither slave nor free, there is neither male nor female; for you are all one in Christ Jesus' (Galatians 3.28). From this basis, and particularly because of the emphasis Christianity placed on others as well as on the self, the new religion promised a new social awareness of limitless potential. In late antiquity Augustine (*C.D.* 9.5) pointed out that the outward-looking objectives of reforming the sinner, freeing the afflicted from sorrowful suffering, and saving those in danger from death were quite at odds with the self-oriented

---

[21] Society as a whole: cf. Ste Croix 1981: 173: slavery was 'omnipresent in the psychology of all classes'. Observe how in Latin curse tablets from Britain, a rather remote area of the Roman world, the division of society into slave and free is as elemental as the division between male and female: see, for example, M. W. C. Hassall and R. S. O. Tomlin, *Britannia* 10 (1979): 343 (no. 3); *Britannia* 12 (1981): 375 (no. 8); *Britannia* 13 (1982): 406 (no. 7). St. Patrick: Thompson 1985: 17–21.

cast of traditional Greco-Roman philosophy. When in the middle of the third century the church at Rome was supporting over fifteen hundred widows and beggars, displaying thereby an altruism glaring in its unconventionality, there could be no doubt of the Christians' ability to combine belief with social action. Despite its myriad forms and troubled beginnings, Christianity unquestionably brought change to the Roman world.[22]

The history of the Christian slave Callistus, however, suggests that by the turn of the third century Christianity had brought little change for good to the Roman slavery system. As a young man Callistus was owned by a certain Carpophorus, himself a Christian, who set Callistus up in business at Rome as a banker. Like one of the slaves the Roman jurists were all too familiar with, Callistus soon set about embezzling sums of money from his bank's depositors, but in the end he panicked and ran away to preempt discovery of what he had done. He made for Portus where he boarded a ship. But realising that Carpophorus had followed him (like a slaveowner in Lucian), he tried in desperation to kill himself by jumping overboard. He was rescued by the ship's crew, however, and taken back to Rome where Carpophorus assigned him to the treadmill (*pistrinum*) in punishment. Believing that Callistus still had some of their money, the depositors later arranged his release. But Callistus had no money, and again he undertook to escape danger in death by concocting a scheme that involved creating a riot in a synagogue. The scheme misfired, and Callistus was instead sentenced to hard labour in the mines of Sardinia by the city prefect. There, no longer so intent on dying, he contrived his release following the powerful interest in setting Christian convicts free shown by the concubine of the emperor Commodus, Marcia. He was then comfortably settled in Antium by the bishop of Rome, Victor, and under Victor's successor Zephyrinus became an ecclesiastical administrator and counsellor of such eminence that on Zephyrinus' death in 217, Callistus, the former slave banker and fugitive, was himself elected pope.[23]

The tale of Callistus is remarkable on many counts. But what is most remarkable is that the relationship between master and slave

---

[22] Basis: for further and later evidence, see Cadoux 1925: 133, 454, 610. Widows and beggars: Eusebius, *Historia Ecclesiastica* 6.43.11.

[23] Hippolytus, *Refutatio Omnium Haeresium* 9.

which it depicts shows no sign of having softened, or altered in any way for the better, under two centuries of Christian influence. Clearly there was no Christian objection to owning slaves, whatever the teachings of the faith on spiritual equality. The Christian slaveowner was concerned to profit from the labour of his slave just like any other slaveowner, and he responded to what he perceived as criminous behaviour in the slave in exactly the same way as his non-Christian counterpart. Following traditional assumptions, he took for granted that the culpable slave, even though a Christian himself, must atone for his misbehaviour with his body. On the other hand, the Christian slave was still making a troublesome property of himself, resorting to time-honoured methods of self-interested sabotage and adopting conventional modes of escape in the face of danger. Ingenuity was still the only guarantee of survival, and opportunities for self-advantage had to be grasped as soon as they appeared. Continuous struggle and tension, therefore, still pervaded the lives of master and slave.

This lack of change is apparent, and dramatically so, in almost every aspect of slave life recorded in Christian sources. Christian slaveowners were well aware that energy had to be devoted to regulating and managing the behaviour of their slaves, and the methods they employed remained the same as they had always been. Cyprian, the third-century bishop of Carthage, for instance, understood (*ad Demetrianum* 8) that the Christian master might enforce obedience to his will in any number of violent ways – beating the slave, depriving him of food and water, giving him nothing to wear, threatening him with the sword, putting him in prison. The bishop might be suspected of rhetorical exaggeration or of referring to unusual capricious violence (there is no way of telling but allowance for the extreme can be made), but shackling and beating obviously raised no serious questions for Christians. A third-century council of bishops meeting at Illiberis (Elvira) in south-eastern Spain ruled that a woman who beat her maidservant (*ancilla*) to death in a fit of anger was to be excommunicated for seven years if the death had been caused deliberately but only for five years if accidentally; excommunication for five years was likewise the penalty for first time adulterers. Nor was any consternation caused by the iron collars used on recaptured runaways: an example from Sardinia, probably of late imperial date, gives the name of the owner of the slave who wore it as 'Felix the archdeacon'. Runaways of course were to be returned to their owners, even if they had taken refuge in monasteries. So prescribed the Cappadocian Basil, bishop of Caesarea in the 370s, in his longer collection of monastic rules (11), with the example of Paul two hundred years earlier firmly in his mind: in prison in Ephesus Paul had converted the fugitive slave Onesimus to the new religion, but because Onesimus was a runaway Paul had sent him back to his master Philemon, as the Roman law required. It did not matter that Philemon was also a Christian: the gospel did not promote or sanction slave resistance.[24]

The passage of time only confirmed the traditional outlook. According to the apologist Lactantius at the turn of the fourth century (*de Ira Dei* 5.12) it was perfectly appropriate that the bad slave should be punished physically, and in exactly the same ways Cyprian had earlier detailed. But towards the good slave, Lactantius said (*Institutiones Divinae* 5.18.14–16), the master was best advised to behave magnanimously, giving him words of praise and increasing his responsibilities as a reward for loyal service. Both courses of action would have an effect upon the household at large: the rewards of submission and the penalties for disobedience would be visible to all and the appropriate lessons learned. Servile compliance did not have to depend on physical repression alone in the Christian slaveowner's mind: a broad psychological control was just as desirable and equally attainable. Yet Lactantius' insights were hardly a revelation. The benefits of manipulating rewards and punishments had been known to Roman slaveowners for centuries.[25]

Lactantius' evidence makes clear that good and bad continued to be the principal designations Christians assigned to their slaves, the choice depending as always in the past on the degree of dutifulness displayed. Longstanding notions of servile inferiority also remained unchallenged. Ignatius, bishop of Antioch in the early second century, maintained in his letter to Polycarp, bishop of Smyrna (4), that slaves' presumptuousness – the sort that followed from treating slaves with some consideration (which Ignatius generally favoured, for male and female slaves alike) – was in no way to

---

[24] Cyprian: cf. Tert. *de Resurrectione* 57. Council: Canons of Illiberis 5, 68. Sardinia: Sotgiu 1973–4. Paul: Philemon 8–16.
[25] Lactantius: cf. *Ira* 17.8–10.

be tolerated. He meant that slaves, even if kindly treated, were always to know their place, which was at the very bottom of the social scale. Later in the second century Clement of Alexandria made the argument (*Paedagogus* 3.6.34) that as human beings master and slaves hardly differed from one another and that in some respects the slave was superior to his master. Yet Clement nonetheless drew on traditional stereotypes of how the slave was popularly conceived when he urged (*Paed.* 2.1.13) that the Christian was to be sure to avoid the slave's table-manners. To the rancorous Tertullian (*ad Nationes* 1.7) slavery was full of opprobrious associations: slaves were all spies who would betray their owners as a matter of course; they were not to be trusted at all.[26]

Well into the fourth century and beyond slavery remained uncontroversial. To the Gallic poet Ausonius (*Ephemeris*) it seemed perfectly natural to rouse the sleepyhead slave who assisted him in his toilet with the threat of a beating just before he offered up his morning prayers; once the prayers were over the slave could bring the master his outdoor clothes as he prepared to visit friends, or be sent to invite guests for dinner; the owner meantime had instructions to give to his slave cook, while if a flight of literary fancy caught him he could at once summon the slave stenographer to take dictation. To Lactantius again (*Ira Dei* 17.16–19) it was perfectly normal for the head of the household to maintain discipline, correct morals and restrain licence among his dependants, not simply among his slaves but among his wife and children too. There is nothing more traditionally Roman than that. After several centuries the new religion had made no major impact on Rome's social attitudes and structures, and as the vitriolic words of a Christian who disowned his children at Antinoopolis in Egypt (they had tried to kill him) show, even at a very late date slavery was still the social benchmark by which all else was judged: 'I reject and abhor you from now to the utter end of all succeeding time as outcasts and bastards and lower than slaves ...'[27]

---

[26] Inferiority: e.g. Tert. *de Patientia* 10.5; Origen, *contra Celsum* 2.47. Clement: cf. *Paed.* 3.12.92.

[27] Ausonius: *Ephemeris* is seemingly a polished version of a school exercise: Dionisotti 1982; cf. Green 1991: 245–6. Impact: Pagels 1988: 52, speaks of Christians taking news of Christian equality 'among the hovels of the poor and into slave quarters, offering help and money and preaching to the poor, the illiterate slaves, women and foreigners'. But she cites no evidence in support. Vitriolic words: *P. Cair. Masp.* 67353.

It would be an error, however, to say that there had been no change at all. Christian teachings on equality clearly had much in common with Stoic theories of cosmopolitanism, Christians, like the Stoic philosophers, taking the view that slavery was a matter of the spiritual or moral domain and that physical, earthly bondage was immaterial to spiritual progress. They agreed that the slave who pursued truth and virtue was not really a slave at all: it was the free person who was enslaved by passion or some other evil who was the true slave. However, whereas the Stoics addressed their message primarily to their social peers and made the self their principal focus of attention, Christian teachers took their good news directly to the slave population. Slaves were addressed in a new way, in their own right, though not with the end of breaking down barriers between slave and free in mind; rather, slaves as in the past were to know their place, but, because eternal life after death was so important, they were now positively instructed by those in authority to stay in it, to be content with it, not to question it:

Slaves, be obedient to those who are your masters according to the flesh, with fear and trembling, in sincerity of heart, as to Christ. (Ephesians 6.5)
Slaves, obey in all things your masters according to the flesh, not with eye-service, as men-pleasers, but in sincerity of heart, fearing God. (Colossians 3.22)

Let as many slaves as are under the yoke count their own masters worthy of all honour, so that the name of God and his doctrine may not be blasphemed. (1 Timothy 6.1)

Slaves, be submissive to your masters with all fear, not only to the good and gentle, but also to the harsh. (1 Peter 2.18)
Were you called while a slave? Do not be concerned about it. (1 Corinthians 7.21)

These injunctions were reiterated time and time again to the slave members of Christian communities all over the Roman world in every generation. The effect was to reinforce the legitimacy of slavery as an institution, not to bring alleviation to those who suffered under it or in any way to promote equality in the church between master and slave.[28]

To the ideology of loyalty and obedience that Roman slave-

---

[28] True slave: cf. Lane Fox 1986: 296. Addressed: the distinction, crucial in my view, is not recongised by Pagels 1988: 74, among others.

owners had always sought to inculcate in their slaves, Christianity brought indeed a novel refinement. It was no longer a question of the master eliciting from the slave by material rewards and incentives a pattern of behaviour the master laid down, but of the slave having to behave as the Master told him to – and coincidentally what master and Master desired was exactly the same. With the argument that obedience was to be given to them 'as unto Christ', Christian slaveowners gave themselves a stronger grip on their slaves than they had ever had before. To pious slaves the teachings on obedience and submission automatically foreclosed all possibility of agitating for freedom, of seeking material improvements, of resisting servitude. Freedom of the spirit and hopes of eternal life, they were repeatedly told, were all that mattered. It was better to be the slave of an earthly master than to be the slave of sin. Slavery was the will of God.[29]

Christianity brought change, therefore, but from the servile perspective it was change not for the better but for the worse. In the past Romans had thought of slavery as a moral evil, full of contagion and horror. Now Christians added a dangerous theological dimension by equating slavery with sin. Slavery was God's punishment for sin, Augustine declared (*C.D.* 19.15), and there was no possibility of error: sin was slavery's first cause. It was a sinister, even pernicious, development. With the promise of spiritual salvation and the threat of eternal damnation at their disposal, Christian slaveowners' psychological domination of their human property was complete. In this sense Christianity did not humanise or otherwise improve the life of the slave; it destroyed it.[30]

The unwillingness of the Christians to tamper with slavery, to call into question its elemental place in the structure of society, is apparent most starkly of all in their adoption of slave imagery to describe and symbolise their relationship with their God. Paul and

---

[29] Cf. Ste Croix 1981: 420: 'Whatever the theologian may think of Christianity's claim to set free the soul of the slave ... the historian cannot deny that it helped to rivet the shackles rather more firmly on his feet.' See also Ste Croix 1975; Brunt 1993: 384–6. The wishes of Christian slaveowners, however, may not always have been secured; see Lane Fox 1986: 297.

[30] Theological dimension: Davis 1966: 90, concluding a chapter on the ancient world, writes: 'For some two thousand years men thought of sin as a kind of slavery. One day they would come to think of slavery as a sin.' To my mind this attributes a mode of thought to classical antiquity that has no basis in evidence and fails to distinguish between Greco-Roman and Christian ways of thinking. For an attempt, however, to draw a moralistic correspondence between Latin *scelus* and Christian sin, see Wallace-Hadrill 1982.

other early Christian leaders quickly styled themselves and their followers 'slaves of Christ' or 'slaves of the Master' or 'slaves of God'. Thus the Epistle to the Philippians opens (1.1) with the words, 'Paul and Timothy, slaves of Jesus Christ ...', while the admonition in the Second Epistle to Timothy (2.24), 'And a slave of the Master must not quarrel but be gentle to all ...', gives an example of the all-encompassing application. English translations tend to prefer 'servants' and 'Lord' for 'slaves' and 'Master' in texts such as these, diluting as a result the forcefulness of the original language (or languages). But to contemporaries there could have been no doubt about the significance of the metaphor. The absolute authority commanded by the object of worship over the worshipper was precisely the same as that commanded by the earthly slave-owner over the slave, while the powerless subjection of the worshipper before God was exactly the same as that characterising the earthly slave's relationship to his owner. To Tertullian (*Apol.* 34.1), the word *dominus* (master) when used of the Christian god meant a god who was omnipotent and omnipotent eternally. It is easy to understand why Augustus in an earlier age should have been so careful to avoid it as a form of personal address.[31]

Because some slaves, in view of the responsible positions they held, had some influence with and ranking before their owners (financial agents, overseers, and so on), the assertion has been made that Paul in particular used the phrase 'slave of Christ' as a title connoting the high authority he held in the early Christian community. But even high ranking slaves were never exempt from physical punishment and other degrading types of maltreatment (as the example of Callistus makes clear), and Paul evidently thought of all Christians as Christ's slaves, not simply Christian leaders like himself. He exhorted slaves to endure their servitude, taking as a norm that slaves were the most downtrodden and unworthy members of society. He knew all the pejorative associations of slavery, taking them over and adapting them to his own purpose. Accordingly there is no room for manoeuvre in understanding the Christian metaphor of slavery. The devotees of the new religion expressed their relationship to their God in the most self-debasing and self-degrading terms that society offered them.[32]

[31] Texts: see Gal. 1.10; Romans 1.1; 6.22; Titus 1.1; Col. 4.12; 1 Pet. 2.16. Augustus: Suet. *Aug.* 53.1.
[32] Assertion: Martin 1990.

It was a remarkable choice, deriving in the first instance from Jewish antecedents. Once taken up, however, the metaphor was never abandoned but became common currency among Christians at all times and in all places regardless of sectarianism, as natural to Eusebius of Caesarea in one generation and to Augustine of Hippo in another as it had been hundreds of years earlier to Paul of Tarsus and others of his age. The logic of Tertullian (*ad Uxorem* 1.1.1; 2.1.1) in addressing his wife as his beloved fellow-slave in the Master (*conserva*) was impeccable. Christians made, therefore, a new addition to the traditional set of asymmetrical relationships between superiors and inferiors that society had always known in the past. Yet as they did so they relied on a spiritual image that bolstered the acceptability of slavery in the real world and increased the ammunition of those who wished to regard it as a natural human institution. In turn the possibility of significant amelioration that Christianity's egalitarian principles theoretically created was closed off by its failure to develop any new intellectual perspective from which slavery might be viewed in a critical light. Roman moralists observed the condition of the slaves around them and retreated from what they saw into abstract intellectualism. Christians made their observations and took refuge in the comfort of their faith. To them change was unnecessary because it was slavery that opened the way to salvation, no matter what misery it entailed along the way. There was no Christian torment, only compromise.[33]

---

[33] Jewish antecedents: see Nock 1928: 83–7; Vogt 1975: 148–9. Eusebius: *H.E.* 4.15.20; 5.1.3. Augustine: *C.D.* 1.2; 5.26.

CHAPTER 8

Slavery and progress

To dream of being beheaded, of being turned to bronze, of blowing a sacred trumpet, of riding a horse through the city, of becoming a king, of flying – these were just a few of the dreams that Artemidorus took to signify that the slaves who dreamed them would at some future point in their lives be set free. There was always a good reason: beheading indicated the impending separation of slave and slaveowner; it was only the free who had bronze statues set up to them, only the free who possessed sacred trumpets and had the privilege of riding through the city on horseback; a king had to be free by definition, and to fly was to resemble a bird, a creature above which there could be no other. This was not all fancy. A slave known to Artemidorus was actually manumitted after dreaming that he had three penises, exchanging his single name for the three names of a Roman citizen. Artemidorus' science was not to be doubted.[1]

The interpretation of slaves' dreams was predicated on the dual assumption that freedom was the greatest benefit that could be bestowed on the slave and that it was a benefit the slave unquestionably wanted to acquire. At one stage indeed (*Onir.* 2.3) Artemidorus speaks of slaves who longed for freedom. Some might well have wondered how they would survive once they were set free and left the protective environment of the *familia* to which they had become accustomed, because henceforward they would have to provide for themselves in a way that had been unnecessary before and for which they were perhaps ill-equipped. But anxiety about the future did not necessarily extinguish the wish to be free. The same dual assumption underlies the practice of manumission, an

---

[1] Artem. *Onir.* 1.35; 1.50; 1.56; 2.30; 2.68; 1.45 (cf. 5.91).

institution characteristic of Roman slavery all through its history and one that on the surface implies in Roman society a certain liberality towards slaves. To what extent, therefore, were manumission and humanity connected and what was their relationship over time?[2]

First the mechanics of the process. Manumission at Rome was either formal or informal. Formal manumission meant that the slave was set free and simultaneously given Roman citizenship – was admitted at once, that is to say, into the Roman civic community, a very radical transformation of status. Informal manumission meant that the liberated slave enjoyed only a *de facto* freedom at the pleasure of the owner and had no citizenship rights whatsoever. Probably in the reign of Augustus informally freed slaves were legally classified as Junian Latins and it then became possible for them to add citizenship to their freedom once certain conditions had been met, if for example they had married and had children.[3]

Informal manumission, conferred perhaps by letter from master to slave or orally in the presence of friends acting as witnesses, was subject to no restrictions of time or process. But it was different with formal manumission. The slaveowner had three options in essence. He could declare the slave free before the censor when a census was taken, so that the slave's name was officially entered on the register of Roman citizens and his slavery thereby ended; he could appear before a magistrate or provincial governor with the slave and a third party who, by collusive arrangement, declared to the official that the slave was really a free person wrongfully held in slavery, whereupon the owner offered no rebuttal and the official declared the slave free; or the owner could set the slave free in his will, the manumission taking place as soon as the will came into effect on the owner's death. All three forms of procedure were very ancient. But in the central period manumission by census must

---

[2] Wondered: see Epictetus 4.1..33–40. The problem was experienced by New World slaves too. John Holmes, one of Benjamin Drew's subjects, said after twenty-four years as a free man that he would have prospered more had he been given an education while a slave, and that many of his peers had to struggle simply to keep going despite their acquisition of freedom (Drew 1856: 173). Liberality: assumed uncritically by Dyson 1992: 80, 132, 200–1.

[3] Junian Latins: the date at which the *lex Junia* was passed is unknown, and may belong to the principate of Tiberius; see Buckland 1908: 533–7; cf. Bradley 1987a: 87. On identifying Junians, see Weaver 1990. Conditions: Gaius, *Inst.* 1.28–35.

have occurred only sporadically, since censuses were infrequent in the late Republic and, although regularly held in the provinces under the Principate, were never held more often than at five-yearly intervals. Which of the other two processes was the more prevalent, if either, it is impossible to decide and meaningless to enquire: they were complementary, not antagonistic, forms of setting slaves free and allowed slaveowners a choice in when and how to reward those they wished to liberate. Documents from Roman Egypt bring life to the theoretical forms. They show for instance how a home-born *ancilla* named Helene was set free 'among friends' ('inter amicos') by her owner Marcus Aurelius Ammonio, how the five-per-cent tax on formal manumissions was collected after freedom had been conferred on the slave Hermes before the prefect of Egypt, how a Roman cavalryman named Antonius Silvanus provided in his will for the manumission, in due course, of his slave Cronio.[4]

Two sets of events, at a great chronological remove from one another, illustrate how manumission underwent the impact of changing historical conditions and offer some sense of what motivated it. First the passage under Augustus of laws that modified previous manumission procedures, and secondly the introduction under Constantine of a new form of setting slaves free.[5]

The Augustan laws were a reforming response to the haphazard manumission practices of the pre-imperial era. As seen in an earlier chapter, the *lex Fufia Caninia* of 2 BC set limits to the number of slaves an owner could set free in his will, the permissible proportion diminishing as the size of the *familia* increased. The *lex Aelia Sentia* of AD 4 set minimum age requirements of twenty for the slaveowner and thirty for the slave before a living owner could formally manumit a slave (though some exceptions were allowed); and the *lex Junia* created the new status of Junian Latinity for informally manumitted slaves, one effect being that ex-slaves had the right to dispose of their property by will when before their possessions had at death automatically reverted to their former owners. These laws

---

[4] Formal manumission: for full details, see Buckland 1908: 457–532. By the time of Ulpian, manumission by census was probably obsolete: Thomas 1975: 19. Very ancient: see Daube 1946; *CAH²* VII.2, 209. Provinces: see Brunt 1990: 329–35. Documents: *CPL* 172, 171, 221 (cf. Macqueron 1945).

[5] Laws: see in general, Buckland 1908: 533–51. New form: see in general, Buckland 1908: 448–51; cf. Barnes 1981: 50, 311 nn. 75, 76.

remained operative for centuries, and from time to time a document appears showing them in force at the local and individual level. Thus from A D 62 a record has survived from Herculaneum of a Junian couple becoming Roman citizens after registering the birth and first birthday of their infant daughter, in accordance with the *lex Junia*. The provisions and ramifications of the laws certainly became the subject of much discussion from the lawyers of the Severan era.[6]

Scholars have debated the purpose of the laws endlessly. On one view they were intended to reduce the numbers of slaves currently being set free, especially slaves of eastern Mediterranean origin who, the theory holds, constituted a threat to Roman racial purity. On another view it was the economic interests of heirs that were at stake, or perhaps the laws betrayed an anxiety on the part of the upper classes about former slaves' willingness to accept traditional ways of life. More probably they were meant to impose public standards for formal manumission and to protect the Roman citizenship by making it available only to those who were properly qualified – proper qualification being a demonstrated commitment on the part of the slave to Rome and Roman values. However, no historian would argue that the laws were intended to increase manumission, to create more opportunities for more and more slaves to be set free or to encourage owners to manumit at the earliest possible moment. To one end or another (or several) the Augustan legislation was restrictive, and to that extent it constitutes rather compelling evidence against notions of growing liberalisation in Roman society, an obvious point though one whose full force has not always been brought out.[7]

Manumission in Christian churches was an innovation of Constantine's early in the fourth century A D. Precisely when it was introduced is unknown, but two rulings from emperor to bishop, the first of which belongs to A D 316, confirm an earlier directive, now lost, that seems to have established the procedure a few years before. The rulings make clear that the new ceremony was to take place before a Christian congregation that included bishops, to whom fell the special responsibility of validating the written record

---

[6] Record: *Herculaneum Tablets* nos. 5, 89. Discussion: e.g. *Dig.* 40.2.12; 40.2.15; 40.2.16; 40.4.27; 40.9.16.

[7] See Bradley 1987a: 84–95; 148–9; 160; Gardner 1991.

of manumission that Constantine required. They show too that manumission in the church conferred citizenship, though its value was far less now than in earlier periods. Constantine also gave permission to Christian priests to free their slaves by a simple deathbed indication of their wish to manumit.[8]

A point of particular interest in Constantine's second ruling is the reference it makes to slaveowners setting free their slaves because of their religious convictions: 'religiosa mente'. This suggests a possible new ideological impetus to manumission that, using the old forms, could well have been at work in the Christian communities long before Constantine's conversion. Certainly something of a demand for the new process must be inferred from the fact that Constantine's rulings were letters responding to petitions received from bishops. However, it has already been seen that the new religion did not include in its mission any goal of ridding the Roman world of slavery, and, whatever the sensibilities of individual Christian slaveowners, it is unlikely that the rate of manumission was significantly raised by Christianity. Christians continued to own slaves century after century, and not all of the slaves were eventually set free. The new form in fact was little more than a convenience for those who wished to manumit and who wished to do so in the context of their religious way of life. It was an adaptation bred of expedience, not a mark of progress, giving slave-owners another of the choices they had always given themselves in the past.[9]

The superstructure of manumission, then, its forms and presentation, could alter from one age to another as the general temper of society changed, but not obviously as a result of tendencies to improve the conditions of slaves at large or because progress towards the final removal of slavery was at work. No doubt there were in every generation any number of slaveowners who freed their slaves from genuine motives of affection, gratitude and good will: the case of Tiro in Cicero's household can stand as an appropriate example. But once the substructure of manumission is examined, that is the circumstances that preceded the event and what they entailed for the slave, humanity emerges as only one of a

---

[8] *Codex Justinianus* 1.13.1; *Codex Theodosianus* 4.22.1 (= *CJ* 1.13.2). Robleda 1976: 146 assigns the lost directive to the period AD 313–15.

[9] Petitions: cf. Millar 1977: 591. To some extent the rise of manumission in the church offsets the decline of manumission by census.

cluster of elements in the total picture. The evidence of the jurists is once more valuable as an illustrative guide.

It appears from the *Digest* (40.2.15.1) that owners were at times prepared to reward their slaves with grants of freedom for particularly meritorious acts of devotion such as coming to the master's aid on the field of battle, protecting him against brigands, securing his recovery from illness, or revealing a plot against his life. It is easy to understand how gratitude in situations like these (none of which was far-fetched) could find a practical outlet and bring benefit to the slave, but the situations themselves were exceptional rather than everyday and can hardly have accounted for the majority of manumissions in any given time or place. They were situations, moreover, that all made very heavy demands on slaves to begin with, including the risk of death, and it is difficult to imagine that most slaves ever had the chance to win freedom this way or were prepared to take the chance when and if it arose.

On other occasions manumission was the result of an agreement between slave and master whereby the slave bought his freedom and so compensated the owner for the loss of property the acquisition of freedom involved. The money could come from any number of sources, the slave's *peculium* (which to be sure strictly belonged to the slaveowner) or, in Ulpian's words (*Dig.* 40.1.41.), 'from profit obtained by chance, or by the kindness or generosity of a friend, or by the slave's carrying a charge to his own account, or giving an undertaking, or accepting a liability or the obligation to pay a debt'. Whatever the circumstance, freedom in exchange for cash was a commercial transaction, governed on the owner's side not by morality or benevolence but by considerations of financial gain and loss. For slaves in occupations that opened up prospects of profit-making or of indirectly controlled assets the system brought advantages, and as Ulpian indicated there was always the possibility that good fortune might intervene in the figure of a beneficent third party – a spouse for instance who had already been set free and had now saved enough money to buy the partner's freedom. The *ancilla* Helene was set free for a price of 2,200 drachmas, a sum of money put up by a certain Aurelius Ales, who was perhaps Helene's husband. In Petronius' *Satyricon* (57.6) the freedman Hermeros says that he paid 1,000 *denarii* for his freedom and that he bought the freedom of his *contubernalis* as well. The doctor P. Decimius Merula, known from an inscription (*ILS* 7812), paid the very considerable sum of HS 50,000 in order to be free. But whether most slaves fell into this category at any particular time or in any particular place, is again a doubtful proposition.[10]

Testamentary freedom seems often to have been awarded not simply after years of faithful service but subject to a condition in the owner's will that offered the heir some form of compensation for a slave who otherwise would have become his to own indefinitely. The condition could be the straightforward one of making a cash payment, either a specified sum or the whole of the slave's *peculium*. But the exchange of cash for freedom was not always a transaction that was swiftly concluded. Owners laid down that the money was to be paid in instalments over a prescribed period of time, three or five years for instance, which meant that the heir reaped a double dividend, cash and labour, while the slave was compelled to wait for freedom well beyond the original owner's death. Alternatively, the condition might be merely to remain in servitude, or to give the heir a certain number of days' work over a period of years – one, three, five, seven, even twelve. Sometimes the conditions were less predictable: building a block of apartments, erecting a statue to the deceased owner, maintaining the owner's tomb, painting a room, building a shop, and there were no limits to what could be demanded: a slave woman might find herself given a guarantee of manumission if she first provided her owner's heir with three new slave infants. Meantime, while these requirements were being met, the position of the slaves concerned did not improve. A new legal status was acquired, that of the *statuliber* (a slave working off a testamentary condition), but for all practical purposes this was meaningless: the *statuliber* was still technically a slave.[11]

The element of manipulation in all of this, using, or rather abusing, servile aspirations of freedom to the economic advantage of the slaveowner's heir but extending the life of the slave in slavery, is not

---

[10] Third party: *Dig.* 40.1.19: a brother or father (a very rare reference to a slave father). Helene: *CPL* 172. Petronius: cf. also *Sat.* 68.8: Habinnas has a multi-talented slave, a cobbler, cook and baker, who came at a cost of 300 *denarii*.

[11] Cash payment: *Dig.* 40.7.3.1; 40.7.8 pr.; 40.7.40.1. Instalments: *Dig.* 40.7.3.14; 40.7.18; 40.4.41.1; 40.7.40.2. Work: *Dig.* 40.7.4.2; 40.7.4.4; 40.7.3.15; 40.7.14.1; 40.7.39.3; 40.4.41 pr. Less predictable: *Dig.* 40.4.13 pr.; 40.4.44; 40.4.13.1. Slave woman: *Dig.* 40.7.3.16 (quoted in n. 12); cf. 1.5.15 with Bradley 1988: 484. *Statuliber*: *Dig.* 40.7.21 pr.; 40.7.29 pr.; see Buckland 1908: 286–91; Watson 1967: 200–17. For very comparable procedures in Brazil, see Queirós Mattoso 1986: 184–9; note that legally the position of the conditionally freed Brazilian slave was better than that of the Roman *statuliber*.

an immediately obvious indication of the widespread presence in Roman society of liberal or humane currents of thought. But the situation could deteriorate further if an unscrupulous heir chose to impede the ability of the slave to fulfil the condition that was supposed to lead to freedom. What, for example, if the heir gave a contraceptive to the woman who had to give birth to three children before she could be set free? (Actually, Ulpian said (*Dig.* 40.7.3.16), the woman should be set free anyway because she was not herself responsible for the lapse of the condition; but consider the implications of conception on demand and involuntary birth-control for trying to understand how slaves lived in antiquity.) What if the heir sold the slave and specified a new condition before manumission became possible? What if the heir prevented the slave from paying money to a third party for his freedom as the original owner had required? Testamentary conditions met the needs of slaveowners in the first instance, and a comment from the Augustan jurist Labeo leaves the matter beyond all doubt. A condition commonly required of slave accountants and managers (*dispensatores, actores*) before they were set free was to give a full reckoning of their accounts: thus Antonius Silvanus wrote in his will that Cronio was to be free only after he had given a full account of everything in his charge and had notified the heir or procurator accordingly. The procedure was delicate and complex in some cases, though it could reasonably be concluded within thirty days. The slave might then find his freedom enhanced by a cash bonus: 'Let my steward Calenus be free and have all that belongs to him plus one hundred, if it shall appear that he handled my accounts with care' (*Dig.* 40.7.21 pr.). Labeo glossed this provision as follows:

The care we should require is that which will have been in the master's interest, not the slave's. This care will be accompanied with good faith not only in the presentation of the accounts but also in the payment of any balance due.[12]

Ulpian's ruling on the slave woman who could not produce three children to win her freedom is a fine legal point. But it suggests that

[12] *Dig.* 40.7.3.16: 'Further, Julian, in the sixteenth book of his *Digest*, wrote that if Arethusa was given freedom subject to the condition of her bearing three children and the heir was responsible for her not giving birth, for example, by the administration of a contraceptive, she would be free at once; for what is the point of waiting? So, too, if the heir had procured an abortion; for she might have born triplets.' Sold: *Dig.* 40.7.9.1. Prevented: *Dig.* 40.7.20 pr. Full reckoning: *Dig.* 40.7.21 pr.; 40.7.40.7; 40.7.40.8. Antonius Silvanus: *CPL* 221. Procedure: *Dig.* 40.7.5 pr.; 40.7.6.7; 40.7.26 pr.; 40.7.28 pr. Bonus: cf. *Dig.* 40.7.40.3.

in some circumstances the law could operate to the advantage of the slave. Indeed, there is considerable evidence that legal judgements were regularly made in favour of slaves whose manumission was obstructed by adverse factors, the operative principle being *favor libertatis*, giving the slave the benefit of the doubt when a claim to freedom was not clear cut. In A D 166 one particular case, occasioned by an interest on the part of the imperial treasury (*fiscus*), came before the emperor Antoninus Pius (*Dig.* 28.4.3). A testator, having drawn up his will, subsequently had second thoughts and erased some of its details, including the names of his heirs, and at his death the *fiscus* intervened to claim the man's estate. Also erased from the will was the name of a slave the testator ordered to be set free, so that the slave's manumission was immediately put in jeopardy. Pius ruled, however, that the manumission was valid, his reason being 'to favour freedom'.[13]

The principle of *favor libertatis* was very old, perhaps, like the convention of conditional manumission, as old as the Twelve Tables. Certainly in A D 19 a *lex Junia Petronia* established that freedom was to be favoured when judges in a suit for freedom were equally divided. The principle was not therefore a product of new enlightenment in the era of the Antonine and Severan emperors, to which most of the evidence about it belongs, and although notable for its leniency it can never have accounted for huge numbers of slaves being set free. By nature it was suited only to occasional applications, functioning as a safety-valve to release the build-up of pressure in the system as a whole.[14]

As long as slavery existed in the Roman world slaveowners were always setting some of their slaves free. The act of manumission was a commonplace. But the common nature of the event does not mean that all slaves had equal prospects of being manumitted, nor does the regularity of manumission mean that most Roman slaves were set free. If owners, moreover, were always freeing some slaves, the implication is that they were always simultaneously creating new slaves, so again the practice of manumission is not in and of itself evidence of the benign for the sake of the benign in Roman

---

[13] Considerable evidence: e.g. *Dig.* 29.2.71; 31.1.14 pr.; 35.2.32.5; 40.4.16; 40.4.17.2; 40.5.24.10. See Crook 1955: 125, for the view that *favor libertatis* gives evidence of 'the slowly leavening process of *humanitas*' on slavery. Antoninus Pius: cf. Millar 1977: 237–8.

[14] Very old: *Dig.* 49.15.12.9. Twelve Tables: Watson 1967: 200. *Lex Junia Petronia*: Buckland 1908: 664.

society. For slaves themselves the surrounding presence of freedmen and freedwomen was visible proof that anyone might be able
to secure release from bondage, and Roman masters were well
aware of the role that the resultant hope played in their slaves'
minds. Discoursing on hope and human survival while exiled on
the coast of the Black Sea, Ovid observed (*Epistulae ex Ponto* 1.6.29–
30) that hope caused even the shackled *fossor* to go on with life
because he would perhaps one day be free from his chains and all
they symbolised. But in reality it was not usually a slave like the
fossor who was set free – or at least it is only the accomplished and
the privileged whom the historian can now see becoming freedmen
and freedwomen: 'My clerk of accounts (*dispensator*), December, my
bailiff (*vilicus*), Severus, and Victoria, my housekeeper (*vilica*) and
Severus's *contubernalis*, are to be free after eight years'; so a fairly
typical testamentary provision (*Dig.* 40.5.41.15). And it is accountants, a cook, a treasurer, a wardrobe-master and a child-minder
who are the slaves set free, together with their wives in some
instances, in the Will of Dasumius, not the hundreds of rural
labourers the testator can be presumed to have possessed.
Manumission at Rome was selective, not generic, and while slaves
such as Tiro could probably afford to nurture realistic expectations
of it, those like Scyphale in the *Moretum* could not.[15]

It is simplistic therefore to think that humanity was the major
factor that controlled manumission, even though the Romans were
willing to add citizenship to the gift of liberty. To varying degrees,
manumission was evident in all the major slave societies of the
Americas, and in some contexts, nineteenth-century Brazil being a
case in point, the manumitted also became citizens. But New
World slavery was not characterised by general tendencies sym-
pathetic to servile interests. There manumission served primarily
the interests of the slaveowners by keeping the slavery system as a
whole intact and in good running order; it was both 'an instrument
to elicit cooperation from slaves by holding it up as a reward that
might ultimately be gained' and 'a powerful instrument of domination' that 'emphasized the completeness of the slave's dependency on his master'. In Rio de Janeiro especially it was common
for owners to set slaves free in return for compensatory payments or

---

[15] Regularity: see Wiedemann 1985. Will of Dasumius: *ILS* 8379a (= Gardner and
Wiedemann 1991: no. 158).

subject to conditions that served the owner's needs, and in 1849 there were well over 10,000 men and women in the city who were former slaves. Nonetheless, society as a whole was not biased towards manumission: almost 80,000 people remained in slavery in that year despite the regularity of manumission in evidence. New World slaveowners could at all times make their own decisions about the extent to which they wished to reward or to dominate. The same was true at Rome. Gratuitous manumission cannot have been the norm.[16]

The motives in a slaveowner's mind for setting a slave free must often have been mixed. It is difficult now in consequence for the historian to untangle them. A kindly slaveowner may well have believed that he was doing the right thing when he manumitted a dying slave and allowed him the satisfaction of ending his life in freedom. Martial (1.101) represents the nineteen-year-old Demetrius as grateful to him for a gesture of this sort and Pliny (*Ep.* 8.16.1) claims that he made a habit of the practice. But it is the poem of Martial and the letter of Pliny that provide the evidence, and precisely what the slaves concerned thought of their owners' generosity is simply unknowable. With Pliny, moreover, there is a sense of self-consolation in his claim for not having conferred freedom on his dying slaves at a more timely moment, and one might well wonder why he waited until sickness brought his slaves to the verge of death before displaying the 'facilitas manumittendi' he wanted his peers to appreciate. Evidence of concern for the slave at Rome is not to be minimised when it appears, but the motives of economic and social self-improvement, of providing for the material security of family members, of promoting compliance in the *familia*, these are rather more noticeable aspects of the record. Furthermore this is true of all periods, which means that it is impossible to discern any progressive tendency towards greater liberalisation of manumission practices from one part of the central period to another. A softening of servile conditions could in fact be satisfactorily proved only if statistics were available to show increased rates of manumission over time in specified regions of the Roman empire. This is not the case. But given the evidence as it is the proposition itself is very dubious.[17]

---

[16] Varying degree: see Patterson 1982: 209–96. Brazil: see Queirós Mattoso 1986: 145–6; 178–9. 'Instrument': Fogel 1989: 194. Rio: Karasch 1987: 66, 335–69 (census figures).

[17] Dying slave: cf. Petr. *Sat.* 65.10. The record: cf. especially Hopkins 1978: 115–30.

The unassailable fact remains that for the owner setting a slave free was an act of *indulgentia*, the conferment of a *beneficium*. For a slave there was never any automatic right to freedom and if he wished the owner could close off the prospect of freedom for ever by banning manumission through an appropriate clause in his will or in a bill of sale. The city prefect and the provincial governor were empowered to uphold such provisions. If it was shown, moreover, that a slave had gained manumission by physically intimidating his master – which is suggestive of the lengths to which some slaves were prepared to go to be set free – the grant was automatically invalidated. The supreme cruelty, not unknown to slaveholders in the New World, was for a testator to give instructions in his will that a slave was to be set free on his, the slave's, deathbed, the owner's intent being to ensure that the slave was never free long enough to enjoy his freedom. But a touch of genuine humanity prevailed: the procedure was ruled invalid, so the slave died a slave and thus cheated the master of the final insult intended for him.[18]

At a trial in 66 BC in which he defended a man named A. Cluentius on charges of murder and attempted murder, Cicero described to the court (*Cluent.* 175–7) how some years previously his client's mother Sassia, in an attempt to fabricate evidence that Cluentius had killed his stepfather Oppianicus, had put to the torture three slaves named Strato, Ascla and Nicostratus. Strato was a slave owned by Sassia, bought in fact from the doctor who had attended Oppianicus, her husband, before his death, and Ascla was also her slave. But Nicostratus had belonged to Oppianicus, a trustworthy individual, Cicero says, who had been in the habit of regularly reporting to his master on Sassia's infidelities and who now belonged to his young son. The examination took place in Rome before witnesses, some of whom were associates of Oppianicus, others of Sassia. The object was to extract statements from the slaves that Cluentius had plotted to poison Oppianicus. But the slaves withstood the ordeal and failed to incriminate Cluentius. At a later date, Sassia tried again. A second examination was conducted

---

[18] *Indulgentia*: *Dig.* 29.5.3.17; cf. Quint. *Inst.* 7.3.27. *Beneficium*: *Dig.* 1.1.4. Intimidating: *Dig.* 40.9.9.1. Close off: *Dig.* 40.1.4.9; 40.1.9; 40.1.12; 40.4.9.1; 40.4.9.2. Supreme cruelty: *Dig.* 40.4.17 pr.; 40.4.61 pr. Note that the *lex Fabia* (*Dig.* 40.1.12) restricting manumission of slaves guilty of *plagium* was operative in Cicero's time: Watson 1967: 200 n.2. Cicero refers to a ban on manumission specifically, at *Att.* 7.2.8.

at which, Cicero continues, 'the most exquisite tortures were rigorously employed'. In the end matters got completely out of hand:

The witnesses protested, unable to bear the sight any longer, while that cruel, savage woman was beside herself with rage to find her scheme by no means turning out as she had hoped. At last, when the torturer and even the instruments of torture were wearied, and still she would not make an end, one of the witnesses . . . declared himself convinced that the object of the inquiry was not to discover the truth, but to compel the slaves to say something untrue. The others agreed: and everyone supported the decision that the inquiry had gone far enough.

Cicero's description is rhetorical and prejudicial. But in spite of the horror of the situation he saw fit to evoke, Cicero did not call into question Sassia's right as a slaveowner to torture slaves for evidence on criminal, or allegedly criminal, matters, nor did he expect his audience to question that right. The procedure was standard at Rome, a means of establishing the truth requiring from established society's point of view no defence or justification. The facilities of torturer and torture-equipment were readily available for Sassia and any other slaveowner to use, throughout Italy as well as in Rome, as an inscription from Puteoli confirms (*A E* 1971.88). There a torture and execution service was operated by a company of undertakers who were open to business from private citizens and public authorities alike. Flogging and crucifixion were standard options, at a flat rate to the user of HS 4 per person involved in the proceedings. It will have been a similar service that Sassia used in Rome.[19]

The Roman practices of flogging, burning and racking the body, evident throughout the central period, do not from a modern perspective evince any redeeming features, especially if the details of what the practices involved are fully understood. The whip (*flagellum*) was meant to make deep wounds as it struck the flesh, and its thongs accordingly had pieces of metal attached to them; as the beating took place the slave was either hung up, his feet weighted down, or else he stood with his arms tied to a beam across his shoulders. Burning meant applying directly to the body boiling pitch, hot metal plates, or flaming torches, while racking, on either the 'little horse' (*eculeus*) or 'lyre-strings' (*fidiculae*), was designed to

---

[19] Standard: see Robinson 1981: 223–7. Inscription: translated in Gardner and Wiedemann 1991: no. 22. Note that Trimalchio had *tortores* on his household staff (Petr. *Sat.* 49.6).

separate limb from limb. These procedures took place publicly, allowing anyone who wanted to spectate to increase the victim's pain. In principle they were far more severe than the punishments sanctioned by the law in the slave society of Brazil.[20]

However, the belief that the truth, when servile testimony was needed, would emerge only following the application of physical pressure was logical. By definition slavery was an institution that began with violence and that was maintained by violence (the sadistic cruelty with which some Roman slaveowners visited their slaves is notorious); and since slaves, as owners of no property, were vulnerable only to the extent that their bodies were vulnerable, it made sense to believe that the habitual lying with which all slaves were credited could only be guarded against by the infliction of bodily pain. The Romans knew of course that principle and practice did not always ride in tandem, and when it was appropriate Cicero (*pro Sulla* 78) was prepared to use a standard rhetorical argument against the value of evidence taken under torture, maintaining without difficulty that the capacity to tolerate pain, both physically and psychologically, varied from individual to individual, as did hopes and fears of what was at issue; indeed, the whole business was open to abuse by the presiding officials. Ulpian understood too (*Dig.* 48.18.1.23–25) that, while some slaves would never tell the truth no matter what tortures they suffered, others would admit anything and everything to escape the agonies confronting them. And care had to be taken, he said (*Dig.* 48.18.7), to ensure that a slave who was put to the torture did not die as a result. In fact, however, the victims of torture died frequently.[21]

In view of this openly recognised ambivalence about torturing slaves, a drive to eliminate it from the Roman judicial system might well have arisen and there certainly were some emperors who took positive steps to discourage its indiscriminate use. Although endorsing it in serious cases, Augustus for example argued against recourse to torture in every conceivable circumstance and recommended against relying on it exclusively. This position was later confirmed by Hadrian, who also ruled that if a slave claimed to be a free person in order to evade the torture with which he was threat-

---

[20] Practices: Wiseman 1985: 5–10. Brazil: Karasch 1987: 117.
[21] Violence: see Hopkins 1978: 118–23; Bradley 1987a: 113–37. Rhetorical argument: *Auctor ad Herennium* 2.10; Quint. *Inst.* 5.41.2. Frequently: *Dig.* 48.19.8.3 (Ulpian).

ened, the claim had to be properly heard before the torture could be applied. Later still Septimius Severus directed that a commonly owned slave could not be tortured for evidence against any of his owners, extending thereby the longstanding point of law that slaves were not to be examined for evidence against their own masters.[22]

These measures, however, can be countered by others that show a completely different thrust. Thus Antoninus Pius, followed later by Septimius Severus, extended the use of torture for evidence to financial cases and, although generally safeguarding slave children below the age of fourteen from examination, made an exception of them in treason cases. Pius also ruled that a slave who was set free expressly to avoid torture would not be exempt, unless the charge were capital. A number of rulings show in addition that slaves' traditional protection against being tortured for evidence against their own masters gradually dissipated in the Antonine and Severan periods. Thus Trajan stated that the slaves of a slaveowner who had already been condemned could be tortured for evidence against him because the fact of condemnation stripped the master of his slaveowning rights. Trajan also allowed the slave of a husband to be tortured in capital cases affecting a wife. Both Marcus Aurelius and Septimius Severus permitted torture against a slaveowner in adultery prosecutions. Ulpian (*Dig.* 48.18.1.6) quotes a rescript from Severus that suggests a considerable erosion of the original principle by the end of the central period:

Since information under torture ought neither to be obtained from slaves against their masters, nor, *if this is done*, should it guide the counsel of the person who is to pronounce sentence, much less should informations laid by slaves against their masters be admitted.

The reference at the end of the rescript was to information volunteered by slaves, which was to be discountenanced; the reason given by the jurist Paul (*Dig.* 48.18.18.5) has a delicious, though unconscious, irony to it: 'it is not right in matters of doubt for the master's well-being to be entrusted to the whim of his slaves'.[23]

Another item on torture from Ulpian (*Dig.* 46.18.1.27) is instruc-

---

[22] Augustus: *Dig.* 48.18.1 pr. Hadrian: *Dig.* 48.18.1.1–2; 48.18.1.12. Severus: *Dig.* 48.18.3. Longstanding point: see Brunt 1980b: 256.

[23] Pius: *Dig.* 48.18.9 pr.; 48.18.1.13. Trajan: *Dig.* 48.18.1.12; 48.18.1.11. Marcus: *Dig.* 48.18.17 pr. Rescript: cf. App. *BC* 4.81: in 43 BC at Patara in Lycia, M. Brutus crucified a slave for presumptuously accusing his owner of concealing gold Brutus needed.

tive for the general Roman view of humanity. It refers to an imperial letter, which Ulpian quotes, enunciating the principle that a person who had been found guilty of a crime on his own evidence should be set free if it subsequently came to light that the person was innocent and had made a false confession; for, Ulpian says, 'sometimes people confess out of fear or for some other reason'. The principle seems to be very enlightened. But the specific circumstances the letter describes create a rather different impression. The letter was written by Marcus Aurelius and L. Verus to the provincial governor Voconius Saxa, probably the Q. Voconius Saxa Fidus who was proconsul of Africa in A D 161/162 (Africa must be the site of the episode accordingly). A slave named Primitivus who was afraid of his master accused himself of murder in order to get away from his owner, and he gave the names of some other people he said were his accomplices. An investigation was held by the governor who, suspecting the story, decided to put Primitivus to the torture to discover the truth. At once Primitivus admitted that he had lied: there were no accomplices, he had made up the whole story. Marcus and Verus, whom Voconius must have informed of the case, subsequently gave instructions that Primitivus was to be sold, but on condition that he not return to his original owner (who could not complain since he was to be compensated financially). In a sense, therefore, Primitivus gained what he had first sought, though he still remained a slave. The striking, if not alarming, detail about the letter, however, is the way Voconius Saxa is commended by the emperors for having proceeded immediately to torture Primitivus to find out the truth, for having acted, as they put it, 'prudently and with the excellent motive of humanity' ('Prudenter et egregia ratione humanitatis'). Even in a situation where some sympathy for the plight of the slave seems to have been felt (and Primitivus must have been desperate indeed to charge himself with murder), the governor did not hesitate to torture the slave, and his course of action was deemed entirely appropriate at the highest level of government. Torture and humanity were clearly not irreconcilable opposites in the Roman mind.[24]

Despite expectations, therefore, it seems unlikely that in the area of judicial torture slave conditions ever improved over time in any

---

[24] Q. Voconius Saxa Fidus: see Syme 1979: 468. On *humanitas* in Roman law, see in general, Bauman 1980: 173–218.

substantive way. On occasion there could be improving modifi-
cations, such as the concession that a pregnant slave woman should
not be tortured for evidence until she had first delivered her child.
But the system itself was never seriously challenged and the practice was unrelentingly maintained. In A D 16 when the young aristocrat M. Scribonius Libo Drusus was accused of treason, his slaves
gave evidence against him despite the ban on slaves incriminating
their own masters in capital cases: the emperor Tiberius simply
had the slaves sold to the state to make sure the law was technically
obeyed. In A D 62 Nero did not balk at torturing his wife's *ancillae*
for evidence of her adultery with a slave (some resisted the attempt
to produce false evidence, others were not so brave), and half a
century later Pliny similarly put Christian slave women to the test
without compunction when investigating the spread of the new
religion in Bithynia-Pontus as provincial governor. Well beyond
the central period emperors continued to assert the centrality of
slave torture in Roman judicial life, to the point at times of near
absurdity. Diocletian, for example, allowed interrogation of *vernae*
to establish their ownership when their owner had no documentary
record of such, and Constantine permitted torture of a slave whose
ownership was disputed between two parties, one of whom claimed
that the slave in question was a fugitive: not only would torture
resolve the issue of ownership, it would also deter other slaves from
running away. It is preposterous that in cases like these it should be
the slave who was ultimately judged most capable of telling the
truth. Any notion of true amelioration, or even softening change,
moreover, runs counter to an indisputable judicial development of
the imperial age that has long been evident, the gradual extension
of the use of torture to extract evidence and confessions from
persons of free status, including (before A D 212) Roman citizens.
Allied to this was a gradual harshening of penalties for those of
socially inferior status convicted of crimes, who although free were
increasingly punished with penalties that had traditionally been
reserved for slaves alone. Under this regime humanity towards
slaves is scarcely to be expected.[25]

Three years after the investigation of Nicostratus, Ascla and Strato,

---

[25] Slave woman: *Dig.* 48.19.3. M. Scribonius Libo Drusus: Tac. *Ann.* 2.30. Nero: Tac. *Ann.*
14.60. Pliny: *Ep.* 10.96.8. Diocletian: *CJ* 3.32.10. Constantine: *CJ* 6.1.6. Gradual extension: see Garnsey 1970. Gradual harshening: see Garnsey 1968; MacMullen 1986.

the implacable Sassia found a pretext to put Strato and Nicostratus to the torture once more. Cicero (*Cluent.* 182–7) again provides the evidence, though his account this time is more allusive than before. Whether the examination was witnessed is unclear, but it seems that there was now little to restrain Sassia: Nicostratus appears to have died under torture and Strato was crucified after his tongue had been cut out to prevent him incriminating Sassia herself. Because of the extreme lengths like this to which individual slave-owners could go in torturing and punishing their slaves, slaves under the Principate were increasingly brought within the purview of Roman criminal law, and the authority of owners to punish absolutely was curtailed and replaced by public forms of coercion. The ease with which the slaveowner could freely abuse the slave was diminished by a sequence of laws that, for example, made murderous masters liable for homicide, proscribed castration, and outlawed *ergastula*; and through recognition of rights of asylum and appeal to magistrates and governors slave victims in the imperial age came to have some means of relief against abusive owners. These were undoubted gains of principle for the servile sector of society.[26]

In practice, however, the gains probably had no more than a small impact on slave life. Anecdotal and random evidence leaves the impression that slaves continued as much as before to be the objects of capricious brutality, while the servile capacity to use the mechanisms of relief available was far from easy to exercise. A fourth-century papyrus from Oxyrhynchus (*P. Oxy.* 903) illustrates both points. It records a wife's catalogue of complaints against a violent husband, as follows:

He shut up his own slaves and mine with my foster-daughters and his agent and son for seven whole days in his cellars, having insulted his slaves and my slave Zoë and half-killed them with blows, and he applied fire to my foster-daughters, having stripped them quite naked, which is contrary to the laws ... and to the slaves when they were being beaten he said, 'What did she [i.e. his wife] take from my house?' and they under torture said, 'She has taken nothing of yours, but all your property is safe.'

In this example distinctions of status obviously had no bearing on the way the husband behaved; his victims were not slaves alone.

---

[26] Roman criminal law: see Robinson 1981. Laws: see Buckland 1908: 36–8; Manning 1989: 1531–3; cf. Bradley 1987a: 123–9. Asylum: see Freyburger 1992.

But in dealing with his suspicions that his wife had stolen from him, the husband was clearly not deterred by Roman imperial legislation from interrogating, battering and incarcerating the slaves of his household as much as he wished, and to the slaves the theoretical rights of appeal to the provincial governor and taking refuge before a statue of the emperor were, in the heat of crisis, useless. The scenario at large was hardly different from that of Sassia torturing her slaves four hundred years earlier.[27]

The piecemeal improvements were, therefore, little more than cosmetic tinkerings with a system that in all essentials remained unchanged throughout the long duration of the central period. They were designed to satisfy the interests of slaveowners rather than those of slaves and to safeguard the well-being of the system itself. Under Constantine, when most of the 'improving' laws had been passed and might be thought to have wrought some alterations of attitude, the branding of slaves on the face was banned because with the new religious sensibilities of the age it was felt that to disfigure the face was to disfigure the image of God. A change for the better, perhaps, though it was still permissible to brand slaves on their arms and legs, and for the slave who was branded under the new rules the pain of molten metal on the limbs can scarcely have been less searing, the humiliation of the scars that afterwards were left as a permanent reminder of the pain suffered any less intense, simply because God's image had not been disfigured and owners were safely relieved of the anxiety of desecration. It is of course impossible to say how many slaves were treated in such a fashion. There may have been very few. But the possibility of the action was never denied. In England in 1102, by contrast, an end was legislated to the trade in slaves, uninterrupted since the Roman withdrawal centuries earlier, by a canon of the Westminster Council. It followed a change in moral consciousness that came to see the traffic in human merchandise as something 'nefarious', comparable to the exchange of 'brute animals'. Slavery in England was not thereby at once extirpated, but a significant turning-point had been reached. In Roman antiquity, a turning-point of that sort was never even perceived.[28]

To think of history as a steady march through time that brings to

---

[27] Small impact: see Watson 1983; Bradley 1987a: 126–9. Note Tert. *Apol.* 27.7 on *ergastula*.
[28] Constantine: *CTh* 9.40.2. England: see Pelteret 1981: 113.

every generation and to all members of society, if only dispro-
portionately, the never-failing increases in material welfare and
cultural sophistication by which social progress is often identified,
is a mode of thought characteristic of the modern era, not of the
distant and certainly not of the Roman past. Indeed, to Romans
with any sense of historical development the growth of materialism
and everything associated with it was synonymous with moral
enervation and social decay, the very opposite of progress in the
modern definition. To assume and to look for progress of a modern
liberalising kind in the history of slavery at Rome is, therefore, to
indulge in anachronism. The mentality of the Romans concerning
slavery was a steady-state mentality, dependent upon deeply
entrenched and unchangeable views of a social hierarchy that was
itself impervious to change. At no time in the central period of
Roman history was there any significant amelioration of the institution and at no time any indication of revolutionary reformist zeal.

CHAPTER 9

To be a slave

In the middle of the first century AD at Phrygian Hierapolis in the Roman province of Asia, a child was born who in adulthood and much further to the west was to achieve lasting fame as a philosopher. He spent a considerable portion of his life in Rome, commingling with members of the Roman elite and studying in the Flavian era with the eminent Musonius Rufus. Subsequently, when Domitian in the early nineties expelled philosophers from the city, he took up residence at Nicopolis in Epirus and there he attracted audiences of Roman officials, among others, who stopped to hear him as they journeyed to and from Rome's eastern provinces. About AD 108 the young L. Flavius Arrianus, a future consul, historian and redactor of the philosopher's teachings, was among the visitors and somewhat later the emperor Hadrian may well have made an appearance too. The child was Epictetus. Yet when he was born there could have been little anticipation of future celebrity or association with the powerful, for Epictetus was born a slave and owed both his early translation to Rome and his introduction there to philosophy to the accident of belonging to the freedman Epaphroditus, who in the reign of Nero was the emperor's secretary *a libellis*.[1]

It was because of slavery that Epictetus became a philosopher – slavery brought Epictetus, that is to say, certain opportunities, perhaps even advantages he might otherwise have never known. But his experiences as a slave are not likely to have been uniformly

---

[1] Epictetus: for the details on his life, see *PIR²* e 74; Millar 1965 (noting that there is no record of his manumission); Syme 1988: 25, 306; Syme 1991: 349. L. Flavius Arrianus: see in general, Stadter 1980; Syme 1988: 21–49. Epaphroditus: see *PIR²* e 69; Millar 1977: 77–8. Secretary: Millar 1977: 249–51.

positive. The long journey from Hierapolis to Rome was typical of the compulsory mobility to which Roman slaves were routinely subjected, the deleterious consequences of which have been seen. In addition, for most of his life Epictetus was lame, the result according to tradition of abuse he had suffered during his years in slavery. At the physical level consequently there would have been even in Nicopolis a constant reminder of the harsher aspects of life in servitude. It is a natural question to ask whether the philosophical discourses that Arrian set down for posterity long after his stay with the philosopher contain reflections of what it had been like to be a Roman slave.[2]

A striking feature of Epictetus' teaching is a preoccupation with freedom, a preoccupation perhaps to be explained by the notion that a philosopher who had once been slave might well have had a far keener appreciation of liberty than one who had not: a Seneca or Musonius, for instance. But as with his Stoic predecessors the freedom that concerned Epictetus was the freedom of the spirit, not the earthly legal status of freedom in the real world that the slave could not by definition know; and despite his origins the most that Epictetus said on this subject was that slaveowners should confine their slaveowning to a moderate scale. Alternatively therefore the preoccupation can be assigned another cause: his knowledge of tyranny in the reign of Domitian.[3]

Yet must the connection between Epictetus' life as slave and his teachings on freedom be so quickly dismissed? It was difficult after all for freedmen ever to forget that they had once been slaves: high society regarded them as servile still and would never allow them or their free descendants to shake off altogether the slavish past. The discourses, as it happens, allude to Epictetus' life as a slave more than once: he was still a slave when studying with Musonius and he knew at that time that he was not safe from being flogged if his owner wished to punish him. Moreover, a useless cobbler in his household had been sold off, who by a twist of fate ended up as cobbler to Nero and so found himself in a position to lord it over Epaphroditus. Manumission did not expunge slavery from the memory, and Epictetus' work, it can be maintained, evinces a

---

[2] *The Discourses of Epictetus* were brought out in the reign of Antoninus Pius: Syme 1988: 47.
[3] Notion: dismissed by Brunt 1977: 24. Moderate scale: Epict. *Encheiridion* 33.7. Tyranny: see Starr 1949.

sensitivity to slave life that points the way to resuming some of the constant elements of living in servitude that affected all Roman slaves, differences in individual circumstances and the complexity of the institution notwithstanding. If Epictetus was 'repelled by the arrogance of high society', it does no harm to associate his remarks with his personal experience.[4]

First, there is the indignity of slavery – the kind of indignity that came from having to work as a body-slave to a wealthy owner or from being bought and sold like a commodity. For Epictetus the slave was a permanent symbol of subjection, ignorance and cowardice, connoting 'sorrows and fears and turmoils', in a positive sense a token only of the slaveowner's prosperity. Secondly, violence – the violence of being reduced from freedom to slavery as a woman or child while the husband and father was simultaneously murdered, or the violence of being forever exposed, in the run of everyday life, to beating after beating (if not the reality then certainly the threat) so that the owner could make sure the slave turned out right. Thirdly, the caprice to which the life of the slave was subject: if a slave who was asked to bring warm water brought water that was not warm enough or if he were not there to perform the service at once, it was inevitable that he should face the slaveowner's wrath. As the owner saw fit or as temperament or emotion dictated, burdens could be lightened or humiliation heaped upon humiliation. From a philosophical point of view, Epictetus makes clear, the slaveowner himself might be answerable to a higher authority just like the slave; but in the world of everyday reality the slave had no claim to independence at all and no choice but to subordinate himself to the master's will. And indignity, violence and caprice were all in and of the world of everyday reality – the world in which the Roman magnate stocked his household with slaves to cater to his every need: slaves to buy his food, slaves to cook his food, slaves to serve his food, slaves to clean up what was left of it once he had eaten, slaves to dress him, slaves to take care of his shoes, slaves to massage him; it was the world in which the praetor presided over manumissions and the manumission tax had to be paid and in which the slaveowner was always worrying

---

[4] High society: Tac. *Ann.* 2.12; Plin. *Ep.* 3.14.1. Allude: Epict. 1.9.29–30; 1.19.19. 'Repelled': Syme 1988: 306.

whether his slaves would steal from him, run away, or simply die before their time.[5]

The anxieties of the slaveowner indicate well enough that slaves were not without all choice in their lives, and Epictetus understood the psychology that lay behind the process of their decision-making. The demands imposed upon slaves might often be abominable, but if met and met well they at least brought food and freedom from painful victimisation. If a beating had been suffered, the memory of the pain provided a basis for not making the same mistake twice. Some control could be gained. More assertively, if commanded to pour oil in the master's bath, why not pour in fish-sauce instead, and pour some of it over the owner's head into the bargain? Or if ordered to bring barley-gruel, why not a bitter concoction of vinegar and fish-sauce (again)? Collusion among three or four slaves in the household could infuriate the owner and his torment was worth the risk of a flogging. A choice could be made. Then there was running away, an enterprise Epictetus knew required great reserves of inner strength: the fugitive had only himself to rely on, he had to live by his wits from one day to the next, he had to make sure he stole some food from the household to last him for the first few days and contrive one scheme after another to find more later on, he had to keep on the run, over land and over sea. To make the philosophical point that great wealth was unnecessary to guarantee human survival, Epictetus claimed that no one had ever seen a fugitive who died of hunger. Yet he knew that the runaway slave could never relax. His image of the fretful fugitive who panicked in the theatre on hearing the word 'master' from the stage – the slave thought his owner had finally caught up with him – has more than a touch of the comic about it. But it is an image evoking a reality of slave life that followed a decision about slavery taken by the slave himself. There was a choice. The impulse behind escape was of course the wish to be free, and that was a wish slaves wanted to come true in their lives at the earliest possible moment. They might have underestimated what it took to fend for themselves once outside the household and they were unaware of the dangers of falling into a worse slavery than the one they hoped to leave behind (the slavery of materialism). Nonetheless it was

[5] See Epict. 1.2.8–11; 4.1.7; 2.2.12–13; 2.14.18; 3.22.45 (cf. 4.6.4); 1.28.26; 3.25.9–10; *Ench.* 12.1; 1.13.2 (cf. 1.18.19); 3.24.75; 3.26.21–2; 2.1.26; 3.26.12.

freedom from slavery that slaves prayed for – actually prayed for, Epictetus noted, and despite his concentration on spiritual freedom his observation must be taken to represent a common fact of life. Perhaps it was a fact of particular significance to him in view of his intimate knowledge of being a slave.[6]

Epictetus' allusions to living in slavery encapsulate the tension that must always have been present in the mind of the Roman slave: the tension between being held in a state of total subjection that denied all sense of personhood on the one hand, and being at the same time a human agent capable of responding to submission in a variety of self-validating ways on the other. To greater or lesser degree, slavery presented all Roman slaves with an unavoidable dilemma – the dilemma of reconciling their active human potential with a social categorisation that in theory denied them all possibility of exercising independent judgement and freedom of the will. How the dilemma was resolved determined the slave's emotional and psychological well-being. This of course is a speculative generalisation, based on imaginative inference from the remaining historical record. But it is a generalisation strongly supported by the evidence of former New World slaves, in which, as earlier chapters have shown, two elements have particular prominence: first the agonies of slavery – the suffering caused by cruel treatment, the pain and humiliation of physical and sexual despoliation, the devastating consequences of family separation, the problems of material and emotional survival; and secondly, the means by which these adversities were endured and overcome, as strategies of accommodation and resistance were deployed, as disadvantage was turned to advantage, as the manipulated became the manipulators. If the stories of Frederick Douglass and Harriet Jacobs are the most celebrated examples of slave narratives that bring these themes together and show how the slave's wish for freedom proved ineradicable, they are stories that in whole or in part were replicated time and time again in the New World: they were neither exceptional nor unique.

The bare record of fact shows that Roman slaves, like those in the Americas, were bought and sold like animals, were punished

---

[6] See Epict. 1.2.8–11; 3.25.9–10; 2.20.29–31 (cf. *Ench.* 12.2); 1.9.8; 3.26.1–2; 1.29.59–63; 4.1.33–40.

indiscriminately and violated sexually; they were compelled to labour as their masters dictated, they were allowed no legal existence, and they were goaded into compliance through cajolery and intimidation. They were the ultimate victims of exploitation. At the same time, however, and again like their modern counterparts, they responded with actions which their owners often condemned as symptomatic of the evil that was generically attributed to them all, but that can be more reasonably recognised as mechanisms by which resistance to exploitation was offered and efforts to assert human individuality made. The Roman slave's perception of these experiences cannot be seen clearly, which is a tragedy. But it can be glimpsed just a little through a string of questions that derive from the factual record. The questions cannot be answered. But merely to pose and to ponder them is to go a little way towards defining the psychological climate under which Roman slaves lived and to understanding the pressures that had to be balanced against one another for the sake of human survival.

What, for instance, was it like to be a captive of the Roman army and to know, at a precise moment in time, that the only future you faced was to be butchered or sold off into servitude, for ever as far as you could tell, having suddenly been deprived of the freedom you had known all your life previously? What did you feel when your wife and children were torn away and handed over to slave-dealers, pernicious men, to be sold on the block and never be seen again? What was it like to feel powerless when the woman you called your wife was stripped naked and mercilessly flogged by the master in full view of the household, and how did you live with the memory of all this afterwards? What was it like to be casually told year after year that you would be set free one day when your owner died, but on condition that you later, and in fact for many years, provided some compensation for this gift? Did you really think it possible to live long enough to be set free? Would it be worth it?

Or what did it feel like to grow up as a slave, perhaps to live well in a rich household, but gradually to come to realise that you were the symbol of everything that the powerful in society thought despicable, rotten and corrupt? What was it like to feel a sense of inferiority hammered into you every day by the food you were given to eat, the clothes you had to wear, the space you were supposed to sleep in? And what was it like to anticipate the lick of the lash, the clasp of the slave collar, the touch of the branding iron? To feel so desperate that you would run away and abandon all family ties and all the security of the household in an attempt to create a better life somewhere else, knowing all the time that you would be hounded, perhaps recaptured and returned to a life more miserable than the one you had left? What was it like to know you had outwitted your owner and had evaded a day's work, had run the risk of stealing from him or defrauding him? What was it like to know you had killed your owner?

Traditionalists will object that to try to penetrate the psychological world of the Roman slave is beyond the historian's sphere, especially if the attempt leans heavily for support on evidence from other times and places. Those satisfied with the conventional themes of classical history are never likely to be dislodged from their reclusive positions of serene superiority. But objections are inadmissible when founded on defective knowledge or false, and even arrogant, beliefs that the unique character of the classical world somehow renders it incapable of profitable comparison with other historical societies. Modern historians and sociologists, knowing full well the need to make every allowance for particular variations in one society after another, have disclosed nonetheless the universalist features of slavery across time and place: to pretend otherwise is futile.[7]

What does it matter, more importantly, to stress the burden of the servile psychological regime? Perhaps the oppression was not all that severe because relevant factors have been glossed over. Ambitious slaves had lots of opportunities to succeed in Roman society, and through industry and application many integrated themselves fully into the established world around them, aided not least by liberal grants of manumission. From an economic point of view slavery was not a vital concern in every time and place covered by Rome's history, its prominence in Italy of the last two centuries BC contrasting with its relatively low economic profile in, for instance, Roman Egypt of the first two centuries AD. What reason is there in any case to dwell on the voiceless and the disempowered when the historian's attention should more properly turn

---

[7] Objections: Yavetz 1988: 153-4, with n. 120. Cf. Dyson 1992: 34; contrast Fogel 1989: 185.

to 'the visible and vocal', those who enjoyed 'freedom of action'? The question is one almost of intellectual propriety.[8]

Perhaps one might pause and wonder. Wonder first if there is not something distressing and disturbing about the assumption that it is only those slaves with ambitions to succeed on lines laid down by established society who deserve attention and approval, as if all the rest were not really fit for anything but the abjection of slavery. Ambitious on whose terms? Wonder also if the slaves of Roman Egypt or of any other place or period for which a relative insignificance of slavery is claimed would have agreed that slavery was unimportant, when it exposed them to a form of social discrimination that shaped and adversely affected every aspect of their lives every minute of the day, no matter what their numbers or the work they did. Important from whose perspective? And wonder finally if there is not in fact rather a lot to be learned about the Roman elite from dwelling on the ways in which they treated and managed and indeed depended upon their slaves, though the unedifying results might not be particularly welcome or palatable to those historians devoted exclusively to the study of high culture, law and the arts of government.

It is a historical, objective reality that slavery was an evil, violent and brutalising institution that the Romans themselves, across a vast interval of time and space, consciously chose to maintain, for which they themselves were responsible, whose justification they never seriously questioned and for which no apology or exoneration can now be offered. Slavery for the Romans was not a peculiar institution but the standard by which all else in society was measured and judged: it was a way of thinking about society and social categorisation. To recognise this is not to depreciate the successes of elite culture or even to assign blame; it is only to bring into proper historical and intellectual focus the incalculable degree of human misery and suffering those successes cost, and to guarantee that a sanitised and distorted version of the past does not prevail.

For the sake of historical understanding as a whole, therefore, it is a matter of considerable importance to make the attempt to understand what it was to be a slave at Rome, to capture something

[8] Ambitious slaves: Dyson 1992: 46, 116, 187, 200, 201. Economic point of view: Jones 1956. Voiceless and disempowered: Syme 1991: 186 (quoted); cf. Syme 1988: 20.

of the slave mentality and the servile point of view. And the results need not always be gloomy. As the consul of 63 BC fumed over the disappearance of a trusted household slave named Dionysius, some time in the mid-forties, and mobilised all the resources available to a Roman senator of his great eminence in order to recover the man, Dionysius himself was safely away across the Adriatic, last spotted on the coast of Dalmatia. Cicero never saw him again.[9]

[9] Dionysius: Cic. *Fam.* 13.77; 5.9; 5.11; 5.10a.1–2, with Bradley 1989: 32–5.

Bibliographical essay

Roman slavery is a subject on which there is an enormous and constantly growing scholarly literature, so that it is probably impossible any longer for even the most conscientious of historians to master it all. Here, however, I am concerned less with the bibliographic needs of professionals than with the needs of readers such as the undergraduates I teach at a medium-sized public university in western Canada. These are students whose general knowledge of classical antiquity is typically very limited (through no fault of their own) but who are quick to seek more and sometimes extensive information about slavery and Roman society once the initial interest has developed (for whatever reason).

HISTORICAL BACKGROUND

A sound introduction to Roman society in the first half of the central period is provided by Mary Beard and Michael Crawford, *Rome in the Late Republic* (London 1985) and in the second half by Peter Garnsey and Richard Saller, *The Roman Empire: Economy, Society and Culture* (Berkeley and Los Angeles 1987). Both books have ample suggestions for further reading. Beard and Crawford assume knowledge of P. A. Brunt, *Social Conflicts in the Roman Republic* (New York and London 1971), which to my mind has the status of a minor masterpiece (even if now over twenty years old) and is indeed essential reading, while Ramsay MacMullen, *Roman Social Relations 50 B.C. to A.D. 284* (New Haven and London 1974) is also very rewarding, if a little idiosyncratic. Students with stamina can follow up Brunt's views on the late Republic in his larger work, *The Fall of the Roman Republic and Related Essays* (Oxford 1988), especially the first chapter, though they must be sure they are not faint of heart. The main problem with books on Roman social and economic history is that they take for granted a working knowledge of Rome's political history. But for most students reference to a standard narrative is obligatory. Michael Grant, *History of Rome* (New York 1978) is the most preferable of the general histories available.

EVIDENCE

An excellent collection of sources on slavery in translation is available in Thomas Wiedemann, *Greek and Roman Slavery* (Baltimore and London 1981) and some extra material has now appeared in Gardner and Wiedemann 1991 (cited in the bibliography below). P. A. Brunt has raised a challenge by claiming that it is impossible to generalise about what he calls the 'lot' of slaves in Roman antiquity, given the inadequacies of the evidence available (Brunt 1987: 706); but for approaches to how the obstacles might be overcome, see M. I. Finley, *Ancient History. Evidence and Models* (London 1985 and New York 1986) and MacMullen 1990: 3–12. The value of law as a source of historical evidence is best learned from J. A. Crook, *Law and Life of Rome, 90 B.C.–A.D. 212* (London and Ithaca 1967), an incomparable book. The law of slavery in particular is introduced in Alan Watson, *Roman Slave Law* (Baltimore and London 1987), but for detail advanced students will still have to consult Buckland 1908 (note that to avoid severe headaches, Buckland should never be read for more than thirty minutes at a time). Marcel Morabito, *Les Réalités de l'esclavage d'après le Digeste* (Nice 1980) facilitates access to slavery material in the *Digest*. For bibliography on law under the Principate, see Gérard Boulvert and Marcel Morabito, 'Le droit de l'esclavage sous le Haut-Empire', *ANRW* II 14 (1982): 98–182. Evidence for slavery in Rome's western provinces is surveyed in E. M. Staerman, V. M. Smirnin, N. N. Belova, Ju. K. Kolosovskaja, eds., *Die Sklaverei in den westlichen Provinzen des römischen Reiches im 1.–3. Jahrhundert* (Stuttgart 1987).

SLAVERY

The three most important books to deal with Roman slavery in recent times are Keith Hopkins, *Conquerors and Slaves*, M. I. Finley, *Ancient Slavery and Modern Ideology* and G. E. M. de Ste Croix, *The Class Struggle in the Ancient Greek World* (cited fully in bibliography below). All are essential reading but all are controversial: Hopkins because of the heavy reliance on sociological methodology, Finley because of the open assault on the 'apologetic' attitude towards slavery represented in the recent age particularly by the German scholar Joseph Vogt, and Ste Croix because of the Marxist missionary zeal which dominates his work. To gain a sense of balance, Joseph Vogt, *Ancient Slavery and the Ideal of Man* (Cambridge, MA and Oxford 1975) can be read alongside Finley, while for Ste Croix and Hopkins two discussions from more conservative historians appear conveniently and consecutively as follows: P. A. Brunt, 'A Marxist View of Roman History', *JRS* 72 (1982): 158–63; E. Badian, 'Figuring Out Roman Slavery', *JRS* 72 (1982): 164–9. Wiedemann's *Greece and Rome* survey (Wiedemann 1987) gives useful guidance on the wider picture of contemporary scholarship. Orlando Patterson, *Freedom*, Volume I: *Freedom in the Making of Western Culture* (New York and London 1991) has much to say on slavery in classical antiquity, but is not as reliable as it is ambitious. Among older works, William L. Westermann, *The Slave Systems of Greek and Roman Antiquity* (Philadelphia 1955) is still worth consulting, but it must be read with the critical review by P. A. Brunt in *JRS* 48 (1958): 164–70. On Greek slavery, the works of Finley and Ste Croix referred to earlier are essential, but see also Yvon Garlan, *Slavery in Ancient Greece*, revised and expanded edition (Ithaca and London 1988), and Ellen M. Wood, *Peasant-citizen and Slave: The Foundations of Athenian Democracy* (London 1988).

For more detailed information on the topics treated in this book, reference can of course be made to the bibliography that appears below and to the bibliographies of the books mentioned above. Advanced students should be aware, however, of the comprehensive *Bibliographie zur Antiken Sklaverei*, edited by Joseph Vogt, Heinz Bellen and Elisabeth Herrmann (Bochum 1983), and of the annual surveys of scholarship that appear in the journal *Slavery & Abolition* (though for antiquity the coverage tends to be spotty and does not replace recourse to *L'Année philologique*).

COMPARATIVE STUDIES

A valuable guide to what comparative history might achieve is Theda Skocpol and Margaret Somers, 'The Uses of Comparative History in Macrosocial Inquiry', *Comparative Studies in Society and History* 22 (1980): 174–97. Kolchin 1987 is a fine example of what can be done. The point of view represented by Yavetz 1988: 154 is unnecessarily pessimistic. A superb introductory survey of New World slavery in regions other than the United States is Herbert S. Klein, *African Slavery in Latin America and the Caribbean* (New York 1986), while for the United States the most recent comprehensive work known to me is Fogel 1989 (see chapter 6 especially for the historiography of American slavery). Although their points of view differ strongly, I regard the following as outstanding pieces of history from which the ancient historian can learn much: Craton 1982 on the British Caribbean, Gaspar 1985 on Antigua, Karash 1987 and Queirós Mattoso 1986 on Brazil (see also Stuart B. Schwartz, *Sugar Plantations in the Formation of Brazilian Society: Bahia, 1550–1835* (Cambridge 1985)), and on the United States, Stampp 1956, Genovese 1972, Blassingame 1979, and Fogel 1989, to which should be added Robert William Fogel and Stanley L. Engerman, *Time On the Cross: The Economics of American Negro Slavery*, 2 vols. (Boston and Toronto 1974). On the more theoretical side, Davis 1966 (augmented reprint 1988) and Patterson 1982 are compulsory for all historians of slavery.

List of works cited

ALFÖLDY, G. (1969) *Fasti Hispanienses*. Wiesbaden
(1988) *The Social History of Rome*. Baltimore
ASTIN, A. E. (1978) *Cato the Censor*. Oxford
BAGNALL, R. S. (1993) 'Slavery and society in late Roman Egypt', in Baruch Halpern and Deborah W. Hobson, eds., *Law, Politics and Society in the Ancient Mediterranean World*, 220–38. Sheffield
BALDWIN, B. (1978) 'Trimalchio's domestic staff', *AClass* 21: 87–97
BARNES, T. D. (1981) *Constantine and Eusebius*. Cambridge, MA and London
BASLER, R. P., ed. (1953) *The Collected Works of Abraham Lincoln*. New Brunswick, NJ
BAUER, R. A. and A. H. BAUER (1942) 'Day to day resistance to slavery', *Journal of Negro History* 27: 388–419
BAUMAN, R. A. (1980) 'The "Leges iudiciorum publicorum" and their interpretation in the Republic, Principate and Later Empire', *ANRW* II 13: 103–233
BELLEN, H. (1971) *Studien zur Sklavenflucht in römischen Kaiserreich*. Wiesbaden
BIËZUŃSKA-MAŁOWIST I. (1977) *L'Esclavage dans l'Egypto gréco-romaine, Seconde partie: Période romaine*. Warsaw
BIRLEY, E. (1953) *Roman Britain and the Roman Army*. Kendal
(1980) 'Law in Roman Britain', *ANRW* II 13: 609–25
BLACKBURN, R. (1988) 'Slavery – its special features and social role', in Léonie J. Archer, ed., *Slavery and Other Forms of Unfree Labour*, 262–79. London and New York
BLASSINGAME, J. W. (1975) 'Using the testimony of ex-slaves; approaches and problems', *Journal of Southern History* 41: 473–92
(1979) *The Slave Community: Plantation Life in the Antebellum South*. New York and Oxford
BÖMER, F. (1957) *Untersuchungen über die Religion der Sklaven in Griechenland und Rom I: Die wichstigsten Kulte und Religionen in Rom und in lateinischen Westen* (2nd edn 1981). Wiesbaden
BOSWELL, J. (1988) *The Kindness of Strangers: The Abandonment of Children in Western Europe from Late Antiquity to the Renaissance*. New York

BOWIE, E. L. (1977) 'The novels and the real world', in B. P. Reardon, ed., *Erotica Antiqua* (Acta of the International Conference on the Ancient Novel, Bangor 1976), 91–96. Bangor

(1985) 'Theocritus' seventh *Idyll*, Philetas and Longus', *CQ* 35: 67–91

BRADLEY, K. R. (1986a) 'Social aspects of the Roman slave trade', *MBAH* 5: 49–58

(1986b) 'Seneca and Slavery', *C&M* 37: 161–72

(1987a) *Slaves and Masters in the Roman Empire: A Study in Social Control.* New York and Oxford

(1987b) 'On the Roman slave supply and slavebreeding', in M. I. Finley, ed., *Classical Slavery*, 42–64. London (= *Slavery & Abolition* 8: 42–64)

(1988) 'Roman slavery and Roman law', *Historical Reflections/Réflexions Historiques* 15: 477–95

(1989) *Slavery and Rebellion in the Roman World, 140 B.C.–70 B.C.* Bloomington, Indianapolis and London

(1990) '*Servus onerosus*: Roman law and the troublesome slave', *Slavery & Abolition* 11: 135–57

(1991) *Discovering the Roman Family: Studies in Roman Social History.* New York and Oxford

BRAUND, D. C. and G. R. TSETSKHLADZE (1989) 'The export of slaves from Colchis', *CQ* 39: 114–25

BROWN, P. R. L. (1988) *The Body and Society: Men, Women and Sexual Renunciation in Early Christianity.* New York

BRUNT, P. A. (1971) *Italian Manpower 225 B.C. – A.D. 14.* Oxford

(1973) 'Aspects of the social thought of Dio Chrysostom and of the Stoics', *PCPhS* 19: 9–34

(1977) 'From Epictetus to Arrian', *Athenaeum* 55: 19–48

(1980a) 'Free labour and public works at Rome', *JRS* 70: 81–100

(1980b) 'Evidence given under torture in the Principate', *ZRG* 97: 256–65

(1987) 'Labour', in J. Wacher, ed., *The Roman World* II 701–16. London and New York

(1988) *The Fall of the Roman Republic and Related Essays.* Oxford

(1990) *Roman Imperial Themes.* Oxford

(1993) 'Aristotle and Slavery', in *Studies in Greek History and Thought*, 343–88. Oxford

BUCKLAND, W. W. (1908) *The Roman Law of Slavery.* Cambridge

CADOUX, C. J. (1925) *The Early Church and the World: A History of the Christian Attitude to Pagan Society and the State Down to the Time of Constantinus.* Edinburgh

CALVERT, B. (1987) 'Slavery in Plato's *Republic*', *CQ* 37: 367–72

CAMBIANO, G. (1987) 'Aristotle and the anonymous opponents of slavery', in M. I. Finley, ed., *Classical Slavery*, 21–41. London (= *Slavery & Abolition* 8: 21–41)

CAMPBELL, J. B. (1984) *The Emperor and the Roman Army 31 BC–AD 235.* Oxford

CARANDINI, A. (1981) 'Sviluppo e crisi delle manifatture rurali e urbane', in A. Giardina and A. Schiavone, eds., *Società romana e produzione schiavistica,* v. 2, 249–60. Rome and Bari

CARTLEDGE, P. A. (1985) 'Rebels & Sambos in Classical Greece: a comparative view', in P. A. Cartledge & F. D. Harvey, eds., *Crux: Essays presented to G. E. M. de Ste. Croix on his 75th birthday,* 16–46. London

CASSON, L. (1984) *Ancient Trade and Society.* Detroit

CHADWICK, H. (1983) 'New Letters of St. Augustine', *JThS* 34: 425–52

CLARKE, J. R. (1991) *The Houses of Roman Italy, 100 B.C.–A.D. 250: Ritual, Space, and Decoration.* Berkeley, Los Angeles and Oxford

COARELLI, F. (1988) *Il foro boario: dalle origini alla fine della repubblica.* Rome

CONRAD, R. E. (1983) *Children of God's Fire: A Documentary History of Black Slavery in Brazil.* Princeton

CORBIER, M. (1989) 'The ambiguous status of meat', *Food and Foodways* 3: 223–64

COTTON, H. M. (1981) *Documentary Letters of Recommendation in Latin from the Roman Empire.* Königstein/Ts
(1986) 'The role of Cicero's letters of recommendation: *iustitia versus gratia?*', *Hermes* 114: 443–60

CRATON, M. (1982) *Testing the Chains: Resistance to Slavery in the British West Indies.* Ithaca and London
(1986) 'From Caribs to Black Caribs: the Amerindian roots of servile resistance in the Caribbean', in Gary Y. Okihiro, ed., *In Resistance: Studies in African, Caribbean, and Afro-American History,* 96–116. Amherst, MA

CRAWFORD, M. H. (1977) 'Republican *denarii* in Romania: the suppression of piracy and the slave-trade', *JRS* 67: 117–24
(1985) *Coinage and Money under the Roman Republic: Italy and the Mediterranean Economy.* London

CROOK, J. A. (1955) *Consilium Principis: Imperial Councils and Counsellors from Augustus to Diocletian.* Cambridge

CURTIN, P. D. (1969) *The Atlantic Slave Trade: A Census.* Madison, Milwaukee and London

D'ARMS, J. H. (1991) 'Slaves at Roman *convivia*', in W. J. Slater, ed., *Dining in a Classical Context,* 171–83. Ann Arbor, MI

DAUBE, D. (1946) 'Two early patterns of manumission', *JRS* 36: 57–75
(1952) 'Slave-catching', *Juridical Review* 64: 12–28

DAVIES, R. W. (1989) *Service in the Roman Army.* Edinburgh

DAVIS, D. B. (1966) *The Problem of Slavery in Western Culture.* Ithaca (augmented reprint, New York 1988)
(1975) *The Problem of Slavery in the Age of Revolution 1770–1823.* Ithaca and London

DEGLER, C. N. (1971) *Neither Black Nor White: Slavery and Race Relations in Brazil and the United States.* New York and London

DESANGES, J. (1976) 'The iconography of the black in ancient North Africa', in Ladislas Bugner, ed., *The Image of the Black in Western Art I: From the Pharaohs to the Fall of the Roman Empire,* 246–68. New York

DIONISOTTI, A. C. (1982) 'From Ausonius' schooldays? A schoolbook and its relatives', *JRS* 72: 83–125

DRESCHER, S. (1986) *Capitalism and Antislavery: British Mobilization in Comparative Perspective.* New York

DREW, B. (1856) *The Refugee: Or the Narratives of Fugitive Slaves in Canada.* Boston

DUCHÊNE, H. (1986) 'Sur la stèle d'Aulus Caprilius Timotheus, *sômatemporos*', *BCH* 110: 513–30

DUMONT, J. C. (1987) *Servus: Rome et l'esclavage sous la république.* Rome

DUNBABIN, K. M. D. (1978) *The Mosaics of Roman North Africa: Studies in Iconography and Patronage.* Oxford

(1989) '*Baiarum grata voluptas*: Pleasures and dangers of the baths', *PBSR* 57: 6–46

DUNCAN-JONES, R. P. (1974) *The Economy of the Roman Empire: Quantitative Studies.* Cambridge (2nd edn 1982)

DYSON, S. L. (1992) *Community and Society in Roman Italy.* Baltimore and London

EDMONDSON, J. C. (1987) *Two Industries in Roman Lusitania: Mining and Garum Production.* Oxford

(1989) 'Mining in the later Roman empire and beyond: continuity or disruption?', *JRS* 79: 84–102

ELTIS, D. (1987) *Economic Growth and the Ending of the Transatlantic Slave Trade.* New York and Oxford

ÉTIENNE, R. (1981) 'Les rations alimentaires des esclaves de la «familia rustica» d'après Caton', *Index* 10: 66–77

EVANS, J. K. (1978) 'The role of *suffragium* in imperial political decision-making: a Flavian example', *Historia* 27: 102–28

(1980) '*Plebs rustica.* The peasantry of classical Italy II', *AJAH* 5: 134–73

FINLEY, M. I. (1973) *The Ancient Economy.* Berkeley and Los Angeles (2nd edn 1985)

(1980) *Ancient Slavery and Modern Ideology.* New York

(1981) *Economy and Society in Ancient Greece.* London

FLORY, M. B. (1978) 'Family in "familia": kinship and community in slavery', *AJAH* 3: 78–95

FOGEL, R. W. (1989) *Without Consent or Contract: The Rise and Fall of American Slavery.* New York and London

FOX-GENOVESE, E. (1988) *Within the Plantation Household: Black and White Women of the Old South.* Chapel Hill and London

FOXHALL, L. (1990) 'The dependent tenant: land leasing and labour in Italy and Greece', *JRS* 80: 97–114

FOXHALL, L. and H. A. FORBES (1982) 'Sitometreia: the role of grain as a staple food in classical antiquity', *Chiron* 12: 41–90

FRAENKEL, E. (1957) *Horace*. Oxford

FRAYN, J. M. (1979) *Subsistence Farming in Roman Italy*. London
(1984) *Sheep-Rearing and the Wool Trade in Italy during the Roman Period*. Liverpool

FREYBURGER, G. (1992) 'Le droit d'asile à Rome', *LEC* 60: 139–51

GARDNER, J. F. (1991) 'The Purpose of the *Lex Fufia Caninia*', *EMC* 10: 21–39

GARDNER, J. F. and T. E. J. WIEDEMANN (1991) *The Roman Household: A Sourcebook*. London and New York

GARNSEY, P. D. A. (1968) 'Why penalties become harsher: the Roman case, late Republic to fourth-century Empire', *Natural Law Forum* 13: 141–62
(1970) *Social Status and Legal Privilege in the Roman Empire*. Oxford
(1988) *Famine and Food Supply in the Graeco-Roman World: Responses to Risk and Crisis*. Cambridge
(1991) 'Mass diet and nutrition in the city of Rome', in A. Giovannini, ed., *Nourrir la plèbe*, 67–101. Zurich

GARNSEY, P. D. A. and R. P. SALLER (1987) *The Roman Empire: Economy, Society and Culture*. Berkeley and Los Angeles

GARRIDO-HORY, M. (1981) *Martial et l'esclavage*. Paris

GASPAR, D. B. (1985) *Bondmen and Rebels: A Study of Master-Slave Relations in Antigua*. Baltimore

GATES, H. L., JR., ed. (1987) *The Classic Slave Narratives*. New York

GENOVESE, E. D. (1972) *Roll, Jordan, Roll: The World the Slaves Made*. New York

GOODMAN, M. (1983) *State and Society in Roman Galilee, AD 132–212*. Totowa, New Jersey

GOW, A. S. F. (1953) *The Greek Bucolic Poets*. Cambridge

GOW, A. S. F. and D. L. PAGE, eds. (1965) *The Greek Anthology: Hellenistic Epigrams*. Cambridge

GRAF, F. (1992) 'Gestures and conventions: the gestures of Roman actors and orators', in Jan Bremmer and Herman Roodenburg, eds., *A Cultural History of Gesture*, 36–58. Ithaca

GREEN, R. P. H., ed. (1991), *The Works of Ausonius*. Oxford

GRIFFIN, M. T. (1976) *Seneca: A Philosopher in Politics*. Oxford

GRISÉ, Y. (1982) *Le Suicide dans la Rome antique*. Montreal and Paris

GRUEN, E. S. (1984) *The Hellenistic World and the Coming of Rome*. Berkeley, Los Angeles and London

GUTHRIE, W. K. C. (1969) *A History of Greek Philosophy: Volume III, The Fifth-Century Enlightenment*. Cambridge

GWYN, J. (1992) 'The economics of the transatlantic slave trade: a review', *Histoire Sociale/Social History* 25: 151–62

HÄGG, T. (1983) *The Novel in Antiquity*. Berkeley and Los Angeles

HARRIS, W. V. (1979) *War and Imperialism in Republican Rome 327–70 B.C.* Oxford (repr. with corrections 1985)

  (1980) 'Towards a study of the Roman slave trade', *MAAR* 36: 117–40

  (1989) *Ancient Literacy*. Cambridge, MA and London

  (1990) 'Roman warfare in the economic and social context of the fourth-century B.C.', in Walter Eder, ed., *Staat und Staatlichkeit in der frühen römischen Republik*, 494–510. Stuttgart

HOLLIS, A. S., ed. (1970) *Ovid, Metamorphoses Book VIII*. Oxford

HOPKINS, K. (1978) *Conquerors and Slaves: Sociological Studies in Roman History, Volume 1*. Cambridge

  (1993) 'Novel evidence for Roman slavery', *P&P* no. 138: 3–27

HÜBNER, R. (1978) 'Four Oxyrhynchos papyri', *ZPE* 30: 195–207

JASHEMSKI, W. F. (1979) *The Gardens of Pompeii*. New Rochelle, NY

JONES, A. H. M. (1956) 'Slavery in the ancient world', *Economic History Review* 9: 185–99 (= M. I. Finley, ed., *Slavery in Classical Antiquity* (Cambridge and New York 1960, repr. with bibliographical additions 1968), 1–15)

JOSHEL, S. R. (1992) *Work, Identity and Legal Status at Rome: A Study of the Occupational Inscriptions*. Norman and London

KARASCH, M. C. (1987) *Slave Life in Rio de Janeiro 1808–1850*. Princeton

KENNEY, E. J., ed. (1984) *The Ploughman's Lunch: Moretum: A Poem Ascribed to Virgil*. Bristol

KIRSCHENBAUM, A. (1987) *Sons, Slaves and Freedmen in Roman Commerce*. Washington, DC

KLEIN, R. (1988) *Die Sklaverei in der Sicht der Bischöfe Ambrosius und Augustinus*. Stuttgart

KOLCHIN, P. (1987) *Unfree Labor: American Slavery and Russian Serfdom*. Cambridge, MA and London

KOLENDO, J. (1981) 'L'esclavage et la vie sexuelle des hommes libres à Rome', *Index* 10: 288–97

LANE FOX, R. (1986) *Pagans and Christians*. New York and London

LEGRAND, PH.-E., ed. (1967) *Bucoliques Grecs II*. Paris

LEPELLEY, CL. (1981) 'La crise de l'Afrique romaine au début du Ve siècle d'après les lettres nouvellement découvertes de Saint Augustin', *CRAI* 1981: 445–63

LEPPER, F. A. and S. S. FRERE (1988) *Trajan's Column: A New Edition of the Cichorius Plates*. Gloucester

LEVICK, B. M. (1990) *Claudius*. New Haven and London

LEVINE, L. W. (1977) *Black Culture and Black Consciousness: Afro-American Folk Thought from Slavery to Freedom*. New York and Oxford

LÉVY-BRUHL, H. (1934) 'Théorie de l'esclavage', in *Quelques problèmes du très ancien droit romain*, 15–33. Paris (= M. I. Finley, ed., *Slavery in*

Classical Antiquity (Cambridge and New York 1960, repr. with bibliographical additions 1968), 151–69)

LEWIS, B. (1990) *Slavery in the Middle East: An Historical Enquiry.* New York
and Oxford

LEWIS, N. (1983) *Life in Egypt under Roman Rule.* Oxford

LOVEJOY, P. E. (1986) 'Fugitive slaves: Resistance to slavery in the Sokoto
Caliphate', in Gary Y. Okihiro, ed., *In Resistance: Studies in African,
Caribbean, and Afro-American History*, 71–95. Amherst, MA

LUTZ, CORA (1947) 'Musonius Rufus: the Roman Socrates', *Yale Classical
Studies* 10: 3–147

MACMULLEN, R. (1986) 'Judicial savagery in the Roman Empire', *Chiron*
16: 147–66 (= MacMullen 1990: 204–17)

(1987) 'Late Roman slavery', *Historia* 36: 359–83 (= MacMullen 1990:
236–49)

(1990) *Changes in the Roman Empire: Essays in the Ordinary.* Princeton

MACQUERON, J. (1945) 'Le testament d'Antonius Silvanus', *RD* 23: 123–
70

MANNING, C. E. (1989) 'Stoicism and slavery in the Roman Empire',
ANRW II 36.3: 1518–43

MARTIN, D. B. (1990) *Slavery as Salvation.* New Haven and London.

MATTHEWS, J. (1989) *The Roman Empire of Ammianus.* London and Baltimore

MCFEELY, W. S. (1991) *Frederick Douglass.* New York and London

MCGINN, T. A. J. (1990) '*Ne serva prostituatur.* Restrictive covenants in the
sale of slaves', *ZRG* 107: 315–53

MCLAURIN, M. A. (1991) *Celia, A Slave.* Athens, GA

MELLON, J., ed. (1988) *Bullwhip Days: The Slaves Remember: An Oral History.*
New York

MILLAR, F. G. B. (1965) 'Epictetus and the imperial court', *JRS* 55: 141–8
(1977) *The Emperor in the Roman World.* London (2nd edn 1992)
(1981) 'The World of the *Golden Ass*', *JRS* 71: 63–75

MILLER, R. M., ed. (1990) *Dear Master: Letters of a Slave Family.* Athens, GA
and London

MONTEVECCHI, O. (1973) *La papirologia.* Turin

NICHOLSON, O. (1989) 'Flight from persecution as imitation of Christ:
Lactantius' *Divine Institutes* IV.18, 1–2', *JThS* 40: 48–65

NICOLET, CL. (1991) *Space, Geography, and Politics in the Early Roman Empire.*
Ann Arbor, MI

NOCK, A. D. (1928) 'Early gentile Christianity and its Hellenistic background', in A. E. J. Rawlinson, ed., *Essays on the Trinity and the Incar-
nation*, 55–156. London (= *Essays on Religion and the Ancient World*
(Oxford 1972), 49–133)

OXÉ, A. and H. COMFORT, eds. (1968) *Corpus Vasorum Arretinorum.* Bonn

PACKER, J. E. (1975) 'Middle and lower class housing in Pompeii and
Herculaneum', in Bernard Andreae and Helmut Kyrieleis, eds., *Neue*

Forschungen in Pompeji und den anderen vom Vesuvausbruch 79 n. Chr. verschütteten Städten, 133–42. Recklinghausen

PAGELS, E. (1988) *Adam, Eve, and the Serpent*. New York

PATTERSON, O. (1982) *Slavery and Social Death: A Comparative Study*. Cambridge, MA and London

PEACOCK, D. P. S. (1982) *Pottery in the Roman World: An Ethnoarchaeological Approach*. London and New York

PELTERET, D. (1981) 'Slave raiding and slave trading in early England', *Anglo-Saxon England* 9: 99–114

PITTS, L. F. (1989) 'Relations between Rome and the German "Kings" on the middle Danube in the first to the fourth centuries A.D.', *JRS* 79: 45–58

PRICE, R., ed. (1979) *Maroon Societies: Rebel Slave Communities in the Americas*, 2nd edn. Baltimore

PRICE, S. F. R. (1986) 'From Freud to Artemidorus', *P&P* 113: 3–37

PUCCI, G. (1973) 'La produzione della ceramica aretina. Note sull' "industria" nella prima età imperiale romana', *DArch* 7: 255–93
  (1981) 'La ceramica italica (terra sigillata)', in A. Giardina and A. Schiavone, eds., *Società romana e produzione schiavistica*, v. 2, 99–121. Rome and Bari

QUEIRÓS MATTOSO, K. M. DE (1986) *To Be A Slave in Brazil 1550–1888*. New Brunswick, NJ

RAMAGE, N. H. and A. RAMAGE (1991) *Roman Art*. Englewood Cliffs, NJ

RAWICK, G. P. (1972) *The American Slave: A Composite Autobiography, Volume I, From Sundown to Sunup: The Making of the Black Community*. Westport, CT

RAWSON, B. M. (1986) 'Children in the Roman *familia*', in Beryl Rawson, ed., *The Family in Ancient Rome: New Perspectives*, 170–200. London and Sydney

RAWSON, E. (1985) *Intellectual Life in the Late Roman Republic*. London and Baltimore

REARDON, B. P. (1991) *The Form of Greek Romance*. Princeton

RICHARDSON, J. S. (1976) 'The Spanish mines and the development of provincial taxation in the second century B.C.', *JRS* 66: 139–52

RICHMOND, I. A. (1953) 'Three Roman writing-tablets from London', *AntJ* 33: 206–8

RICKMAN, G. E. (1980) *The Corn Supply of Ancient Rome*. Oxford

RIPLEY, C. P., ed. (1986) *The Black Abolitionist Papers, Volume II, Canada, 1830–1865*. Chapel Hill and London

ROBERTS, J. W. (1989) *From Trickster to Badman: The Black Folk Hero in Slavery and Freedom*. Philadelphia

ROBERTSON, D. S. and P. VALLETTE, eds. (1965) *Apulée: Les Métamorphoses II*. Paris

ROBERTSON, N. (1987) 'The Nones of July and Roman weather magic', *MH* 44: 8–41

ROBINSON, O. F. (1981) 'Slaves and the criminal law', *ZRG* 98: 213–54

ROBLEDA, O. (1976) *Il diritto degli schiavi nell' antica Roma*. Rome

ROSE, W. L., ed. (1976) *A Documentary History of Slavery in North America*. New York and London

ROSSI, L. (1971) *Trajan's Column and the Dacian Wars*. London

RUDD, N. (1966) *The Satires of Horace*. Cambridge

RUTHERFORD, R. B. (1989) *The Meditations of Marcus Aurelius: A Study*. Oxford

SACKS, K. S. (1990) *Diodorus Siculus and the First Century*. Princeton

STE CROIX, G. E. M. de (1975) 'Early Christian attitudes towards property and slavery', *Studies in Church History* 12: 1–38

(1981) *The Class Struggle in the Ancient Greek World from the Archaic Age to the Arab Conquests*. London and Ithaca

SALLER, R. P. (1982) *Personal Patronage under the early Empire*. Cambridge

(1987) 'Slavery and the Roman Family', in M. I. Finley, ed., *Classical Slavery*, 65–87. London (= *Slavery & Abolition* 8: 65–87)

(1991) 'Corporal punishment, authority, and obedience in the Roman household', in Beryl Rawson, ed., *Marriage, Divorce, and Children in Ancient Rome*, 144–65. Canberra and Oxford

SAMSON, R. (1989) 'Rural slavery, inscriptions, archaeology, and Marx: a response to Ramsay MacMullen's "Late Roman Slavery"', *Historia* 38: 99–110

SCHLAIFER, R. (1936) 'Greek theories of slavery from Homer to Aristotle', *HSPh* 47: 165–204 (= M. I. Finley, ed., *Slavery in Classical Antiquity* (Cambridge and New York 1960, repr. with bibliographical additions 1968), 93–132)

SHAW, B. D. (1984) 'Bandits in the Roman Empire', *P&P* 105: 3–52

(1990) 'Bandit highlands and lowland peace: the mountain of Isauria-Cilicia', *JESHO* 33: 199–233, 237–70

SHELTON, K. J. (1981) *The Esquiline Treasure*. London

SHERWIN-WHITE, A. N. (1966) *The Letters of Pliny: A Historical and Social Commentary*. Oxford

SILVERMAN, J. H. (1985) *Unwelcome Guests: Canada West's Response to American Fugitive Slaves, 1800–1865*. Millwood, NY, New York and London

SNOWDEN, F. M., JR. (1976) 'Iconographical evidence on the black populations in Greco-Roman antiquity', in Ladislas Bugner, ed., *The Image of the Black in Western Art I: From the Pharaohs to the Fall of the Roman Empire*, 133–245. New York

SOTGIU, G. (1973/1974) 'Un collare di schiavo rinvenuto in Sardegna', *ArchClass* 25–26: 688–97

SPEIDEL, M. D. and S. PANCIERA (1989) 'From the North and Black Sea shores: Two new gravestones for boys of the "equites singulares Augusti"', *Chiron* 19: 119–26

SPURR, M. S. (1986) *Arable Cultivation in Roman Italy c. 200 B.C.–c. A.D. 100*. London

(1990) 'Agriculture and the *Georgics*', in Ian McAuslan and Peter Walcot, eds., *Virgil: Greece and Rome Studies*, 69–93. Oxford

STADTER, P. A. (1980) *Arrian of Nicomedia*. Chapel Hill

STAMPP, K. M. (1956) *The Peculiar Institution: Slavery in the Ante-Bellum South*. New York

STARR, C. G. (1949) 'Epictetus and the tyrant', *CPh* 44: 20–9

STEFANELLI, L. P. B., ed. (1990) *Il bronzo dei Romani: arredo e suppellettile*. Rome

STRASBURGER, H. (1965) 'Poseidonios on problems of the Roman Empire', *JRS* 55: 40–53

SYME, R. (1979) *Roman Papers I & II*. Oxford

(1988) *Roman Papers IV & V*. Oxford

(1991) *Roman Papers VI & VII*. Oxford

TCHERNIA, A. (1983) 'Italian wine in Gaul at the end of the Republic', in Peter Garnsey, Keith Hopkins, and C. R. Whittaker, eds., *Trade in the Ancient Economy*, 87–104. London

(1986) *Le Vin de l'Italie romaine*. Paris and Rome

TEMPERLEY, H. (1972) *British Antislavery: 1833–1870*. Columbia, SC

THOMAS, J. A. C. (1975) *The Institutes of Justinian*. Amsterdam and Oxford

THOMPSON, E. A. (1957) 'Slavery in early Germany', *Hermathena* 89: 17–29 (= M. I. Finley, ed., *Slavery in Classical Antiquity* (Cambridge and New York 1960, repr. with bibliographical additions 1968), 191–203)

(1985) *Who Was St. Patrick?* Bury St Edmunds, Suffolk

THOMPSON, L. A. (1989) *Romans and Blacks*. London and New York

TOYNBEE, J. M. C. (1971) *Death and Burial in the Roman World*. London

TREGGIARI, S. M. (1969) *Roman Freedmen during the Late Republic*. Oxford

(1973) 'Domestic staff at Rome during the Julio-Claudian period', *Histoire Sociale/Social History* 6: 241–55

(1975) 'Jobs in the household of Livia', *PBSR* 43: 48–77

VAN HOOFF, A. J. L. (1990) *From Autothanasia to Suicide: Self-Killing in Classical Antiquity*. London and New York

VERSNEL, H. S. (1970) *Triumphus: An Enquiry into the Origin, Development and Meaning of the Roman Triumph*. Leiden

VEYNE, P. (1987) 'The Roman Empire', in Philippe Ariès and Georges Duby, eds., *A History of Private Life I: From Pagan Rome to Byzantium*, 5–234. Cambridge, MA and London

VLASTOS, G. (1941) 'Slavery in Plato's Thought', *The Philosophical Review* 50: 289–304 (= M. I. Finley, ed., *Slavery in Classical Antiquity* (Cambridge and New York 1960, repr. with bibliographical additions 1968), 133–49)

VOGT, J. (1975) *Ancient Slavery and the Ideal of Man*. Cambridge, MA

WADE, R. C. (1964) *Slavery in the Cities: The South 1820–1860*. New York

WALBANK, F. W. (1979) *A Historical Commentary on Polybius, Volume III*. Oxford

WALLACE-HADRILL, A. (1982) 'The golden age and sin in Augustan ideology', *P&P* 95: 19–36

(1988) 'The social structure of the Roman house', *PBSR* 56: 43–97
(1991) 'Houses and households: sampling Pompeii and Herculaneum', in Beryl Rawson, ed., *Marriage, Divorce, and Children in Ancient Rome*, 191–227. Canberra and Oxford
WATSON, A. (1967) *The Law of Persons in the Later Roman Republic.* Oxford
(1968) 'Morality, slavery and the jurists in the later Roman Republic', *Tulane Law Review* 1968: 289–303
(1975) *Rome of the XII Tables: Persons and Property.* Princeton
(1983) 'Roman slave law and Romanist ideology', *Phoenix* 37: 53–65
WEAVER, P. R. C. (1972) *Familia Caesaris: A Social Study of the Emperor's Freedmen and Slaves.* Cambridge
(1990) 'Where have all the Junian Latins gone? Nomenclature and status in the early Empire', *Chiron* 20: 275–304
WELWEI, K.-W. (1988) *Unfreie im antiken Kriegsdienst, III: Rom.* Stuttgart
WHITTAKER, C. R. (1987) 'Circe's pigs: from slavery to serfdom in the later Roman world', in M. I. Finley, ed., *Classical Slavery*, 88–122. London (= *Slavery & Abolition* 8: 88–122)
WIEDEMANN, T. E. J. (1985) 'The regularity of manumission at Rome', *CQ* 35: 162–75
(1987) *Slavery: Greece and Rome*, New Surveys in the Classics, no. 19. Oxford
WIGHTMAN, E. M. (1971) *Roman Trier and the Treveri.* New York and Washington, DC
WILSON, L. M. (1938) *The Clothing of the Ancient Romans.* Baltimore
WINKLER, J. J. (1985) *Auctor & Actor: A Narratological Reading of Apuleius's The Golden Ass.* Berkeley, Los Angeles and Oxford
WISEMAN, T. P. (1985) *Catullus and His World: A Reappraisal.* Cambridge
YAVETZ, Z. (1988) *Slaves and Slavery in Ancient Rome.* New Brunswick, NJ and London
YELLIN, J. F., ed. (1987) *Incidents in the Life of a Slave Girl.* Cambridge, MA and London

Index

Note: well-known Roman names are indexed in the familiar forms used in the body of the book, e.g. 'Cicero' rather than 'Tullius Cicero, M.'.

197